THE NEW FRONTIERS OF
SOVEREIGN INVESTMENT

———

THE NEW FRONTIERS OF SOVEREIGN INVESTMENT

EDITED BY

Malan Rietveld
and Perrine Toledano

COLUMBIA UNIVERSITY PRESS

NEW YORK

Columbia University Press
Publishers Since 1893
New York   Chichester, West Sussex
cup.columbia.edu

Library of Congress Cataloging-in-Publication Data
Names: Rietveld, Malan, editor. | Toledano, Perrine, editor.
Title: The new frontiers of sovereign investment / edited by
Malan Rietveld and Perrine Toledano.
Description: New York : Columbia University Press, [2017] |
Includes bibliographical references and index.
Identifiers: LCCN 2016046841 (print) | LCCN 2017003118
(ebook) | ISBN 9780231177504 (cloth : alk. paper) |
ISBN 9780231543484 (electronic)
Subjects: LCSH: Sovereign wealth funds. |
Investment of public funds.
Classification: LCC HJ3801 .N49 2017 (print) |
LCC HJ3801 (ebook) | DDC 332.67/252—dc23
LC record available at https://lccn.loc.gov/2016046841

∞

Columbia University Press books are printed on permanent
and durable acid-free paper.
Printed in the United States of America

Cover design: Jordan Wannemacher

CONTENTS

ACKNOWLEDGMENTS

The editors would like to acknowledge the support and assistance of a number of individuals and organizations that made this book possible. First, we wish to thank all the contributors for their hard work and patience during the editing process and for their willingness to share their expertise and insights. We would also like to thank PGIM, the global investment management business of Prudential Financial, Inc. and KPMG for their sponsorship of the book. A special word of thanks goes to the Ford Foundation, whose support for the Columbia Center on Sustainable Investment over the past few years has enabled the center to continue its work on resource-based development, particularly in the area of natural resource funds and U.S. state permanent funds.

We would also like to thank Lisa Sachs from the Columbia Center on Sustainable Investment for her support of the project. Finally, we wish to acknowledge the hard work and assistance of our editor, Bridget Flannery-McCoy, and editorial assistant, Ryan Groendyk, at Columbia University Press.

Malan Rietveld and Perrine Toledano
Editors

Arunma Oteh
Vice President and Treasurer
The World Bank

Inclusive growth, both across and within countries, is an essential contributor to peace and to harnessing human potential. Leaders today face a
complex set of issues in a fast-changing environment. We have to persist
and invest together in the future to overcome the skeptics.

Achievement of the Sustainable Development Goals, agreed upon by
world leaders in September 2015, will shape the future of our world and
will impact the lives of billions of people. The Sustainable Development
Goals are ambitious, and they equally demand from us ambition
in leveraging public and private sources of capital. In particular, this
would require countries to break the observed pattern in which natural
resource revenues have many times been more of a curse than a blessing
for resource-rich countries.

It is in this context that I warmly welcome this book, which brings the
most current academic perspectives and practical experiences to contribute to the current toolkit of policy makers.

Sovereign wealth funds are uniquely positioned to partner with both
public and private sectors to contribute to development in a broad sense:
directly in the form of financing and indirectly through policies that foster sustainable and equitable development. Two of their main attributes
certainly should contribute to this desirable outcome: their long-term
horizons and their lack of obsession with daily liquidity levels.

For many oil-producing countries in particular, the afflictions of the
resource curse are real and substantial: By some estimates, despite their
vast oil wealth, per capita gross national product (GNP) decreased by
1.3 percent per year on average in the countries of the Organization of
the Petroleum Exporting Countries (OPEC) between 1965 and the end

of the twentieth century, compared with over 2 percent growth in all lower- and middle-income countries over the same period. A number of current leading indicators of long-run economic performance are worrisome for resource-rich countries. In particular, there is an empirical link between resource abundance and the erosion of countries' human capital and educational outcomes. This is particularly troubling, considering that it is a country's citizens and their skills that are among the key drivers of long-term economic growth and prosperity. As such, resource management is not an isolated issue of financial optimizations but is deeply interconnected with social and economic development and with most of the Sustainable Development Goals. And the greater the level of equitable growth, the greater is the potential for shared prosperity.

The fact is that the resource curse remains a deplorable reality, as is particularly illuminated with the impact of the current downturn in commodity prices on many countries. Decades of accumulated knowledge and awareness of the subject are not a substitute for action. And as various contributors of this book reinforce, there are no clear-cut, easy-to-implement, one-size-fits-all solutions to the long-term challenge of the transformation of resource abundance into national wealth—especially when country-specific legacies, contexts, and risk appetites are taken into account. This book advances the current debate and discusses the practical implications for countries working through these policy challenges at times when the traditional approaches have been contested.

In recent years, sovereign wealth funds have become fashionable, and, as with any such trend, one needs to see whether such a fund suits the particular individual circumstances well. Indeed, the economic objectives of these funds can be multifaceted: countries establish them to facilitate fiscal stabilization, invest in infrastructure, accumulate long-term savings, generate alternative sources of fiscal revenue in the form of investment income—or, more recently, combine several of these objectives. Against this backdrop, one of the major contributions of this edited volume is a sharing of perspectives—as well as evidence and practical experience—on an evolving and more flexible understanding of sovereign wealth funds, particularly the advantages and pitfalls of assigning at least a partial role for sovereign funds in domestic investment.

While it is difficult to establish causality, sovereign wealth funds can be models for institution building and thus catalysts in improving overall governance, which continues to be one of the key challenges impeding the development of resource-rich poor countries. I participated in the Presidential Committee that first worked on the establishment of the Nigeria Sovereign Wealth Fund in 2008, which has a triple mandate and organization structure focused on savings, stabilization, and domestic investment. The Committee was set up by late President Umaru Yar'Adua, who recognized the importance of saving for future generations. Nigeria made the decision to have one of its sovereign wealth funds focus on infrastructure, which serves as an important example of responding to the needs of each country. Of course, there are challenges associated with the establishment and design of such funds. Nigeria has faced some but has been able to overcome them. While recognizing these difficulties, I am also convinced that often these funds can add value and facilitate an important discussion around the trade-offs between catering to short-term needs and investing and saving for the future.

One of the most striking features in the global community of sovereign wealth funds is the enormous economic, political, and institutional diversity among countries with these types of fund. For example, sovereign wealth fund assets under management can range from hundreds of billions of US dollars in high-income countries, such as Kuwait, Norway, and Singapore, to less than a billion in low-income and small countries, such as Rwanda and Kiribati. Sovereign wealth funds are, therefore, an institutional response to the challenges of resource revenue management that has been embraced by countries across the whole spectrum of economic development as a tool for sharing prosperity across generations.

The slump in commodity prices that started in late 2014 underscores the importance of sovereign wealth funds and the role they have in stabilizing volatile revenues, supporting domestic infrastructure investment, and transforming a depleting resource into a more stable, permanent one. It is important to note that all established sovereign wealth funds have significantly changed since their inception, with their mandates and structures evolving over time as circumstances change. This again lends credence to the observation that they must suit the needs of the stakeholders, which ultimately are the citizens.

The design of sovereign wealth funds should be sensitive to local needs and realities—moreover, even the best-designed sovereign wealth fund is only part of prudent and growth-enhancing fiscal and economic development policies. But, the bottom line is that they have proven to be an invaluable tool for an increasing number of countries and, at times, a catalyst for complementary reforms.

At this time, when the global community has affirmed its strong commitment to eliminating extreme poverty and promoting shared prosperity through the endorsement of the Sustainable Development Goals, sovereign wealth funds are part of the solution. They clearly can meet the challenge for resource-rich countries of balancing short-term expedience with the aspiration for long-term benefits for their citizens.

I would like to commend the Columbia Center on Sustainable Investment, its sponsors, and the contributors to this book for their important and timely analysis of the role sovereign wealth funds may play in meeting this challenge. Without a doubt, it requires discipline—and sacrifice—to achieve the transformation of resource-based economies for the sake of future generations. In reflecting on this challenge, I am reminded of a great proverb: "A society grows great when wise men plant trees whose shade they know they shall never sit in."

PART I

The Evolution of Sovereign Wealth Funds
Mandates and Governance

CHAPTER 1

Introduction

Malan Rietveld and Perrine Toledano
Columbia Center on Sustainable Investment

The rise of sovereign wealth funds (SWFs) as global investors is reflected not only in the increase in the size of the assets under their management, but also in the proliferation of new funds established in recent years. Although exact numbers are hard to come by owing to the lack of transparency and differences in how funds are classified, estimates using a broad definition suggest that SWFs held approximately $7.25 trillion in assets as of September 2015.[1] In September 2010, it was estimated that these funds held $4.1 trillion, implying an increase in assets under management of 77 percent in only five years.

The growth of sovereign wealth has been equally striking in terms of the number of funds. By some estimates, which are again somewhat imprecise, the number of commodity-based funds has doubled from around thirty at the start of the twenty-first century to around sixty today; non–commodity-based funds have similarly doubled in number from around five to ten over the same period.[2]

While the current slump in global commodity prices will likely lead to a decline in the growth of both the number of new funds and the size of assets under management of existing funds, the long-term prospects for the growth of SWFs remain compelling. In recent years, major resource discoveries in a number of developing countries have bolstered interest in SWFs there. Further, the shale revolution in the United States has led new oil- and gas-producing states to study the permanent funds of established resource-producing states, where these funds have helped ensure fiscal stability and laid the foundations for spreading the benefits from finite resources over successive generations. New natural resource funds have been proposed in at least twenty national and subnational jurisdictions, including the Bahamas, Bolivia, Colombia, Guyana, Israel, Kenya, Lebanon, Liberia, Mozambique, Myanmar, Niger, Peru, Tanzania, Uganda, and Zambia, as well as a number of American states and Canadian provinces and territories, such as West Virginia, Pennsylvania, Saskatchewan, and the Northwest Territories (Bauer, Rietveld, and Toledano 2014).

While their size and proliferation make SWFs a worthy subject of study in their own right, there is also an increasing sense that the coming decade of sovereign wealth management is unlikely to be as conducive to growth for SWFs as the previous one. The period between 2004 and 2013 was characterized by rising SWF assets (owing to generally increasing commodity prices and, in the case of Asian funds, trade surpluses and national savings) and—with the notable, but ultimately transitory, exception of the global financial crisis—rising asset prices and increasing political and intellectual support for the SWF model. In many ways, this was the golden era for SWFs.

Today, the outlook is considerably less promising, given concerns over weakening returns and economic dynamism in traditional investment destinations, a secular decline in commodity prices and revenue, and political and economic pressure on the management of SWFs as well as calls on their assets. These emerging realities are bringing the new frontier of sovereign investment into sharper focus. In this book, we primarily attempt to inform and stimulate debate around what this frontier might look like. As we argue in the final chapter, it is important to recognize that the emerging challenges pertain to a number of dimensions in the management of SWFs, including macroeconomic policies, investment operations, investment strategies, and internal and external governance.

SOVEREIGN WEALTH FUNDS: DEFINITIONS AND EVOLUTION

It is important to clarify what SWFs are and what the deep drivers are behind their continued evolution. A universally accepted definition for SWFs has remained elusive in both the academic literature and policy discussions of SWFs. According to the broadest definitions, SWFs are "special purpose investment funds or arrangements, owned by the general government" (International Working Group of Sovereign Wealth Funds 2008) or entities "owned or controlled by the government [that] hold, manage, or administer assets primarily for medium- to long-term macroeconomic and financial objectives" (International Monetary Fund 2008).

These definitions are, by the admission of their authors, very broad and best employed in the most general discussions of sovereign investors. More focused discussions require granular and precise definitions and a demarcation of different kinds of sovereign investors. The contributors of this volume have a common understanding of SWFs as extra-budgetary mechanisms holding a (generally natural resource–based) fiscal or foreign exchange reserve surplus.

As a number of authors of this volume argue, SWFs often share important characteristics with other public investors, including central banks, public pensions, pension reserve funds, and national development banks. However, these similarities have resulted in a tendency to clumsily lump together a range of public investors under the SWF banner. Indeed, SWFs differ from other extra-budgetary mechanisms, such as pension funds and development banks, in the sense that some of the money is invested in foreign assets for macroeconomic and sometimes governance purposes. Truman (2010) refines the definition of SWFs as "large pools of government-owned funds that are invested in whole or in part outside their home country"—importantly, Truman includes subnational funds, an approach we also adopt in this book. With this definition in mind, the oldest fund is the Texas Permanent University Fund, set up in 1876, whereas at the national level, the first established fund was the Kuwait Investment Board, established in 1953 and a predecessor of the Kuwait Investment Authority.

Even if we agree on a single definition, we should not forget that SWFs are a highly diverse group, reflected in the wide range of economic contexts in which they operate: from some of the world's richest (e.g., Canada, Norway, and the United States) and poorest (e.g., Nigeria, Papua New Guinea, São Tomé and Príncipe, and Timor-Leste) economies.

THE RISE OF SOVEREIGN DEVELOPMENT FUNDS

If earlier debates regarding the exact definition and classification of SWFs were complicated by a blurring on the lines between them, central bank reserve managers, and public pension funds, today the situation is complicated by the seemingly inexorable rise of sovereign development funds. The emergence of sovereign development funds is undoubtedly a major—we would argue *the* major—overarching feature of the new frontier of sovereign investment and one to which the majority of contributors to this volume devote considerable attention.

While most of the contributors to this volume discuss sovereign development funds in some form, Dixon and Monk, in chapter 6, and Gelb, Tordo, and Halland, in chapter 8, in particular will help readers define and classify sovereign development funds relative to the wider group of sovereign funds, whereas Gratcheva and Anasashvili, in chapter 7, discuss the results of a survey of sovereign development funds that provides much needed data and a comparative perspective on these institutions. Suffice to say that the debate continues regarding whether and how to include these funds—with a mandate to invest in the domestic economy, in pursuit of both commercial and noncommercial objectives—in the fluid and evolving categorization of SWFs.

Although it should be noted that, despite the rise of sovereign development funds, the overwhelming share of sovereign wealth fund assets are still managed according to the principles of providing economic and fiscal stability in the face of resource volatility and transforming a share of finite revenues from a depleting asset into a permanent financial endowment, there is no doubt that the emergence of sovereign development funds has raised new challenges in terms of the governance and operations of sovereign funds.

TOWARD THE NEW FRONTIER OF SOVEREIGN INVESTMENT

While the rise of sovereign development funds and a discussion of the unique governance and operational challenges they bring to the fore occupy a prominent place in this volume, a range of additional challenges and opportunities that confront more traditional or established sovereign wealth funds is also discussed. In the first part of this book, we analyze the evolving mandates of the SWFs, with particular emphasis on their unique characteristics and governance imperatives.

In chapter 2, Corinne Deléchat, Mauricio Villafuerte, and Shu-Chun Yang underline the fact that establishing an SWF with a stabilization and savings mandate is merely a small and partial step to creating sound fiscal policies for resource-rich countries. Their analysis shows how an SWF can be incorporated into (and subordinated to) a sound overall fiscal framework, under different assumptions and based on different economic requirements. They argue that if such integration with a robust public financial management framework is absent, SWFs alone have little chance of improving fiscal policy (and, indeed, could harm it).

In chapter 3, Adrian Orr, the chief executive officer of the New Zealand Superannuation Fund, discusses the governance and investment framework of the SWF he oversees. In particular, he outlines the central tenets of the fund's much-admired "double arm's length" governance structure that ensures independence from government—an arrangement that the fund's management has reciprocated by establishing exceptionally high levels of transparency and accountability. He also explains in detail how the fund realizes the opportunities offered by its long-term investment horizon.

In chapter 4, Robert Ohrenstein and James White consider the strategic, operational, and governance implications for the increasing preference of SWFs for direct investing, particularly through allocations to private markets, including real estate, infrastructure, and private equity.

In chapter 5, after recalling the good governance rules of SWFs, Andrew Bauer warns against the dangers of direct domestic investment by SWFs in contexts in which the broader governance framework is weak. Bauer explains that direct domestic investment by the SWF is often accompanied by both bypassing the formal budget process rules and undermining the macroeconomic objectives for which the SWF was established. If there is under-investment in the domestic economy, he argues, a far better approach, rather than expecting too much from a potentially unaccountable sovereign development fund, is to enact fiscal rules that allocate fiscal revenues more appropriately between the budget and an SWF. In this regard, his message shares much with that conveyed in by Corinne Deléchat, Mauricio Villafuerte, and Shu-Chun Yang in chapter 2. With this recommendation, chapter 5 sets the scene for part II, which delves into the question of direct domestic investment.

Part II begins with Adam Dixon and Ashby Monk's qualified and sympathetic critique of the emergence of sovereign development funds. Chapter 6 presents a categorization of two distinct types of sovereign development funds and considers how local financial, investment, and institutional capacity affect which type is appropriate in a given context. They discuss in detail how the scope and ambition of sovereign development funds must align with practical considerations of costs and the gradual development of internal investment expertise.

In chapter 7, Ekaterina Gratcheva and Nikoloz Anasashvili argue that the debates around sovereign development funds is hampered by a lack of data on the governance, policy frameworks, and mandates of these funds—even at an aggregate level. The authors help address this shortcoming by drawing on the results of the global survey conducted by the World Bank Treasury's Reserves Advisory and Management Program in 2015, with support from the International Forum of Sovereign Wealth Funds. Their chapter considers a wide range of issues around the investment practices and governance processes for domestic investment.

In chapter 8, Alan Gelb, Silvana Tordo, and Håvard Halland focus on the distinctions between commercial and quasi-commercial domestic investments by SWFs in resource-driven countries. They seek to establish a guiding framework and distinct investment assessment criteria for both types of investment and explore the conditions that affect an SWF's ability to be an efficient and prudent investor while fostering local economic diversification and the mobilization of private capital.

In chapter 9, Corinne Deléchat, Mauricio Villafuerte, and Shu-Chun Yang build on the framework presented in chapter 2, applying it in pursuit of fiscal frameworks and rules that are particularly relevant for resource-rich developing countries. Using Liberia and Kazakhstan as illustrations, the authors' model simulations demonstrate how an SWF can serve as a saving tool and fiscal buffer to help smooth government spending into the domestic economy in the context of volatile revenue flows.

In chapter 10, Uche Orji and Stella Ojekwe-Onyejeli describe the practical experience of a highly promising SWF operating in the context of significant infrastructure investment needs and a history of institutional weakness in the management of resource revenues. The Nigeria Sovereign Investment Authority has been granted a three-pronged SWF mandate that combines stabilization, saving, and domestic investment objectives—a model that a number of other African (and indeed non-African) developing countries are emulating. Orji and Ojekwe-Onyejeli describe the process that led to the establishment of the Nigeria Sovereign Investment Authority and the three SWFs under its management, as well as the policies and governance arrangements that have been put in place to promote the authority as a world-class sovereign investment institution.

Part III concludes with a consideration of a number of ideas and practices regarding issues that are just now emerging on the radar of SWFs but are likely to be an important part of their future: operationalizing environmental, social, and governance (ESG) investment, finding innovative ways to deploy return-seeking capital to the infrastructure needs of developing countries, a transition to more cyclically dynamic fiscal rules for resource-based funds, and the emergence of "sovereign venture funds."

In chapter 11, Alison Schneider details how the Alberta Investment Management Corporation (AIMCo), the institutional investment manager of the Alberta Heritage Savings Trust Fund, defines and implements its mandate for responsible investment. Schneider considers both what this means for engagement with external fund managers and firms the fund invests in as well as for AIMCo's internal investment process, assessed through an ESG lens.

Sanjay Peters argues in chapter 12 that there is an in-principle fit between the long-term, intergeneration mandates of SWFs and the length of infrastructure investment horizons—SWFs can be providers of the "patient capital" required to make long-term infrastructure investments (something that is in increasingly short supply at the global level). Peters also makes a bold proposal for a new platform to intermediate and "de-risk" infrastructure investments in order to attract sovereign capital.

In chapter 13, Malan Rietveld notes that the North American energy revolution has led to strong interest in the establishment of subnational resource funds in Montana, North Dakota, West Virginia, Saskatchewan, and the Northwest Territories, as well as other American states and Canadian provinces. Rietveld identifies lessons learned from the successes and failures of an older generation of North American subnational funds in Alaska, New Mexico, Texas, Wyoming, and Alberta and suggests a number of policy and governance reforms to retool established North American permanent funds for a potentially lengthy period of lower resource revenues.

In chapter 14, Javier Santiso describes how sovereign funds are increasingly investing in innovation and technology, broadly defined, following the slowdown in private-sector "venture capital" funding as a result of the global financial crisis. In particular, this trend has resulted in allocation of capital to tech firms, startups, and growth funds. Santiso discusses the available data and evidence on SWF investment in innovation and technology—and explains why this type of investment is both a logical exercise of these funds' mandate and likely to be a growing trend over the coming decade.

The book concludes with chapter 15, by Malan Rietveld and Perrine Toledano, who summarize the key contributions of the volume to the ongoing debates around SWFs. Even as the SWF golden era potentially fades from view, it is nevertheless clear that SWFs will remain important actors at the global and national levels in the management of excess resource revenues and other forms of public savings. The collected wisdom and practical experience of the contributors to this volume is intended to help scholars and practitioners alike navigate the new frontier of sovereign investment.

NOTES

1. Data from Statista: http://www.statista.com/statistics/276618/volume-of-managed -assets-in-sovereign-wealth-funds-worldwide/.

2. Based on data collected by the Columbia Center on Sustainable Investment and the Natural Resource Governance Institute (2014) and the Sovereign Wealth Fund Institute.

REFERENCES

Bauer, A., M. Rietveld, and P. Toledano. 2014. "Managing the Public Trust: How to Make Natural Resource Funds Work for Citizens," edited by A. Bauer. New York: Columbia Center on Sustainable Investment and Natural Resource Governance Institute. http://ccsi.columbia.edu/files/2014/09/NRF_Complete_Report_EN.pdf.

International Monetary Fund. 2008. "The Statistical Work on Sovereign Wealth Funds," Twenty-First Meeting of the IMF Committee on Balance of Payments Statistics, BOPCOM-08/19. Washington, DC: International Monetary Fund.

International Working Group of Sovereign Wealth Funds. 2008. "Sovereign Wealth Funds: Generally Accepted Principles and Practices ('Santiago Principles')," www .iwg-swf.org/pubs/eng/santiagoprinciples.pdf.

Truman, E. 2010. *Sovereign Wealth Funds: Threat or Salvation?* Washington, DC: Peterson Institute for International Economics.

CHAPTER 2

"Best-Practice" Sovereign Wealth Funds for Sound Fiscal Management

Corinne Deléchat, Mauricio Villafuerte, and Shu-Chun S. Yang

Institute of Economics, National Sun Yat-Sen University, Taiwan; International Monetary Fund

INTRODUCTION

Since the early 2000s, sovereign wealth funds (SWFs) have proliferated, and financial resources under their management have increased exponentially. During this period, much of the focus has been on analyzing the impact of SWFs on global capital flows and developing asset management practices (Truman 2010; Das, Mazarei, and van der Hoorn 2010). These issues were clearly at play when SWFs became a source of concern for the more developed countries that were recipients of SWF investments and in the subsequent formulation of Generally Accepted Principles and Practices (GAPP; the so-called Santiago Principles) by an international group of SWFs.

The majority of SWFs have been created as instruments to support the implementation of fiscal policy by their owner governments. In this context, it is critical to place SWFs in the broader context of public financial management (PFM) to make their operations consistent with standard PFM principles. In particular, with a few exceptions (China, Ireland, Korea, New Zealand, and Singapore), most SWFs have been established by governments to manage revenue from nonrenewable natural resources (e.g., oil and minerals; see table 2.1). The owner governments of SWFs tend to be highly dependent on such resources, which, in some cases, represent as much as 90 percent of total annual government revenues.[1] Because of the inherent volatility and exhaustibility of natural resources, the revenue from these resources can significantly complicate fiscal management and may force governments to revise their macroeconomic objectives from time to time (e.g., expenditure paths, net asset accumulation). Sovereign wealth funds can be an effective tool to help resource-rich countries manage these revenues so as to maintain macroeconomic stability and long-term fiscal sustainability.

Another challenge is that many SWFs, particularly in recent years, have been established in developing countries with substantial expenditure needs and relatively weak PFM and financial systems. As documented elsewhere in the literature (Gelb 1989; Sachs and Warner 1999), resource-rich developing countries tend to have weak political systems and are prone to rent-seeking capture. At the same time, resource revenue represents an unprecedented opportunity for these countries to invest in physical and human capital to reach a higher growth path. However, escaping the resource curse has historically proved to be quite challenging in less-developed economies, making it all the more important to set SWF operations in a broader PFM context.

Against this background, in this chapter, we establish the key normative principles for a "best-practice" SWF. In particular, we stress that a best-practice SWF ought to (a) be fully integrated within the fiscal framework, with the accumulation and decumulation of assets mirroring fiscal surpluses and deficits, respectively; (b) be fully integrated within the government's budget, with no spending autonomy; and (c) have clear governance structures, with robust accountability and transparency procedures.

SWFs AND FISCAL MANAGEMENT: NORMATIVE CONSIDERATIONS

BASIC DEFINITIONS AND THE IMPORTANCE OF PUBLIC FINANCIAL MANAGEMENT PRINCIPLES

A review of the more common objectives pursued by SWFs makes it apparent that the majority of them are fiscal in nature, reinforcing the importance of the PFM perspective (see table 2.1 for a detailed list of SWFs and their objectives):

Fiscal and macroeconomic stabilization. The so-called stabilization funds are designed to help smooth public spending and contribute to short-term macroeconomic stability in the face of volatile revenue. Countries such as Algeria, Chile, Mexico, and Mongolia have stabilization funds in place linked to oil and mineral fiscal revenues.

Intergenerational equity. Savings funds are designed to build up and manage financial assets for future generations and to address long-term fiscal sustainability issues. This focus is particularly relevant for exhaustible sources of government revenue (e.g., nonrenewable commodities) and large future expenditure commitments (e.g., pension liabilities). Norway's Government Pension Fund Global, Funds for Future Generations in Gulf Cooperation Council (GCC) countries, and Ireland's Strategic Investment Fund fall into this category.

Undertaking of domestic development activities. Some SWFs (i.e., development funds) have been tasked with spending on social or public investment programs or investing in domestic firms or sectors. Temasek Holdings in Singapore is a prominent example, but SWFs in Angola and Nigeria also fall into this category.

Higher financial returns on public assets. Many SWFs explicitly aim to improve returns on financial assets (subject to prudent degrees of risk). Apart from savings funds, reserve investment funds that manage part of central banks' international reserves are salient examples of SWFs focusing on this objective (e.g., the China Investment Corporation in China and the Korea Investment Corporation in South Korea).

Enhanced visibility of fiscal policy management and its accrued (net) assets. Transparency and disclosure can be fostered if the general public finds it useful, or easier, to focus on the flows and balance of an SWF as summary indicators of fiscal policy, particularly in resource-rich countries.

SWFs are typically characterized by two types of rules addressing how the fund acquires and releases its assets and how its assets should be invested:

Inflow–outflow rules govern the size of an SWF, how it accumulates assets, and under what circumstances it may use its assets. There are different forms of funding rules:
- *Contingent rules* are price- or revenue-contingent deposit or withdrawal rules. Many oil stabilization funds (e.g., those in Algeria, Mexico, and Trinidad and Tobago) specify a threshold price for oil revenue (e.g., $80 per barrel), with any excess (shortfall) above (below) the threshold being transferred to (from) the fund.
- *Revenue-share rules* are formulated as a predetermined share of revenue (e.g., 10 percent of oil revenue). Some savings funds (e.g., the ones in Gabon and Kuwait) operate under this modality.

- *Financing funds* have a very different formulation for SWF inflows and outflows, directly linking them to the government's overall balance (net inflows are equivalent to the overall fiscal balance or a fraction of it), making them mirror images of the country's fiscal position. The SWFs of Chile, Norway, and Timor-Leste use this modality, complemented by fiscal rules.

Strategic asset allocation (SAA) provisions stipulate how a government invests its assets to achieve (or, more realistically, to support the achievement of) its objectives. Different SAAs are usually selected for different investment tranches.

Critically, these provisions should be classified as *operational rules* and not confused with "fiscal rules," which are permanent constraints on budgetary aggregates to guide the implementation of the whole of fiscal policy. Unfortunately, the belief that SWF inflow and outflow provisions are the same as fiscal rules is a common misconception that would work only in the presence of binding liquidity and borrowing constraints (i.e., if a government could not borrow and/or reduce deposits at the same time, inflows into the SWF would need to be "offset" by lower spending, leading to an overall fiscal surplus). If, by contrast, a government could, in fact, borrow, an accumulation of financial assets through the SWF could be accompanied by a simultaneous increase in financial liabilities, creating a potentially problematic situation, as will be discussed in more detail in the next subsection. The latter assumption is overly restrictive, as complete isolation from financing markets is not realistic, and, at a minimum, countries could resort to payment arrears or just ignore any SWF inflow and outflow rules. In this context, the typical prescription of "The government of country X is going to receive large revenue flows from natural resources, so it must create an SWF to help manage the challenges associated with those revenue flows" is overly simplistic, or even wrong, as it overemphasizes the role of SWFs. The SWFs should be considered simply a complementary tool for fiscal policy implementation.[2]

The previous discussion sets the stage for a discussion of the relevant PFM principles that should apply in the management of SWF public assets. There are two overarching tenets of PFM. First, a government must have comprehensive control of its finances to ensure that it can, in fact, achieve its fiscal objectives. Second, a government's budget should be the tool to allocate government resources in a coordinated manner.

On this basis, best-practice PFM emphasizes the following elements: a unified budget, integrated asset–liability management, and the broadest possible coverage of government.

PFM PRINCIPLES FOR SWFs

In this subsection, we propose some normative principles for the design and operation of "fiscal" SWFs along three key dimensions: (i) integration with the fiscal framework; (ii) integration with the budget; and (iii) cohesion of institutional control and accountability procedures (a theme further discussed in chapters 5, 8, and 11). The principles proposed here are supported by examples of both good and problematic practice. In addition, some "second best" but acceptable features are highlighted.[3]

I. INTEGRATION WITH THE FISCAL FRAMEWORK

The following principles can help ensure that SWFs are properly integrated with the overall fiscal framework: (a) governments should run surpluses (i.e., save) during resource revenue boom years to accumulate wealth in their SWFs; (b) rules driving inflows to and outflows from SWFs should be consistent with the fiscal rules driving fiscal policy management; (c) the operation of SWFs should be subordinated to the ultimate fiscal policy objectives; and (d) the operations of SWFs should be articulated within a holistic asset-liability management.

FISCAL SURPLUSES SHOULD DRIVE SWF ASSET ACCUMULATION: This is a basic principle that implies that the SWF balance will grow (fall) as the government records fiscal surpluses (deficits)—that is, the government's net wealth increases (falls). The SWF is then a sort of mirror image of the financial position of the government. Importantly, the durability of an SWF hinges on its owner government's capacity to generate surpluses over time (or from time to time). In fact, if a government permanently runs deficits, it won't be able to make deposits into the fund, or it will have to borrow to make them (i.e., make leveraged deposits). In the latter scenario, gross financing needs will be larger (to cover the deficit, debt amortizations, and deposits into the SWF), complicating fiscal management, in part through an increase in financing costs. In such a context, it is highly likely that the government will decide to ignore (e.g., Mexico and Peru have tended to withdraw mandatory contributions to the SWF) or eliminate the SWF (e.g., Chad's Fund for Future Generations and Ecuador's oil stabilization fund). This is unfortunately a common risk, as many resource-rich countries narrowly focus on earmarking a fraction of resource-related revenue to an SWF irrespective of surpluses or deficits (e.g., SWFs in Ghana and Mongolia).

A one-to-one link between an SWF's net inflows and overall fiscal balances is not an absolute necessity. For instance, part of the fiscal surpluses could be used to reduce government debt rather than to accumulate SWF financial assets, especially when a country faces high borrowing costs. Conversely, inflows into an SWF could continue under fiscal deficits if the deficits could be more than fully financed by long-term debt, as in the case of multilateral project financing. Australia's Future Fund is a case where only a fraction of the surpluses must be transferred to the fund, whereas withdrawals are linked or earmarked to explicit future pension liabilities (superannuation payments). Countries in the GCC, such as Kuwait, have run very large fiscal surpluses, and revenue-share rules allocating a percentage of oil revenue to an SWF have meant, in practice, that a fraction of fiscal surpluses is saved in the form of SWF assets.

While leverage is a normal feature of private investors' portfolio management, the applicability of a "borrow-to-save" strategy for (fiscal) SWFs is a very different matter. This strategy can work in a few scenarios, including when fiscal deficits can be more than fully financed by long-term debt, as explained above. Another possibility is if contributions to the SWF and overall fiscal deficits are limited, as projected in the case of Panama's recently created SWF.[4] However, the situation can be quite different for countries that are highly dependent on volatile resource revenues. In their case, access to financing is very procyclical, and negative shocks tends to be quite large. Accruing leveraged deposits in "good" times (e.g., for stabilization purposes) might be of limited use because these deposits might need to be repaid. Finally, depending on earnings from SWF investments to more than offset borrowing costs is risky, since assets might have to be liquidated quickly in the face of sharp fiscal revenue drops.

CONSISTENCY OF SWF FLOW RULES WITH THE OVERALL FISCAL POLICY FRAMEWORK: The relationship of an SWF to the overall public finances is defined by the SWF's inflow and outflow rules. International experience suggests that flexible funding rules (financing funds) are better in terms of integration with the fiscal policy framework, as changes in an SWF's assets are correlated with the government's overall net financial asset position.

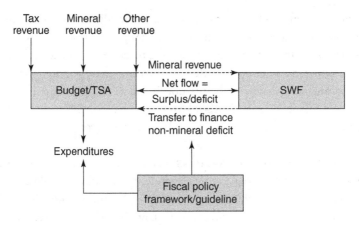

Figure 2.1   A sovereign wealth fund fully integrated with the fiscal policy framework. SWF, sovereign wealth fund; TSA, Treasury Single Account.

By contrast, rigid funding rules (contingent or revenue-share) tend to complicate fiscal policy management (e.g., the "leveraged deposits" problem) and tend to conspire against the durability of the SWF (Davis et al. 2001; Ossowski et al. 2008). In addition, a financing fund is more transparent, since its wealth reflects the summary outcome of fiscal policy. The deposit and withdrawal rules for a financing SWF will in principle be the same under any fiscal policy framework (figure 2.1).

Chile's stabilization fund is a clear example of a fund that has been well articulated within the country's fiscal framework. It works as a mirror image of the implementation of a structural balance rule: It received fiscal surpluses during the "boom" years in copper prices, and those surpluses were then used to undertake countercyclical fiscal policies when the fiscal position shifted to deficits after the global financial crisis. The key feature of Chile's framework is the structural balance rule, with the stabilization fund complementing it effectively. Panama's revamped SWF is another good example, underpinned by a fiscal framework based on targets defined in terms of the nonfinancial public sector overall balance.[5]

SUBORDINATION OF SWF OPERATIONS TO FISCAL POLICY OBJECTIVES: The objectives of most SWFs are typically articulated in terms of important fiscal objectives: stabilization of spending, spreading finite fiscal resources over several generations, and undertaking development initiatives. This principle goes beyond these objectives in stressing that the management of a government's financial assets needs to be aligned with overarching fiscal policy objectives, which might change in response to varying circumstances. Ireland provides a relevant recent example, as its SWF had to be mobilized to achieve a different objective than providing for future pension outlays, namely to help smooth the fiscal adjustment path after the recent financial crisis. In Kazakhstan and Russia, SWF resources were also reallocated to help stabilize a weak financial system.

ARTICULATION OF SWF OPERATIONS WITHIN HOLISTIC ASSET-LIABILITY MANAGEMENT: Countries highly dependent on nonrenewable commodities have particular challenges in ensuring well-functioning SWFs within sound fiscal policy frameworks. As clearly shown by the recent drastic fall in oil prices, commodity prices are very volatile and, importantly, uncertain (i.e., cannot be assumed to fluctuate around a predictable mean/trend). Within a holistic asset-liability framework, an immediate response to a fall in oil prices would be to rely on standard government's Treasury instruments (i.e., Treasury bills and bonds, Treasury deposits, bank overdrafts). In addition, resources from the so-called stabilization funds could be mobilized to help smooth government spending (or to help bridge toward a fiscal adjustment that usually takes time to be put in place). To this effect, it is critical for those countries to estimate the optimal size of a stabilization buffer, which should be based on country-specific characteristics, in particular the volatility of fiscal revenue and the degree of dependency on it (e.g., through value-at-risk analysis like in Bartsch [2006] for Nigeria). In certain circumstances, resources from the savings portfolio could be used to finance spending or to replenish the liquid/stabilization portfolio, options that would need to be carefully specified in advance taking into account the costs of liquidating long-term assets. Finally, if the price shock is deemed to be mostly permanent, a fiscal adjustment will need to be implemented.

II. INTEGRATION WITH THE BUDGET

To ensure that the national budget remains the institution deciding the allocation of government resources and setting the fiscal policy stance, **SWFs should not have authority to spend**, but should instead be designed to transfer resources to the budget when needed. While several reasons have been proposed to grant SWFs off-budget spending authority (e.g., SWFs as "islands of excellence" with enhanced evaluation, selection, and procurement procedures for more efficient domestic investments), the reality is that such power undermines the integrity of the budget and has the potential to create conflict with other fiscal processes. For instance, direct (extra-budgetary) spending by an SWF signals that the budget can be bypassed, leads to the duplication of budget activities, fragments fiscal policy, rechannels spending pressures to the SWF, and complicates macroeconomic policy coordination. Similar problems would arise if an SWF were to provide transaction support domestically through guarantees, loans, and equity participation, if those operations were (or could become) hidden quasi-fiscal activities.

With the best option being that an SWF is limited to funding budget activities, some "second best" options may be considered in response to a strong need to show that SWF assets are directly contributing to contemporaneous social welfare:

A limited earmarking of total SWF outflows to specific spending initiatives or investment projects properly appraised and selected through the budget process (operationally, this could be equivalent to having a "virtual fund" as a way to make the use of resources linked to the SWF more visible); and

Introducing pilot projects with enhanced PFM procedures to be later applied to all budgetary projects.

In any case, even if the SWF is given authority to spend separately from the budget, its spending operations should be consolidated in (ex-ante and ex-post) budget documentation.

Regarding a trend toward increased SWF investment in domestic financial assets (e.g., Angola, Nigeria) on grounds of diversification or a desire to foster private capital markets and close infrastructure gaps, there are important PFM-related concerns to consider. For instance, public policy priorities, or even incentives to bypass the national budget, could be imposed on the SWF over standard portfolio allocation criteria. Allowing domestic investment can make SWFs the target for rent-seeking capture, a latent risk in resource-rich countries with weak institutions that are not accountable to a strong and/or cohesive stakeholder group (e.g., pensioners). This suggests the danger of taking Temasek Holdings (Singapore) or Australia's Future Fund as a relevant benchmark in this area for SWFs in resource-rich developing countries. If an SWF were to undertake domestic financial investments, they should be restricted to commercial projects (with public policy–motivated projects undertaken through the national budget) and be subject to strong governance criteria and transparency requirements, as highlighted in chapters 8 and 11.[6]

III. COHESION OF INSTITUTIONAL CONTROL AND ACCOUNTABILITY PROCEDURES

The following PFM-oriented principles help ensure proper institutional control over, and accountability of, SWFs: (a) clear roles and responsibilities; and (b) robust accountability and transparency procedures.

CLARITY OF ROLES AND RESPONSIBILITIES: Clear roles and responsibilities are essential to enhance the legitimacy, performance, and accountability of an SWF. Governments should be able to control or exercise ownership over "fiscal" SWFs, whereas an SWF should have the capacity to manage its financial assets at arm's length from the government. Therefore, an SWF's institutional and organizational structures should clearly distinguish decision making by the owner government (which should set the strategic investment and accountability directives) from operational execution. Among various options, two models are deemed best practice from a PFM perspective: (a) the SWF as an account or pool of assets (e.g., Chile, Norway); and (b) the SWF as a separate legal entity for the management of financial assets only (e.g., Australia, New Zealand).

ROBUST ACCOUNTABILITY AND TRANSPARENCY PROCEDURES: The success of an SWF depends in large part on the quality of its management, proper oversight, and the transparency of its operations, as recognized in the Santiago Principles. From a PFM perspective, the following elements are worth highlighting:

Oversight carried by several agencies and operational units (i.e., internal auditors, private independent auditing firms with a solid international reputation, external custodians);

An annual report and accompanying financial statements on the SWF's operations and performance, in accordance with recognized international standards; and

An annual audit of the SWF's operations and financial statements in line with international standards or equivalent national auditing standards. In many cases, the external audit report should be prepared by, or ultimately certified by, the auditor general and tabled in Parliament.

KEY ELEMENTS OF A BEST-PRACTICE SWF

For a best-practice SWF, inflows would be composed of the following:

Designated starting capital;

Automatic receipts of any actual fiscal surplus, which would be established through the application of a fiscal framework or rule designed to achieve the desired fiscal policy, including intertemporal redistribution; and

Other extraordinary sources, designated by the government.

The uses of SWF wealth would include the following:

Financing any actual fiscal deficit, which in turn should result from the application of the fiscal framework or rule (in line with the budget and supplementary budgets);

Extraordinary withdrawals consistent with escape clauses under the fiscal framework; and

Long-term objectives of savings assets such as pension liabilities; asset–liability operations designated by the government such as the prepayment of debt, and budget support following the depletion of commodity resources.

These withdrawal provisions would permit the complete depletion of the SWF if circumstances requiring it arose. If the government wanted to limit depletion (e.g., because of a commitment to preserve a proportion of the starting capital of the fund), a minimum level should be specified in advance, and operation of the fund should be suspended once it falls to this minimum. If such a point were reached, the fund would cease to operate, and budget deficits would need to be funded through extra borrowing.

CONCLUSION

The fact that the majority of SWFs have been created as instruments to support the implementation of fiscal policy by their owner governments makes it essential to align the design and operation of SWFs with standard PFM principles. Doing so ensures that the funds are subordinated to the ultimate fiscal policy objectives. For instance, the recent commodity "boom" years that led to an exponential growth in SWF financial assets

Table 2.1 Sovereign wealth funds and their objectives

Country	Name	Source of inflows	Objective
Algeria	Revenue Regulation Fund, 2000	Petroleum revenue	Stabilization
Angola	Angola Sovereign Fund, 2012	Petroleum revenue	Saving, development
Australia	Future Fund, 2006	Fiscal surpluses	Saving
Azerbaijan	State Oil Fund of the Republic of Azerbaijan, 1999	Petroleum revenue	Stabilization, saving
Bahrain, Kingdom of	Future Generations Reserve Fund, 2006	Petroleum revenue	Stabilization, saving
Botswana	Pula Fund, 1994	Mineral revenue	Saving
Brunei Darussalam	Brunei Investment Agency, 1983	Petroleum revenue	Saving
Canada (Alberta)	Alberta Heritage Savings Trust Fund, 1976	Petroleum revenue	Saving
Chad	Fund for Future Generations, 1999[a]	Petroleum revenue	Saving
Chile	Economic and Social Stabilization Fund, 2007	Mineral revenue	Stabilization
	Pension Reserve Fund, 2006	Mineral revenue	Saving
China	China Investment Corporation, 2007	International reserves	Reserve investment
Ecuador	Oil Stabilization Fund, 1999[a]	Petroleum revenue	Stabilization
Equatorial Guinea	Fund for Future Generations, 2002	Petroleum revenue	Saving
Gabon	Sovereign Fund of the Gabonese Republic, 1998	Petroleum revenue	Saving
Ghana	Petroleum Funds, 2011	Petroleum revenue	Stabilization, saving
Iran, Islamic Republic of	Oil Stabilization Fund, 1999	Petroleum revenue	Stabilization
Ireland	Ireland Strategic Investment Fund, 2014	Fiscal surpluses	Saving
Kazakhstan	National Fund of the Republic of Kazakhstan, 2000	Petroleum revenue	Stabilization, saving
Kiribati	Revenue Equalization Reserve Fund, 1956	Phosphates	Saving
Korea	Korea Investment Corporation, 2005	International reserves	Reserves investment
Kuwait	General Reserve Fund, 1960	Petroleum revenue	Stabilization, saving
Libya	Libyan Investment Authority, 2006	Petroleum revenue	Saving
Mexico	Oil Revenues Stabilization Fund, 2000	Petroleum revenue	Stabilization

Table 2.1 *(continued)*

Country	Name	Source of inflows	Objective
Mongolia	Fiscal Stability Fund, 2011	Mineral revenue	Stabilization
New Zealand	Superannuation Fund, 2001	Fiscal surpluses	Saving
Nigeria	Sovereign Investment Authority, 2011	Petroleum revenue	Development
Norway	Government Pension Fund Global, 1990	Petroleum revenue	Stabilization, saving
Oman	State General Reserve Fund, 1980	Petroleum revenue	Saving
Panama	Trust Fund for Development, 1995	Privatizations	Saving
	Panama Savings Fund, 2012	Panama Canal revenue	Saving
Papua New Guinea	Mineral Resource Stabilization Fund, 1974[a]	Mineral revenue	Stabilization
	Sovereign Wealth Fund, 2011	Gas (liquefied natural gas) revenue	Stabilization, development
Peru	Consolidated Reserve Fund, 1996	Privatizations	Saving
	Fiscal Stabilization Fund, 1999	Fiscal surpluses	Stabilization
Qatar	Qatar Investment Authority, 2005	Petroleum revenue	Saving
Russian Federation	National Wealth Fund, 2008	Petroleum revenue	Saving
	Reserve Fund, 2008	Petroleum revenue	Stabilization
Singapore	Government of Singapore Investment Corporation, 1981	International reserves	Reserve investment
	Temasek Holdings, 1974	Fiscal surpluses	Saving
Timor-Leste	Petroleum Fund, 2005	Petroleum revenue	Stabilization, saving
Trinidad and Tobago	Heritage and Stabilization Fund, 2000	Petroleum revenue	Stabilization, saving
United Arab Emirates	Abu Dhabi Investment Authority, 1976	Petroleum revenue	Saving
United States (Alaska)	Alaska Permanent Fund, 1976	Petroleum revenue	Saving
Venezuela, Bolivarian Republic of	Macroeconomic Stabilization Fund, 1998	Petroleum revenue	Stabilization
	National Development Fund, 2005	Petroleum revenue	Development

[a] No longer operational.

might have led to a focus on asset management and long-term invest-ments. However, the recent sharp drop in commodity prices should trans-late into large government financing needs, with accrued financial savings in SWFs an obvious source of financing. Against this background, in this chapter, we laid out key normative principles for a best-practice SWF in terms of financial flows (i.e., integrating SWF asset accumulation with underlying fiscal surpluses or deficits), proper fiscal roles (e.g., ensuring there is no authority to spend from SWFs), and governance (through clearly established responsibilities and accountability and transparency procedures).

NOTES

1. The Panama Savings Fund was established in 2012 to save additional revenue from the expanded Panama Canal, a renewable natural resource but one that is sus-ceptible to commodity price fluctuations and structural changes in the international shipping industry.

2. Chapter 9 discusses alternative fiscal rules for resource-rich developing countries and their links with SWFs.

3. This subsection is largely based on the work of Cheasty and Villafuerte (forthcoming).

4. The numerical fiscal targets from 2018 onward are consistent with a non-Canal deficit of 4 percent of gross domestic product (GDP) and a cap in the overall deficit of 0.5 percent of GDP. Projections suggest that the debt-to-GDP ratio will continue to decline to 25 percent whereas the SWF will accrue up to 9 percent of GDP in assets by 2025.

5. Baunsgaard et al. (2012) provide a comprehensive analysis of fiscal frameworks suited for resource-rich countries.

6. Gelb et al. (2014) offers some more detailed prescriptions in this area.

REFERENCES

Bartsch, U. 2006. "How Much Is Enough? Monte Carlo Simulations of an Oil Stabi-lization Fund for Nigeria," IMF Working Paper 06/142. Washington, DC: Inter-national Monetary Fund.

Baunsgaard, T., M. Villafuerte, M. Poplawski-Ribeiro, and C. Richmond. 2012. "Fiscal Frameworks for Resource Rich Developing Countries," IMF Staff Discussion Note 12/04. Washington, DC: International Monetary Fund.

Cheasty, A., and M. Villafuerte. Forthcoming. "Fiscal Issues in Designing Sovereign Wealth Funds".

Das, U., A. Mazarei, and H. van der Hoorn. 2010. *Economics of Sovereign Wealth Funds*. Washington, DC: International Monetary Fund.

Davis, J., R. Ossowski, J. Daniel, and S. Barnett. 2001. "Stabilization and Savings Funds for Nonrenewable Resources: Experiences and Fiscal Policy Implications," Occasional Paper 205. Washington, DC: International Monetary Fund.

Gelb, A. 1989. *Oil Windfalls: Blessing or Curse?* A World Bank Research Publication. New York: Oxford University Press.

Gelb, A., S. Tordo, H. Hallard, N. Arfaa, and G. Smith. 2014. "Sovereign Wealth Funds and Long-Term Development Finance: Risks and Opportunities," World Bank Policy Research Working Paper 6776. Washington, DC: World Bank.

Ossowski, R., M. Villafuerte, P. A. Medas, and T. Thomas. 2008. "The Role of Fiscal Institutions in Managing the Oil Boom," Occasional Paper 260. Washington, DC: International Monetary Fund.

Sachs, J. D., and A. M. Warner. 1999. "The Big Push, Natural Resource Booms and Growth," *Journal of Development Economics* 59, no. 1: 43–76.

Truman, E. 2010. *Sovereign Wealth Funds: Threat or Salvation.* Washington, DC: Peter J. Peterson Institute for International Economics.

CHAPTER 3

Sovereign Wealth Funds as Long-Term Investors

TAKING ADVANTAGE OF UNIQUE ENDOWMENTS

Adrian Orr
Guardians of the New Zealand Superannuation Fund

While attracting considerable political and regulatory scrutiny and often being a source of controversy, sovereign wealth funds (SWFs) are simply pools of nationally owned financial assets that are managed or invested for specific economic purposes (see Epstein and Rose 2009; Cata Backer 2010). These include intergenerational transfers; retaining, growing, and diversifying wealth arising from temporary commodity revenue windfalls; stabilization funds established to assist the balancing of short-term fiscal positions for a government; and special-purpose buffer funds designed to save for a specific purpose in the future. Sovereign wealth funds provide the opportunity for increased global economic integration, intergenerational wealth sharing, capital market development, and the promotion of responsible investment practices.

Two structural developments over the past decade have led to a much wider acceptance of the role of SWFs in twenty-first century global financial markets. First, the global financial crisis suddenly generated a sharp increase in demand for the type of long-term, countercyclical, and contrarian capital that SWFs can provide. Second, knowledge and understanding have grown between host and recipient nations of SWF capital, assisted by the voluntary development of the Santiago Principles) for SWF investment behavior, operations, and governance. These published principles are championed and overseen by the International Forum of Sovereign Wealth Funds, whose members are expected to implement the principles to the maximum extent possible. The Guardians of the New Zealand Superannuation Fund (the Guardians) contributed to the development of the Santiago Principles and implement and report on the New Zealand Superannuation Fund's (NZSF's) compliance with the relevant Santiago Principles.

The NZSF is an SWF that was established in 2001 to save and invest public money to help meet the future costs associated with providing universal superannuation (public pension benefits) to the citizens of New Zealand. In this chapter, I draw on the experience of the Guardians, the investment manager of the NZSF, to provide insights into how SWFs can develop investment strategies that take advantage of the unique endowments of SWFs. While the endowments I discuss in this chapter are specific to the case of the NZSF, the general lesson is that SWFs—like all other institutional investors—are endowed with particular characteristics (and subject to particular constraints) that shape their investment philosophies, strategies, and models. Understanding what these endowments are, and how to capitalize on them, is the key to fulfilling the mandate SWFs are tasked with achieving.

THE NEW ZEALAND SUPERANNUATION FUND: A BRIEF OVERVIEW

All New Zealanders aged sixty-five and over, subject to basic residency criteria, receive New Zealand superannuation (pension) payments. Currently, these are paid for entirely by today's taxpayers—that is, through "pay-as-you-go" funding. Over the next few decades, New Zealand's population will age significantly: Statistics New Zealand (2014) predicts that, by the late 2020s, the population aged sixty-five and over will surpass one million (more than 20 percent of the population). In 2009, this figure was 550,000 (around 13 percent of the population). By the late 2050s, it is estimated that one in every four New Zealanders will be aged sixty-five or older.[1] This means New Zealand will soon have more people of retirement age as a proportion of the population than ever before—and fewer working-age people to pay tax to fund the greater cost of retirement income.

The NZSF helps smooth the cost of superannuation as borne by today's taxpayers and those of future generations through "save-as-you-go" funding. The fund is legally constituted as a pool of assets on the Crown's balance sheet. Between 2003 and 2009, the government contributed NZ$14.88 billion (roughly US$10.61 billion)[2] to the NZSF. In the aftermath of the global financial crisis, these contributions were suspended but are scheduled to resume in 2020–2021. As of May 2016, the fund stood at NZ$30 billion (roughly US$21.40 billion). From around 2032–2033, the government will begin to withdraw money from the fund.

The NZSF is, however, expected to continue growing until it peaks (as a share of gross domestic product) in the 2080s.

The NZSF's status as an SWF bestows a number of important benefits: It focuses expectations and public understanding on the fund's long-term orientation; it positions the fund as a co-investor of choice, both inside and outside New Zealand; it receives certain international tax treatment benefits; and, as an active member of the international community of SWFs, the fund has opportunities to discuss investment practices with its peers.

THE GOVERNANCE OF THE NZSF: "DOUBLE ARM'S LENGTH" INDEPENDENCE

The Guardians are a Crown entity, operationally independent from Parliament, charged with managing the fund. The Guardians, a 115-person investment organization based in Auckland, invest government contributions—and returns generated from these investments—in New Zealand and internationally in order to grow the size of the NZSF over the long term.

The Guardians must invest the NZSF on a prudent, commercial basis. We are required to do so in a manner consistent with the following principles:

- Best-practice portfolio management;
- Maximizing return without undue risk to the NZSF as a whole; and
- Avoiding prejudice to New Zealand's reputation as a responsible member of the world community.

We are responsible for establishing investment policies, standards, and procedures for the NZSF. This includes determining the proportion of funds allocated to various types of investments and appointing external investment managers to manage different parts of the portfolio. As an autonomous Crown entity, we are accountable to the government, but enjoy operational independence in making investment decisions, and are overseen by an independent board.

The governor general appoints board members on the recommendation of the minister of finance. The minister's recommendation follows nominations from an independent nominating committee in consultation with representatives of other political parties in Parliament.

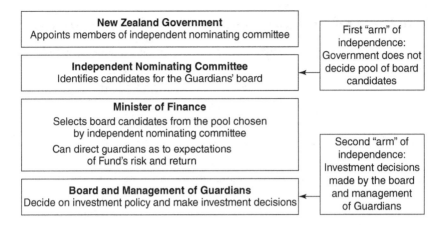

Figure 3.1   The "double arm's length" independence of the Guardians and the New Zealand Superannuation Fund.

This gives rise to the "double arm's length" independence of the Guardians and the NZSF (figure 3.1). At any given time, the board must consist of five to seven members, chosen for their experience, training, and expertise in the management of financial investments. Each board member is appointed for a term of up to five years, after which they may be reappointed.

The minister of finance may give directions to the Guardians regarding the government's expectations of fund performance—as long as such directions are consistent with the legislated duty to invest the fund on a prudent, commercial basis. All such directions must be tabled in Parliament. We are also subject to monitoring from the New Zealand Treasury and subject to regular reviews from auditors on behalf of the government. Every five years, an independent review of our performance is conducted and a report presented to Parliament. The minister of finance establishes the terms of the review and appoints an independent reviewer. The most recent report, by Promontory Financial Group, was published in 2014.[3]

The legislation establishing the NZSF and the Guardians enables an intergenerational investment vehicle to operate beyond a three-year election cycle. The fund's "double arm's length" separation between the government and the Guardians enables the government to delegate authority in exchange for accountability, while the Guardians are empowered to make independent, commercial investment decisions with a long-term perspective.

UNDERSTANDING AND BENEFITTING FROM ENDOWMENTS

Different investors have different attributes or endowments, which are intrinsic characteristics that typically lie outside the investor's control and are not a matter of choice. These endowments enable the exploitation of widely agreed-upon and deeply held investment beliefs. They prevent investors from pursuing unanchored, and therefore unfruitful, strategies. Being fully cognizant of a fund's particular endowments is an essential contributor to long-term success, as these endowments establish the broad parameters, opportunities, and constraints regarding how the fund invests to meet its objectives and mandate (Ang and Kjaer 2012).

By making full use of the NZSF's endowments, the Guardians are confident of adding many billions of dollars to national savings over the coming decades. This expectation is based on economic logic, long-term historical investment performances, and the modeling of likely future outcomes.

The NZSF's endowments can be summarized as follows:

1. **Sovereign status:** The NZSF is a pool of financial assets wholly owned by the Government of New Zealand. First, this establishes a beneficial taxation position for the fund. Second, counterparties tend to regard an investor's sovereign status favorably, which positions the NZSF as a potential co-investor of choice.

2. **Independent investment authority:** The Guardians' investment mandate requires that decisions be made on a purely commercial basis. The government may direct us only about its expectations of the NZSF's overall risk and return. This investment independence enables us to enter into investment arrangements that best suit the fund's purpose, with minimum agency risk. By "agency risk," we mean the risk that the fund's owner may suddenly decide to withdraw and force us into unanticipated liquidity situations and fire sales. The legislated investment mandate requires that the NZSF be managed in a transparent manner, with regard for environmental, social, and governance (ESG) standards.

3. **Defined liquidity profile:** The flow of cash into and out of the NZSF is governed by a public funding formula. This creates a certainty around the timing of cash flows, which enables us to invest in assets that other investors may eschew. The NZSF can buy assets when other market participants are constrained or have been forced to sell to meet their own liquidity demands.

4. **Long investment horizon:** In addition to having a defined liquidity profile, the investment structure of the NZSF is designed to exist for many decades. This long horizon affords us the flexibility to undertake investments with longer-term return characteristics, such as private equity. In addition, it means that the fund has tolerance for market volatility.

The endowments of the NZSF allow investments in illiquid assets; for example, forestry, infrastructure, and private (unlisted) companies. The fund's endowments enable exposure to risk premiums in equilibrium (as expressed through the fund's reference portfolio), as well as execution of value-adding contrarian strategies. The legislation and governance structure for the fund further confers operational independence to the Guardians, which economizes on agency risk.

ADVANTAGES AVAILABLE TO LONG-TERM INVESTORS

The legislation establishing the NZSF and the Guardians enables an intergenerational investment vehicle to operate beyond a three-year election cycle. Intergenerational fairness and setting wealth aside for future generations do not come naturally to the political economy of a society. It is common for current generations to want instant gratification and enjoy wealth now. Also, future generations do not get to vote for current governments, meaning their voice is never heard. Time inconsistency, myopia, and principal–agent problems all drive inappropriate risk taking and insufficient financial provisioning for the future. Not saving now to meet a known demographic challenge implies an assumption that the challenge can be met successfully at some future unknown date and interest rate.

Investing for the long term is largely concerned with the ability to control the deployment of risk capital at all times, and especially at times of market dislocation and turmoil. In other words, the long-term investor must have the resources (particularly human capital) and discipline to resist short-term forces that could cause a deviation from the long-term strategy. However, the term "long-term" does not have the same meaning for everyone and must be considered in the context of a particular set of goals, endowments, beliefs, and capabilities. The Guardians consider a long-term investor to be one that can hold any *investment strategy for as long as they wish.*

The NZSF is a true long-term investor, able to invest in a counter-cyclical and contrarian way across economic and financial cycles—and benefitting from its stable risk appetite. The Guardians are able to maintain necessary control because certain institutional characteristics are at the fore: a government and beneficiary that have granted a commercially focused mandate to a board that then decides independently on a desired risk–return profile and investment strategy for the fund; the board's support of management in the execution of the strategy; limited claims on capital; sufficient liquidity; and generally low levels of peer and agency risk.

The first advantage available to long-term investors is the ability to ride out much of the shorter-term volatility in financial market prices and not be forced to sell assets when their holdings are worth the least. Long-term investors should have a stable risk appetite and profit from the fact that markets suffer from periods of extreme risk aversion (that is, a nonstable or dynamic risk appetite) or outright panic (Barton and Wiseman 2014). The NZSF sets out its equilibrium risk appetite in its reference portfolio (box 3.1).

The second advantage for long-term investors is that a long-term investor can pursue more illiquid investment opportunities. Long-term investors should hold assets for as long as it remains prudent to do so and should not be forced to sell when doing so is not in their interest. The NZSF has demonstrated its ability to take on illiquid investments with long return horizons with the confidence that it has bought into the asset at a good price and will be paid a deserved illiquidity premium by owning assets that more short-term investors cannot.

A third advantage is that long-term investors are, in principle, not driven by reputational or career concerns derived from short-term return comparisons. For example, the NZSF has used its ability to sell insurance effectively when other investors have not been able to manage volatility. The fund's investments in catastrophe reinsurance and life settlements, and its various arbitrage strategies, have simply leveraged its stable risk appetite, investment horizon, and liquidity profile—generating higher long-term returns given the inability of other, more short-term–oriented investors to do the same.

The NZSF and other long-term investors have not only provided superior risk-adjusted returns to their owners, but, in doing so, have also increased stability in global financial markets. This is best illustrated by considering the alternative. The Guardians could have chosen *not* to use the full benefits of their operational independence and investment

Box 3.1: The Reference Portfolio—Benchmark and Reflection of Equilibrium Risk Appetite

The Guardians' board establishes the reference portfolio, and the fund's management implements it and tries to add value through active strategies. The fund's actual portfolio is the combination of these activities.

The reference portfolio benchmarks the performance of its actual portfolio and assesses whether the fund's active investment strategies are adding value. The reference portfolio, which is capable of meeting the fund's objectives over time, is a shadow, or notional, portfolio of passive, low-cost, listed investments suited to the fund's long-term investment horizon and risk profile. As table 3.1 shows, the reference portfolio has an 80/20 split between growth (equities) and fixed-income investments. Foreign-currency exposures are entirely hedged back to the New Zealand dollar.

The reference portfolio can change over time if the fund's purpose or endowments (e.g., its long-term investment horizon or its liquidity needs) change. Similarly, structural market developments may mean that a narrower or wider set of representative market exposures can be accessed passively and at a low cost. Finally, the board's beliefs about the equilibrium risk–return attributes of risk factors could change fundamentally in light of new evidence and experiences. All of these (and similar) developments could mean that the mix of assets in the reference portfolio no longer reflects what the board believes is an appropriate balance of risk and return, given the fund's endowments. Our aim, as an active investor, is to add more value after all costs to the fund than the simple adoption of the low-cost reference portfolio would. In order to generate returns over and above the reference portfolio, we employ a number of active strategies that bring a higher expected return and/or offer diversification benefits, albeit with more complexity and cost. These strategies include (i) investing in a range of illiquid assets—including infrastructure, private equity, and timber; (ii) undertaking extensive due diligence and external manager monitoring to ensure we choose the most effective and skilled investment managers; and (iii) periodically adjusting the fund's exposure to various asset classes in the actual portfolio, using its long-term horizon to take advantage of market volatility (also known as strategic tilting).

The reference portfolio provides a clear and transparent way for us to (i) estimate the fund's expected returns; (ii) benchmark the value added by active investment returns generated by the Guardians net of all costs (i.e., the deviations from the reference portfolio made through the actual portfolio and dynamic strategies); and (iii) be clear about the hurdles active investments need to overcome in order to justify our existence and strategies.

The reference portfolio approach encourages an emphasis on the underlying economic drivers of risk, returns, and correlations (such as economic growth, inflation, liquidity, and agency risks) rather than on asset classes per se. Allocating capital through these lenses can improve the true level of diversification of the NZSF, relative to a more traditional strategic asset allocation approach. The reference portfolio also encourages greater separation and delegation of value-adding activities from the board to internal management. This approach allows the board to focus on governance regarding the risk allocation and investment process and allows management to focus on adding value to the portfolio.

Table 3.1   The New Zealand Superannuation Fund reference portfolio

Asset class	Percentage of reference portfolio
Global equities	75%
New Zealand equities	5%
Total growth	80%
Fixed income	20%
Total	100%
Foreign currency exposure	0%

mandate by adopting a path of less overall financial risk exposure (and, by definition, lower long-term investment returns). Likewise, they could have chosen simply to invest passively and avoid strategies such as exploiting an illiquidity risk premium and investing in a contrarian, countercyclical manner. Such an investment approach involving, for example, government bonds, selling equity as the global share markets declined, or adhering to a predetermined benchmark (to which the responsibility for poor performance can then be attributed) is an easier approach for fund managers to implement. Such an investment model would significantly reduce the scope for criticism in light of the extensive public scrutiny that the Guardians are under, given the monthly, quarterly, and annual reporting on NZSF performance, their relative lack of local long-term investor comparisons, and their disclosure obligations as a Crown entity.

By contrast, the NZSF and other similar investors *do* take advantage of their longer investment horizons, which has a stabilizing impact on global financial markets. The majority of market participants are unable, for fundamental or behavioral reasons, to invest in a countercyclical way. Consequently, they tend to sell assets and risk exposures when prices are falling and vice versa. A study by the International Monetary Fund investigated the causes of the observed procyclical behavior of institutional investors during the global financial crisis and identified the destabilizing effects of "institutional herding" (Papaioannou et al. 2013). Institutional herding occurred, with growing concerns about so-called "capital preservation" as the crisis intensified. Several investors responded by abandoning long-term investment strategies, reducing risk exposures, and switching to safer asset classes, usually with the intention of switching back as soon as market conditions improved.

These actions were generally misguided for reasons that could have been predicted at the time. First, market prices had already plummeted before the decision-making capability of most institutions could have reacted—hence, investors were selling procyclically and therefore locking in losses. Second, the residual fear in the market and the "blamestorming" among boards meant that many investors did not get back into risk assets until well after the global recovery in asset prices was underway. The net outcome is that institutional herding destroyed wealth, increased financial market volatility, and led to the demise of many sensible long-term investment strategies. The temptation to concede to short-term market fluctuations is a trap that significant swathes of the global investment community consistently fall into.

Fortunately, for investors able to maintain a long-term focus, these oft-repeated mistakes increase their competitive advantage. Bearing this in mind, at the height of the crisis, we consciously chose to remain committed to the NZSF's long-term investment horizon and actively sought opportunities arising from the short-termism of other investors. In doing so, we avoided the perils of underutilizing the NZSF's investment mandate and endowments or adjusting our risk appetite to suit the prevailing climate of investor paranoia. During the crisis, we asked ourselves three critical questions. First, have our investment beliefs been challenged (e.g., will markets not normalize and revert to their respective means in the long run, as previously believed)? Second, is our strategy correct (i.e., buying more of an asset when its price has fallen and expected returns have therefore risen)? And third, do we have the capability to manage day-to-day financial operations in an unprecedented credit environment?

Both operational independence and governance clarity were critical to our capacity to stay the course, setting the NZSF apart from a large number of its peers. The Guardians' global recognition as a leader in long-term investing, especially among SWFs, lies in its ability to design and implement an investment framework that essentially institutionalizes contrarian and countercyclical investment, based on the NZSF's endowments, in particular its long-term orientation. In the following section, I discuss how this framework evolved, how it is implemented, and the NZSF's track record in implementing it.

EMBRACING A CONTRARIAN STRATEGY

The NZSF has experienced a volatile economic and investment environment since it started investing government contributions in September 2003. This period included the recovery from the collapse of the dot-com bubble, an international credit crunch, a full-blown global financial crisis, the rise of emerging and frontier markets, a global commodity boom, the near demise of the European currency union, and record-low interest rates. Underlying these short-term fluctuations is an incredible transformation of the global economy in terms of demographics, urban migration, and rising per capita incomes. Long-term investors must understand and prepare themselves to benefit from such underlying trends. Throughout its initial years, the NZSF has demonstrated an ability not only to withstand inevitable short-term volatility (both in rising and falling asset prices), but also benefit from that volatility along the way. It has demonstrated an ability to rebalance its portfolio back to target risk levels during periods of volatility. Rebalancing implies investing in a contrarian manner when extreme risk aversion is evident in asset prices and the behavior of other investors.

Thirteen years is a short period for measuring the success of a long-term investor such as the Guardians, whose confidence in forecasted returns peaks at periods of two decades ahead, when it expects to generate an average return of at least the risk-free rate plus 2.5 percent. A period of more than twenty years is long enough to reap the rewards of taking on ownership (equity) risk as an investor, as the rewards to owners of capital will generally outperform those of lenders (debt providers), as long as they are patient and responsible investors. As noted, the relative inability of most investors to wait this long is why long-term investors, such as the Guardians, can be even better rewarded. Evidence throughout economic history supports such long-term returns. Since 1926, returns to investors in the U.S. equity market have outperformed those of U.S. Treasury bills in every consecutive twenty-year period and the U.S. borrowing rate by over 2.5 percent about 90 percent of the time. These historical return characteristics inform the NZSF's investment model, which includes a clear (long) investment horizon, a well-diversified global portfolio, and an embedded investment discipline to "stay the course" during volatile times—and indeed to take advantage of volatile times, when other investors cannot.

Around two-thirds of the fund is invested passively, in line with the reference portfolio. We undertake active investment only when we are confident that doing so will, over the long term, be better than investing passively—either by improving the fund's returns, reducing risk, (e.g., through diversification), or both.

During our first years of investing, the fund's return expectations were often tested but ultimately vindicated, as returns remained within the confidence intervals initially established. Since inception, the NZSF has generated an average annual return of 9.57 percent (as at May 31, 2016, after costs and before New Zealand taxes). This is 5.15 percent ahead of the risk-free rate of return—that is, more than double the cost of government debt (as measured by the 90-day Treasury bill return). Table 3.2 outlines the fund's returns history and compares this to the risk-free rate of return and our own passive benchmark set out in the reference portfolio.

A focus on medium-term averages, however, masks the month-to-month and year-to-year volatility experienced by this type of growth-oriented fund. For example, during the height of the global financial crisis, the fund lost 29.84 percent in the twelve months to February 2009. Amid this global uncertainty, Crown capital contributions to the NZSF were halted as the government turned its priority to debt reduction. However, the NZSF has benefited in the years following the global financial crisis. It has grown rapidly, returning 15.8 percent per annum (as at May 31, 2016) since the trough. These returns were the result of the fund

Table 3.2   The New Zealand Superannuation Fund's performance since inception

Performance as at May 31, 2016	Since inception (September 30, 2003)
Actual Fund return	9.57% p.a.
NZ Treasury bill return	4.43% p.a.
Net return (actual Fund return minus NZ Treasury bill return)	5.14% p.a.
Estimated $ earned relative to NZ Treasury bills	NZ$13.547 billion
Reference Portfolio return	8.29% p.a.
Value added by active investment (actual Fund return minus Reference Portfolio return)	1.28% p.a.
Estimated $ earned relative to Reference Portfolio	NZ$4.382 billion

Abbreviation: p.a., per annum.
Source: New Zealand Superannuation Fund Monthly Performance and Portfolio Report, May 2016.

taking advantage of global asset prices that fell far below their medium-term value in the aftermath of the global financial crisis.

The NZSF's strategy and performance has demonstrated that it can be sensible, given the right endowments, for debt and investment to coexist. A degree of caution around debt is appropriate for individual families with mortgages, career risk, health risk, and the need to access cash for day-to-day requirements—and for institutions facing massive income shocks and uncertain liabilities. However, for a diversified and sovereign-backed investor like the NZSF, with its liquidity profile and its unusually long investment horizon, investment returns can comfortably exceed, and have exceeded, the cost of capital.

The most fundamental aspect of any countercyclical investment strategy is that the investor's appetite for risk should remain stable throughout the economic and financial cycle. Accordingly, the NZSF's risk appetite remained constant throughout its turbulent first decade of investing. Rebalancing policies, which ensure that the portfolio retains the targeted level of risk and balance of risk exposures even when asset prices (and perceived risk) move, are an important reflection of the fund's constant risk appetite. For example, if the fund seeks to hold at least 50 percent in global equities, it will purchase more of these assets as the value of equities falls with a mark-to-market price decline, while selling other assets whose value has risen (and vice versa).

ACTIVE INVESTMENT STRATEGIES AND IMPLEMENTATION

The Guardians introduced a number of active contrarian, or counter-cyclical, investment strategies, such as strategic tilting, selling rather than buying insurance, and being opportunistic in direct investing in private markets when there is a clear gap between the current price and an asset's long-term value. With these simple investment strategies, it joined a minority group of disciplined contrarian, or countercyclical, investors.

The Guardians do not purport to forecast market troughs or peaks, which it regards as a futile practice that too often leads to procyclical investment behavior and missed opportunities. Instead, as a long-term investor, we maintain a focus on the NZSF's horizon and liquidity profile, and on our investment beliefs. We consciously focus on the NZSF's robustness to financial volatility and seek to ascertain how the fund could gain from the shorter-term fads, fashions, and procyclical investment strategies of other investors that dominate the global financial environment. We are particularly focused on ensuring our investment strategies align with our overarching investment beliefs (table 3.3). Long-term and contrarian investing often requires the allocation of capital in times of considerable uncertainty, because these are the times when expected returns are the most attractive, even after adjusting for the higher risk. In doing so, we reiterate the central importance of anchoring the NZSF's strategy in its purpose, capabilities, and, ultimately, its managers' beliefs about the drivers of long-term returns.

The Guardians have adopted a "single-fund view," which is different from how most global funds and large institutional investors operate, with their emphasis on sticking to traditional asset-class allocations. The latter approach can lead to mechanistic and rigid "bucket filling" (in each asset class) and significant remuneration complexity as each asset-class expert demands their specific allocated portion.

We use risk budgets to ensure we allocate active risk consistently over baskets of investment opportunities. We believe risk budgets are the best means to ensure a single-portfolio focus for the whole team, rather than simply meeting an asset-class quota. Within a board-approved overall active risk budget for the fund, various investment opportunities with similar underlying drivers are grouped together into baskets by our investment committee. The investment opportunities in each basket have similar risk characteristics (e.g., diversifiers, market pricing, or asset pricing).

Table 3.3 The Guardians' investment beliefs

Investment decision	Investment beliefs	Investment facts
Governance and investment objectives	Clear governance and decision-making structures that promote decisiveness, efficiency, and accountability are effective and add value to the Fund.	It is important to be clear about investment objectives for the Fund, risk tolerance, and the time frame over which results are measured.
Asset allocation	Asset allocation is the key investment decision.	Risk and return are strongly related.
	Investors with a long-term horizon can outperform more short-term–focused investors over the long run.	There are varied investment risks that carry premiums or compensations. Illiquidity risk is one such premium.
		Investment diversification improves the risk-to-return (Sharpe) ratio of the Fund.
Asset class strategy and portfolio structure	Asset class expected returns are partly predictable, and returns can revert toward a mean over time.	Investment markets are competitive and dynamic, with active returns very difficult to find and constantly changing source.
		Market volatility tends to cluster over short horizons but reverts to the mean over longer horizons.
		Investment risks can be unbundled to make the fund more efficient. This includes the separation of market (beta) and investment-specific (alpha) investment manager skills.
Manager and investment selection	True skill in generating returns in excess of a manager's benchmark (i.e., pure alpha) is very rare. This makes it hard to identify and capture consistently.	The more efficient a market is, the more difficult it is for a manager to generate a return in excess of their benchmark.
	Some markets or strategies have characteristics that are conducive to a manager's ability to generate excess return.	The research signals and methods used by managers tend to commoditize over time through market forces.

Table 3.3   *(continued)*

Investment decision	Investment beliefs	Investment facts
	These characteristics tend to evolve slowly over time, although the shorter-term opportunity set available in any market or strategy can vary through the cycle.	In some cases, synthetic exposure to a market or factor can provide a guaranteed additional return to the fund; this represents an additional hurdle that an active manager must overcome.
	Most active return is driven by a combination of the research signals the manager is using, the conduciveness of their market to generating active returns, beta factors, and luck.	
	Responsible investors must have concern for environmental, social, and governance (ESG) factors because they are material to long-term returns.	
Execution		Managing fees and ensuring efficient implementation can prevent unnecessary cost.

The investment committee allocates the overall risk budget across these baskets. Teams of investment professionals monitor investment opportunities relating to a given basket, making risk allocation recommendations and informing investment and divestment activities.

Risk budgets help us assign capital judiciously, allowing investment professionals who are deeply familiar with investment opportunities to be closely involved in decision making. Our investment teams are partly incentivized and remunerated on how much value the NZSF as a whole added relative to the reference portfolio (over a four-year moving average period). This is partly why we chose a reference portfolio over a more elaborate strategic asset allocation (figure 3.2). The latter is a mixture of passive and active investment decisions, which can blur ownership of the risk and mask active investments that may not make economic sense.

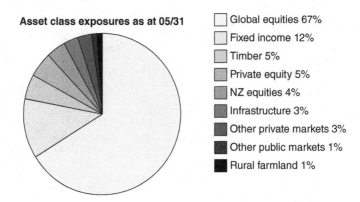

Asset class exposures as at 05/31

- Global equities 67%
- Fixed income 12%
- Timber 5%
- Private equity 5%
- NZ equities 4%
- Infrastructure 3%
- Other private markets 3%
- Other public markets 1%
- Rural farmland 1%

Figure 3.2 The New Zealand Superannuation Fund's actual portfolio (as of May 2016).

Source: Guardians of New Zealand Superannuation, "Monthly Performance and Portfolio Report—May 2016."

CONCLUSION

It is increasingly understood that SWFs are an important institutional commitment to achieving the difficult task of long-term investment. The NZSF is an SWF that has gained some recognition for its governance, transparency, and innovation. The NZSF experience may offer insights into the investment strategies that can position SWFs to benefit from both anticipated and unanticipated future developments.

First, the NZSF experience underlines the importance of understanding and capitalizing on the unique endowments of a fund. In the case of the NZSF, the most important endowments are its sovereign status, its enabling legislation and governance model that establish a "double arm's length" independence from the government owner, a long investment horizon, and a defined liquidity profile. These endowments allow the NZSF to be a true long-term investor, able to invest in a countercyclical and contrarian way across economic and financial cycles—and benefitting from its stable risk appetite. Second, the NZSF example highlights the importance of having an agreed-upon and clearly articulated set of investment beliefs—to ensure the disciplined selection of investment strategies and to use as a compass for decision making in times of market stress.

NOTES

1. For the latest projections, see Statistics New Zealand's (2014) *National Population Projections*, released in November 2014.

2. Using the exchange rate of NZ$1.40 = US$1 as of May 2016.

3. See "Final Report—Review of the Guardians of New Zealand Superannuation," available at www.nzsuperfund.co.nz/sites/default/files/documents-sys/2014%20 Independent%20Review%20by%20Promontory.pdf.

REFERENCES

Ang, A., and K. Kjaer. 2012. "Investing for the Long Run," Netspar Discussion Paper No. 11/2011-104. Tilburg, Netherlands: Network for Studies on Pensions, Aging and Retirement.

Barton, D., and M. Wiseman. 2014. "Focusing Capital on the Long Term," *Harvard Business Review* January–February.

Cata Backer, L. 2010. "Sovereign Wealth Funds as Regulatory Chameleons," *Georgetown Journal of International Law* 41, no. 2: 428–429.

Epstein, R., and A. Rose. 2009. "The Regulation of Sovereign Wealth Funds: The Virtues of Going Slow," *University of Chicago Law Review* 76, no. 111: 111–134.

Guardians of New Zealand Superannuation. 2016. "Monthly Performance and Portfolio Report—May 2016." Auckland, New Zealand: New Zealand Superannuation Fund. www.nzsuperfund.co.nz/sites/default/files/documents-sys/May_2016 _Performance_Report.pdf.

Papaioannou, M., J. Park, J. Philman, and H. van der Hoorn. 2013. "Procyclical Behavior of Institutional Investors During the Recent Financial Crisis: Causes, Impacts, and Challenges," IMF Working Paper WP/13/193. Washington, DC: International Monetary Fund.

Statistics New Zealand. 2014. "National Population Projections." Wellington, New Zealand: Statistics New Zealand. www.stats.govt.nz/browse_for_stats/population /estimates_and_projections/NationalPopulationProjections_HOTP2014.aspx.

CHAPTER 4

The Governance Implications of the Increasing Levels of Direct Investment of Sovereign Wealth Funds

Robert Ohrenstein and James White
KPMG

Over the past decade, there has been an extraordinary level of development among sovereign wealth funds (SWFs), as well as an increased awareness of their presence and activities. The more established SWFs have gradually moved into new asset classes and collectively manage a rising share of their assets in house rather than relying on third-party managers. A number of the larger and more established SWFs have evolved into sophisticated investors, capable of executing direct investment strategies, particularly in private (or unlisted) markets around real estate, infrastructure, and private equity. This chapter examines how a number of key trends around these developments have impacted the governance of SWFs.

Any meaningful discussion of SWF governance needs to include an awareness that these public institutions operate within the prevailing political environment of their home countries. Sovereign wealth funds generally, and particularly with respect to their activities in direct private investments, are discreet, even in comparison to the private equity industry, which has itself faced criticism from investors, politicians, and regulators for its lack of transparency. As such, there is a shortage of publicly available data, where even specialist information providers with extensive research capabilities are unlikely to capture a complete picture of all direct investments by sovereign investors. (See chapter 7 for a discussion of the lack of available data on SWF investments in domestic markets, much of which are also direct investments in private markets.) In this chapter, we make use of some data sources on the direct investments of SWFs but also draw largely on our general observations.[1] Similar to the analysis in chapter 7, we also draw on the experiences of other state or public investment vehicles (e.g., state pension funds and wholly government-owned state investment companies) that, while not strictly meeting the defining criteria of SWFs, nevertheless possess certain similar characteristics and provide a wider base for comparison.

THE EVOLUTION OF SOVEREIGN WEALTH FUND INVESTMENT STRATEGIES

Sovereign wealth funds pursue vastly different investment strategies, driven by their respective investment objectives or mandates, available human capital, relative organization maturity, and sophistication. As a number of contributors to this volume point out, it is also important to recognize that some SWFs have objectives beyond purely financial returns, such as promoting economic and social development, encouraging industrial or geographical diversification, or supporting government policy in such areas as environmental sustainability.

In order to facilitate the consideration of governance issues, it is helpful to make some general observations on the usual evolution of investment strategies. Typically, when an SWF is created, and in its early stages, third-party fund managers will be used with a high proportion of assets being held in equity and fixed-income securities traded on recognized and liquid public markets. This is a relatively straightforward model to govern, as it does not rely on building extensive internal resources and allows for an easier deployment and monitoring of considerable amounts of capital. As SWFs mature and develop their internal expertise, more capital is often gradually managed in house, and exposure to other more complex alternative asset classes is sought, again using third-party fund managers while potentially retaining some discretion over asset allocation. The final stage of development is to make direct investments, often initially as sizeable minority positions in publicly quoted companies, then as co-investors in private investments, typically alongside an alternative investment manager, and ultimately as a lead investor. In the main, only the more established funds that have accumulated considerable capital, both financial and human, have substantial direct private investment programs. It is this last stage of development that requires the greatest step change in governance within an SWF. (See chapters 6 and 14 for related discussions of the governance and organizational implications of introducing more complex investment strategies.)

The propensity of an SWF to make direct private investments is also dependent upon the nature and objectives of the fund. The strategic rationale of SWF funds can broadly be characterized into four most common types: (i) stabilization funds protecting against commodity or currency volatility; (ii) development funds assisting the development or diversification of the host economy; (iii) pension reserve funds for future pension provision; and (iv) savings funds investing commodity profits or currency surpluses in financial assets to ensure the benefits of these surpluses can be shared intergenerationally. A single fund may have more than one aim. Stabilization funds typically require a more liquid investment portfolio and hence have a relatively low allocation to direct investments. Development funds investing in infrastructure or industrial development tend to have a greater propensity toward direct investment, as an SWF may be encouraged to act as cornerstone investor to initiate such projects. Pension reserve funds and savings funds have the capacity to carry more illiquid investments owing to their longer-term investment horizon and may therefore have somewhat broader investment mandates, giving management more flexibility and independence over asset allocation.

DIRECT INVESTMENTS BY SOVEREIGN WEALTH FUNDS: TYPES AND TRENDS

Direct investments can take a number of forms: the first distinction is between direct investments in public and private markets, and then, within private markets, whether the investment is made on an individual basis or is structured as a co-investment (with the SWF acting as a senior or junior partner to third-party managers, investors, or corporations). The most common type of direct investment by SWFs is large strategic investments (but usually minority) in listed companies. These are distinguished from holdings forming part of an overall listed equity portfolio by their significant size and the pursuit of a concentrated overweight exposure to a particular asset or security. While these investments are direct, they are also somewhat passive: although they may come with a nonexecutive board seat, they do not demand active participation in the investee company's underlying management or governance processes. For investments in public companies, the role is typically limited to providing limited, high-level guidance and influence, without any direct involvement in executive management. These investments, while

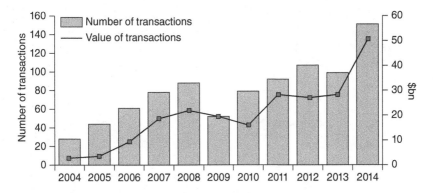

Figure 4.1   The direct investment transaction volumes and values of sovereign wealth funds, 2004–2014.

Source: Sovereign Wealth Center transaction database (as of June 2015).

possibly large in the context of the portfolio of assets, are less challenging from a governance perspective. Figure 4.1 shows how the annual level of direct investment has risen consistently and substantially in recent years, as more SWFs have undertaken direct investments and the more established funds that have been undertaking direct investment for many years have further increased the depth and capacity of their existing direct investment teams.

Complexity, and therefore demands on the governance structure, is added when direct investments are made in private companies. Here, the investment necessarily becomes illiquid and, depending on the level of shareholding, usually includes provisions for the shareholder to participate in management supervision through board participation (regardless of whether this is actually taken up). A further distinction of this type of investment depends on whether these investments are made solely by an SWF or structured as a joint venture or co-investment alongside an asset manager. Examples of the latter include co-investments in buyouts alongside private equity managers or other fund managers, such as real estate managers, and joint ventures with corporate partners. Typically, third-party managers will take the lead on structuring the transaction and will subsequently participate in and oversee the operational management team. However, SWFs are frequently active participants in both processes, allowing them to leverage the specialist skills and experience of co-investees, which correspondingly reduces operational risks.

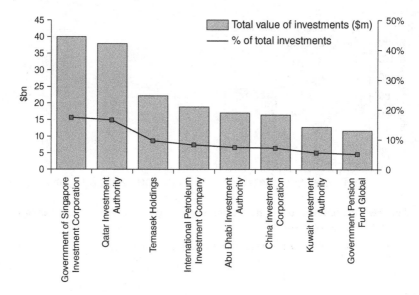

Figure 4.2   Direct investments undertaken by leading sovereign wealth funds (2004–2014) and the proportion of these direct investments relative to the overall funds.

Sources: Sovereign Wealth Center transaction database (as of June 2015); Preqin Sovereign Wealth Fund Review, 2015.

Demands upon an organizational structure are clearly highest when an SWF leads the investment in a directly controlled private transaction, as here the SWF must manage its investment structuring and active shareholder participation in house.

As shown in figure 4.2, a relatively small number of SWFs have substantial levels of direct investments (i.e., more than 5 percent of their portfolios): of the 774 recorded direct foreign investments, 73% were undertaken by the eight most active investors. Further, these investments (ignoring holdings of "national assets"; that is, where the SWF holds shareholdings of strategically important companies, such as airlines and telecommunications networks, on behalf of the government) still account for relatively modest proportions of their portfolios—the largest share of direct investments, managed by the Government of Singapore Investment Corporation, still accounts for only an estimated 17.4 percent of its portfolio. Figure 4.3 illustrates the nature of investments being undertaken and whether capital was deployed domestically or outside the SWF's host nation.

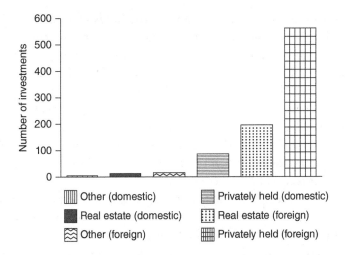

Figure 4.3   Domestic versus nondomestic direct investments by sovereign wealth funds (2004–2014).

Source: Sovereign Wealth Center transaction database (as of June 2015).

EXTERNAL PRESSURE FOR ENHANCED GOVERNANCE

Prior to the global financial crisis that began in 2008, there was a general unease concerning direct investment by SWFs within the Organisation for Economic Co-operation and Development (OECD) community, particularly concerning whether investments were being made for noneconomic strategic reasons. This concern was manifest in some governments reacting negatively to the prospect of direct investments being made by SWFs, particularly with regard to companies those governments deemed strategically important (Thatcher 2013). The most publicized example is the American government's blocking of Dubai Ports World's (owned by Dubai World) planned acquisition of a number of port facilities in the United States. Although a subsequent study by Avendaño and Santiso (2009) found no empirical evidence of this, perception seems to have overridden reality. Concerns were also expressed regarding the transparency and governance of SWFs. In response to these pressures, twenty-four of the largest SWFs chose to address this by signing on to the Santiago Principles.

Full compliance with these principles is by no means universal, and some commentators suggest that, in fact, they do not set a particularly high bar (Gelpern 2010). However, this is not surprising given the widely differing domestic political systems of the funds that established them: political reality dictates that disclosure and governance practices are going to differ among democratic countries, countries with political monopolies, and countries with absolute monarchies. The robustness, or otherwise, of how SWFs have dealt with implementing the Santiago Principles also varies considerably. However, the transparency of SWFs has generally increased, as illustrated by the generally upward trend scores assigned by independent monitoring authorities, notably the Sovereign Wealth Fund Scoreboard published by the Peterson Institute for International Economics (Bagnall and Truman 2013).

To a large extent, external regulatory and political pressure on SWF governance and transparency has abated. As the economic environment deteriorated at the height of the financial crisis, capital became significantly scarcer; and, consequently, previous sensitivities regarding SWF investment appeared to fall away rather quickly as these funds became one of the few sources of substantial liquidity. As a result, governments and corporates alike increasingly courted SWFs, reducing the external pressure for more transparent governance and disclosure.

DOMESTIC DRIVERS OF GOVERNANCE

The domestic political environment of the sponsoring country is also a factor influencing SWF governance. More democratic countries face higher levels of public scrutiny and consequently pressure for transparent governance of public funds. Interestingly, transparency may in some circumstances be a disadvantage, as organizations can be more flexible and responsive to opportunities outside the public limelight. Sovereign wealth funds also have to comply with applicable domestic law and generally accepted codes of corporate governance in host countries. This may encourage an SWF not only to have robust governance within the fund itself, but also to require that certain standards of governance be maintained within its key investee companies.

Any governance framework obviously must exist within the bounds of the legal structure of the fund. A country's government or leadership ultimately sits at the top of the governance structure of all SWFs as owner of the assets on behalf of its people. The government is therefore ultimately responsible for setting the investment mandate. There are various approaches to the structure of the fund manager and how assets are held. One approach is for the ministry of finance to have management responsibility whereby the fund becomes integral to government and is essentially run by public employees. However, many governments have chosen to adopt alternative structures, such as the ministry of finance forming a separate legal entity to manage the fund's assets or possibly going a step further by legally transferring the assets to a wholly state-owned investment company. The relative proximity of the assets and the manager of the fund to government is one of the factors that may affect the influence of the government on the day-to-day management of the fund over and above that prescribed by the investment mandate.

Domestic direct investments, in particular those made by funds with a national development mandate, may have different governance considerations (also discussed in chapters 5, 6, 7, and 8). In these circumstances, it may be appropriate for the government to have a more direct influence over the investment decisions of a fund to ensure coordination with wider government policy. These investments often have additional investment criteria beyond pure financial return. This wider national interest may also be evident in times of economic stress, when an SWF may be seen by a government as a readily available form of liquidity to support broader domestic policy. The presence of noneconomic factors beyond fund returns and the safeguarding of fund assets makes commenting on governance in these circumstances somewhat more subjective. We therefore focus on economic investing, where the emphasis is on measurable financial returns.

GOVERNANCE IMPLICATIONS OF DIRECT INVESTMENT

Direct investment increases the demands on governance in that such investments are sizeable and, in the case of private transactions, typically illiquid and highly bespoke structured transactions. These latter transactions are far more complex to execute than direct investments in or trading of listed public securities; hence, our analysis concentrates on direct investments in private markets. Although capable of generating high returns and potentially adding to portfolio diversification from market risk, these investments also have considerable risks attached to them, including the concentration of capital and high execution complexity.

Consequently, the first governance challenge in this situation is deciding whether to have a direct private investment strategy at all—which is typically determined by the host government. One of the largest SWFs, managed by Norges Bank Investment Management, has adopted a relatively conservative position in this regard. For many years, its investments were limited to listed securities, and only in recent years has the fund been permitted to make direct investments. Moreover, direct investments are presently only in real estate assets, which typically carry lower operational risk.

For smaller SWFs in particular, direct investments may not make sense, as building the capability internally to make these investments may not be financially beneficial, unless enough capital can be allocated and the potential return premium (after taking into account the additional running costs) over other investment classes is sufficient. Research by Bortolotti and co-authors (2009) into the direct investment returns of SWFs suggests that returns have underperformed appropriately benchmarked returns, although the study focused on direct investments in public companies owing to limitations in data availability.

Assuming a direct investment strategy in private markets is mandated and deemed appropriate, the governance challenges can be broken down into two broad areas: first, deciding on an appropriate strategy, and, second, implementing that strategy effectively. Broadly, these are the respective responsibilities of what could be termed the strategic oversight board and the operational oversight provided by executive management.

STRATEGIC GOVERNANCE FRAMEWORKS

The initial task of those charged with governance is to decide on an appropriate direct private investment strategy. Key inputs into this decision are risk appetite and the extent to which it is possible to hire expertise or develop skills internally. A progressive approach is generally advisable. If we consider the direct private investment landscape, potential areas of direct investment vary in their risk, benchmark returns, and operational complexity. At the lower end of the spectrum is real estate investing in developed assets that, at the premium end of the market, offer more stable cash flows for a relatively low level of operational risk. Infrastructure assets have similar characteristics, albeit in most cases with more operational complexity. Direct private investments in commercial enterprises can offer higher potential returns but usually attract the most operational risk. Such risk may be better managed through co-investing alongside an institutional private equity investor. Given these risk profiles, and the maturity stage of many of the funds, it is perhaps unsurprising to find direct investments more prevalent at the lower end of the risk spectrum and nondomestic direct investments at the higher end, often made alongside private equity firms in co-investment strategies to leverage the expertise of specialist managers.

From a strategic governance perspective, it therefore makes sense to start a direct investment strategy at the lower-risk end of the direct investment spectrum. This is likely a contributing factor to the fact that real estate (and high-end hospitality) assets have long been a favorite with sovereign investors. This is an area that has seen substantial direct investment activity, frequently at the premium end of the market;[2] with their comparatively low levels of operational risk and complexity, steady income streams, and potential for long-term capital appreciation, these types of assets are highly suited to the long-term objectives of SWFs.

As the larger SWFs have developed, they have increasingly moved into other asset classes, but relatively few have substantial allocations to investments in private commercial companies. Almost three-quarters of all private direct investment captured by the Sovereign Wealth Center database was undertaken by the top eight SWFs most active in this area. Many investors have preferred to place funds with private equity managers and then seek co-investment on a selective basis in their portfolio companies. This approach reduces overall management fees and the cost of carried interest (the private equity manager's share of the capital profits on investments) and allows SWFs to leverage the expertise of external managers, while building their own internal capabilities. A similar model involves having an individual "managed account" with a private equity manager, which enables the investor to access various platforms and investments run by the private equity manager, affording the investors greater discretion than the normal approach under the typical structured private equity fund. (Under the latter model, once a commitment is made to a fund by the investor, there is usually no subsequent discretion exercisable over how those funds are deployed.)

Both strategies offer progression toward direct investing. However, some research has suggested that, even with the cost advantage of partially disintermediating private equity managers and leveraging their expertise, there is material execution risk. For example, a study that considered all co-investment and not just that undertaken by SWFs, found that the returns of co-investments of individual assets may not match the returns generated by a portfolio of the funds themselves (Auerbach and Pradhan 2015). There could be a number of factors explaining this outcome, such as general partners not offering co-investment in the best deals, investors not picking the right deals, or the private equity funds doing a better job of timing investments over the economic cycle.

Widely cited research by Bernstein, Lerner, and Schoar (2013) suggests that SWFs have a greater propensity to invest when prices are higher, which would lead to suboptimal performance over economic cycles. Additionally, the best private equity managers identify investment trends (and hence opportunities) earlier and may have a greater appetite for risk and contrarian investment theses in comparison to SWFs, who may be more conservative given their fiduciary duties over public funds. Whatever combination of factors is prevalent, for some funds, particularly those other than the largest funds, it is likely that the risks and costs of establishing and building a direct private investment team with a focus outside real estate are outweighed by the benefits of using private equity managers to obtain exposure in this investment area.

Consequently, governance decisions hinge on which types of investments SWFs should be allowed to make (e.g., sector, geography, size) and ensuring that the skills and capabilities of the team in place are sufficient to effectively manage the complexities of the types of investments being undertaken. The latter point is particularly interesting from a governance perspective, as returns in direct private investing may be heavily dependent on the talents of a few senior decision makers. Here, it makes sense to build skills progressively. More experienced direct private investors, such as Singapore's Government of Singapore Investment Corporation and Temasek Holdings and Abu Dhabi's Mubadala Development Company, now have deep levels of expertise across multiple strategies, whereas others are still developing in this regard. Other similar public, but not strictly sovereign, wealth fund organizations have reached similar levels of expertise; for example, Canadian pension investors, such as the Canada Pension Plan Investment Board and the Ontario Municipal Employees Retirement System.

The more complex the underlying assets, the more difficult it is likely to be to recruit the best people. Skills are more specialized, supply is shorter, and, for the most part, competition for talent is with private equity partnerships and similar direct investment organizations. (See chapters 6 and 14 for related discussions on the human resource implications of introducing more complex investment strategies). Rewards in the large or successful private equity partnerships can be substantial, and more senior staff are hard to recruit and retain, given the lucrative carry arrangements on funds with ten- to twelve-year life spans that effectively lock in senior staff for extended periods. Structuring remuneration packages is also likely to be critical. Insufficient overall packages are unlikely to attract the best talent, and paying market-based compensation could create issues in countries where public-service remuneration levels are relatively low. One solution is to have a high variable compensation component, but this in itself can influence investment behavior (as discussed in chapter 6). At the extremes, too high a variable component based on investment profitability may encourage low bidding for assets that could hinder capital deployment, and too low a variable component based on deal execution could encourage excessive pricing with consequential risk issues.

OPERATIONAL GOVERNANCE CHALLENGES

With direct investing in private markets, individual investment decisions become critically important, given illiquidity and high transaction costs. Systems for monitoring the underlying portfolio company performance and participating in its management oversight are required, as is a robust independent system to value assets periodically for reporting purposes. One of the key governance challenges is balancing exposure to different geographies, sectors, and investment vintages, and, in the case of direct investing in the domestic market, the risks of high concentrations of investments relative to the size of the economy. As discussed, many SWFs (such as those from Botswana, Chile, and Norway to name just a few) have mandates limiting domestic investment (as explained in chapter 5), whereas some funds, particularly those with a development mandate, are necessarily overweight in domestic investment. Getting this balance right given the long holding periods is clearly challenging. As evident in the case of Dubai, high concentrations of leveraged domestic investment can lead to high concentrations of risk. Sovereign wealth funds should also monitor sector concentration, particularly if they act as a holding vehicle for large national assets such as telecommunications, airline, banking, or utility companies.

The detailed investment appraisal and evaluation process in the context of direct private investment is significantly more complex than for most public investments and therefore requires a steep change in organizational capacity. The private nature of transactions enables vendors to make more detailed corporate information available to a limited number of potential acquirers or investors. This information then needs to be subject to thorough due diligence from a variety of perspectives, such as accounting, legal, commercial, and tax, and possibly also pensions, information technology, and regulatory. Most transactions also necessitate bespoke structures and extensive legal documentation. These all take time, money, and expertise either to perform or manage on an outsourced basis. Adequate controls and processes are required for all these procedures to ensure that opportunities and risks are adequately understood in order that an informed judgment can be made regarding whether an investment meets appropriate risk-adjusted returns criteria. These detailed processes are both costly and complex and hence challenging to manage and govern.

In respect of the broader governance around investment decisions, it makes sense to follow the private equity model of processes established to get a proposed investment to the point of signing, including, in particular, an investment committee that approves potential individual transactions at various stages in the acquisition process (rather than approving specific market exposure for broader portfolios of traded assets). An investment committee provides a review forum that ensures the wider system of checks and balances has been complied with and, ultimately, that the investment risks are understood and have been mitigated or managed to the extent possible.

It is important that the investment committee has the authority, independence, experience, and diversity of opinion to ensure rigorous debate. For a debate to be effective, a potential investment needs not only advocates supporting it, but also robust independent challenge. Regarding the suggestion of several empirical studies that returns from direct investing by SWFs underperform, the former chief investment officer and head of the private equities department of the Abu Dhabi Investment Authority suggests that one factor contributing to this may be that certain sovereign investors have an overreliance on—or do not adequately challenge—the investment theses underpinning deals originated on their behalf by investment banks (Sudarskis 2011). The much reported derivatives transaction between the Libyan Investment Authority and Goldman Sachs may be an example: The Libyan SWF had alleged that Goldman Sachs took advantage of its limited in-house capabilities to arrange complex derivative trades, which subsequently lost nearly all their value (Croft 2014).

Given investment banking fees are often fully contingent when investment banks advise SWFs on acquiring assets, respective economic incentives are not aligned. Consequently, a clear challenge is required to the key investment hypothesis and underlying assumptions. This challenge must be provided through robust due diligence, and here the research implies there may be some subtle differences in approach and execution between private equity houses and some sovereign investors. The inherent suggestion is that some SWFs may also make less use of external diligence providers and do more work internally. While this does not necessarily mean this work is compromised, two potential benefits of making use of external advisors need to be considered. First, specialized external suppliers can provide a greater depth of expertise in target sectors or the individual asset owing to their greater resources and hence ability to specialize. In addition, external consultants are objectively independent, whereas the degree of independence of internal diligence teams from those advocating the transaction may be less clear.

Once investments have been made, the organization has to establish a governance protocol to monitor and, depending on the structure and terms of the investment, participate in the oversight of the investee company. This is especially the case where the investment thesis itself may envisage some active changes in direction or strategy of operations. As active investors, SWFs will have to play a greater role in ensuring the success of their investments and will therefore need to acquire the appropriate skills to understand company performance and be effective board participants.

A critical element of this governance protocol is an effective risk management "middle office," whose task is to monitor the execution of the investment thesis and allow the early identification of issues or below-plan performance in portfolio companies. Efficient identification of issues enables early intervention and participation in the formulation of remedial action plans by company management. However, this process is not all about traditional risk management: it is just as important that the investor brings value-added skills to ensure that identified upsides in the investment theses are realized and that the shareholder return is maximized. Generally, SWFs are not yet well recognized for their ability to input strategically into their private investments. This is probably a factor of many of these investments still being minority investments that are, by their nature, more passive or being in relatively less complex asset classes, such as real estate. As the trend toward increased direct SWF investment in private markets continues, SWFs will need to recruit or develop these skills in house.

As for many investors, there were deep ramifications arising from the global financial crisis for SWFs. The sustained period of economic growth from the early 1990s until 2008 coincided with a large increase in aggregate assets under management of these funds and also some movement toward direct investing. These rapid changes posed developmental challenges for SWFs: For many, the sophistication of governance and risk management regimes lagged behind their capacity to deploy capital. Since the financial crisis, however, there has been a clear recognition that these functions were falling short of best practice in the wider investment management industry, and many have sought to address this perceived shortfall. In respect to direct investment, we have seen funds upgrading management information systems and processes for monitoring exposures in portfolio companies, resulting in higher-quality reporting and compliance controls. These efforts should lead to more effective supervision of investee companies and improved overall risk management.

The valuation of illiquid private investments is key in appraising the performance of a portfolio of private investments and is naturally highly judgmental and subjective. It is therefore critical that clear governance structures are established around the process with allowance for independent challenge. Methodologies should be clear and consistently applied, with best practice recommending the use of external guidelines, such as the International Private Equity and Venture Capital Valuation Guidelines. Such methodologies should be subject to scrutiny by management, independent of the deal and portfolio teams, and preferably by an independent external auditor.

Ultimately, exiting or realizing direct private investments are in some ways a greater governance challenge within the SWF community than for other direct investors. Most alternative asset managers operate closed-end funds with fixed lives of ten years, typically extendable for a further two, as well as fee arrangements that, in normal circumstances, usually encourage turnover of the underlying assets. In contrast, as evergreen funds, SWFs have no such considerations. This enables some SWFs to hold strategic domestic assets, such as airline and telecommunications companies, on an ongoing basis. While this ability could be a source of competitive advantage, it does have potential governance issues in that longer or permanent hold periods are possible. Moreover, there are further implications in terms of designing incentive schemes for direct investment teams: These may need to be more complex, as there may not be realizations upon which to base carried-interest–type incentive payments.

Incentive plans based on valuations may offer an alternative, although best practice would be to have a mechanism in place capable of adjusting for when valuations fall.

PORTFOLIO COMPANIES: GOVERNANCE AND COMPLIANCE

Sovereign wealth funds typically want to ensure governance structures in their portfolio companies are consistent with their own governance regimes and policies, which in turn reflect the policies of the sponsoring government. This goal can be achieved in a variety of ways, most commonly by an assessment of governance and corporate policy in the investment appraisal process and subsequently monitoring compliance. Some governments restrict investment in certain areas that are seen as incompatible with general government policy. Once an investment is made, the ability of the SWF to influence governance is dependent on its shareholding. Many SWFs, for example, have a preference for keeping ownership of nondomestic assets below 50 percent so that they do not legally control a portfolio company and therefore cannot be held directly accountable for unethical behavior or business decisions that may cause unwanted negative publicity in the host country. This issue can be challenging to manage, particularly if SWFs hold a portfolio company that is independently managed. This is often the case when an SWF acts as a holding entity for national strategic assets, such as airlines or natural resources.

Environmental, social, and governance (ESG) policy is one area in which some state investors, particularly some of the European public pension funds, have been influential in generating a shift in corporate behavior, governance, and disclosure. This shift initially manifested itself through pressure exerted on fund managers to ensure they had an active ESG program to monitor investee companies. ESG policy is now seen as a lever to drive effective policies within the companies in which SWFs directly invest (also discussed in chapter 11).

CONCLUSIONS, FUTURE TRENDS, AND POLICY IMPLICATIONS

While direct investment by SWFs has certainly grown over the last decade, this growth has been selective. A nondomestic direct investment policy may not suit all SWFs but tends to attract the larger funds with longer-term investment horizons and suitable resources to implement such an investment remit. In this chapter, we have analyzed what the shift toward larger direct investment programs requires in terms of more sophisticated investment and risk management processes, the skills and expertise of internal investment teams—and, as an overarching requirement for all SWFs pursuing this course, considerable investments in governance.

Overall levels of governance within the SWF community have continued to improve. Like many investors, they have had to confront a harsher investment environment in the aftermath of the global financial crisis. They have also reacted to concerns raised by governments, nongovernmental organizations, and the wider investment community. Those that have direct investment programs have likewise generally improved the governance of these asset classes. Recruitment of senior staff from some of the larger established private equity funds has improved expertise, and some funds have also made significant investments in their governance infrastructures.

However, within this general improvement, there is significant variation among SWFs in terms of the size (both relative and absolute) of direct investment programs—and the quality and sophistication of the governance processes around them. A small number of SWFs exhibit close to what can be regarded as best practice in the wider investment management and alternative asset communities. Unsurprisingly, larger funds with more direct investment experience are further along this journey than others. Certain SWFs have had well-publicized challenges with their direct investments over the past few years. However, it would likely be an oversimplification to attribute all these problems solely to governance failings. These issues must be put into context, since a number of privately held funds and alternative asset managers have also suffered significant losses. What these problems have done, however, is to act as a timely reminder that, following a long period of rising asset prices, direct investments remain inherently risky—especially when leveraged—and that best-practice governance has a strong role to play in mitigating and managing an acceptable level of risk.

We expect most SWFs to maintain relatively modest direct investment programs in terms of overall asset allocation. Co-investment models that leverage expertise from private equity managers are likely to be a popular model for many funds looking to raise the share of direct investments in their overall portfolio. Real estate is also likely see greater levels of direct investment from SWFs, given the favorable fit between the fundamental characteristics of the asset class and the mandates and requirements of SWFs, and the comparatively lower levels of operational risk associated with directly held real estate.

A major issue for SWFs (and indeed other long-term investors) seeking to increase direct investment is origination. Although the majority of large direct investment deals today are intermediated by investment banks familiar with SWFs, most sellers and management teams have not yet had significant dealings with these funds. In addition, most SWFs have not yet established reputations as value-enhancing active owners. These factors, along with strong competition for a presently limited supply of transactions, are likely to result in SWFs not always being on top of existing owners' preferred investors. That said, SWFs do have a number of unique differentiating features as substantial equity investors, including most notably a long-term investment horizon (and a reduced risk of exit determined by fund expiration owing to fixed-duration private equity funds or other fund performance management issues). This patient capital is attractive for many investors (as discussed in chapters 12 and 14). Sovereign wealth funds may also be attractive partners for those looking to expand operations into the host country or region or business owners who want to retain control of their businesses and sell a substantial minority, rather than majority, stake.

There has been an ongoing debate in the investment management industry as to whether these very significant investors are ultimately going to contribute towards disintermediating specialized fund managers, such as private equity and real estate managers. In our view, this is unlikely to happen in the short to medium term, as we expect that changes in the types of investments made by SWFs will be neutral to positive for third-party, alternative-asset fund managers. We anticipate more state investors making increased allocations to alternative asset classes via third-party fund managers than those reducing exposure to these managers by undertaking more direct investing activities in house. For some of the larger funds, if substantial capital allocations were to be invested directly in house, it would be hard to envisage these SWFs being able to scale expertise and capacity to a sufficient level, given that doing so would suggest running pools of capital well in excess of the largest global private equity managers (the larger SWFs have assets under management of several hundred billion dollars).

While some SWFs will use co-investment and managed accounts to gain direct investment experience and reduce management fees, for most, it will still make sense to retain a strong and mutually beneficial relationship with these managers. From a private equity manager's perspective, although co-investment may have some fee impact, it may also help managers to do deals on a larger scale than their committed capital may otherwise allow. Sovereign wealth funds may also seek further ways of cooperating with private equity funds to take advantage of differing returns expectations and holding periods. Providing opportunities for private equity fund managers to sell down stakes in assets prior to full exit is one strategy. In the future, this could develop into the acquisition of tails of portfolios from private equity managers where funds are approaching the end of fixed lives. These often contain companies that are steady rather than star performers and are therefore not attractive for secondary buyouts owing to lower growth prospects, and likewise may not have obvious trade buyers. This would enable the private equity manager to close out a fund and give an SWF some long-term stable assets with which they are familiar and that yield a decent, if not private equity–benchmarked, level of return.

Looking across the wider public funds management landscape, relatively few other players have developed significant direct investment capability. Of those that have, some of the Canadian pension funds are noticeable leaders, the Canada Pension Plan Investment Board, the Ontario Municipal Employees Retirement System, and the Ontario Teachers' Pension Plan Private Capital being the best known. A number of established SWFs are looking to evolve in this direction. The Abu Dhabi Investment Authority is known to be investing heavily in their direct investment capabilities, and it is possible that, in the future, Norges Bank Investment Management will expand its direct investment capabilities beyond real estate. Others will no doubt follow the lead of these and other more established direct SWFs, notably Singapore's Government of Singapore Investment Corporation and Temasek Holdings. This approach will, however, not suit the risk–reward criteria and liquidity requirements of all SWFs. Direct private investment poses significant challenges in building skilled capability and capacity to undertake successful investments. Moreover, it necessitates a different approach to governance that is far deeper and more complex than equivalent indirect and publicly traded investment models.

NOTES

1. KPMG would like to thank and acknowledge the assistance of the Sovereign Wealth Centre for its provision of data. While every effort has been taken to verify the accuracy of this information, KPMG International Cooperative ("KPMG International") cannot accept any responsibility or liability for reliance by any person on this information. The views and opinions expressed within the publication are those of the authors/participants and do not necessarily represent the views and opinions of KPMG International or KPMG member firms. KPMG International serves as a coordinating entity for a network of independent firms operating under the KPMG name. KPMG International provides no client services. Services are provided solely by member firms (including sublicensees and subsidiaries) in their respective geographic areas. Each KPMG firm is a legally distinct and separate entity and describes itself as such.

2. Taking London as an example, sovereign investors have interests in many of the capital's upper-end developments, including Canary Wharf (Qatar Investment Authority), Regent Street (Norges Bank Investment Management), the "Walkie-Talkie" at 20 Fenchurch Street (China Investment Corporation and Qatar Investment Authority), and the Shard (Qatar Investment Authority). Similar trends are noted in other major global cities, such as New York, Paris and Hong Kong.

REFERENCES

Auerbach, A., and P. Pradhan. 2015. "Making Waves: The Cresting Co-Investment Opportunity." Boston: Cambridge Associates.

Avendaño, R., and J. Santiso. 2009. "Are Sovereign Wealth Funds' Investments Politically Biased? Comparison with Mutual Funds," OECD Development Centre Working Paper 283. Paris: Organisation for Economic Co-operation and Development.

Bagnall, A., and E. Truman. 2013. "Progress on Sovereign Wealth Fund Transparency and Accountability: An Updated SWF Scoreboard," Policy Brief RB13-19. Washington, DC: Peterson Institute for International Economics.

Bernstein, S., J. Lerner, and A. Schoar. 2013. "The Investment Strategies of Sovereign Wealth Funds," *Journal of Economic Perspectives* 27, no. 2: 219–238.

Bortolotti, B., V. Fotak, W. Megginson, and W. Miracky. 2009. "Sovereign Wealth Fund Investment Fund Patterns and Performance," Nota di Lavoro 22.2009. Milan, Italy: Fondazione Eni Enrico Mattei. www.feem.it/getpage.aspx?id=1880& sez=Publications&padre=73.

Croft, J. 2014. "Libya–Goldman Clash Sheds Light on Formerly Secretive Fund." *Financial Times*, October 20. www.ft.com/intl/cms/s/0/0828bbd8-4ef7-11e4-b205 -00144feab7de.html#axzz3xQx2VR6P.

Gelpern, A. 2010. "Sovereignty, Accountability, and the Wealth Fund Governance Conundrum," *Asian Journal of International Law* 1, no. 2: 289–320.

Sudarskis, G. 2011. "Direct Investments by Sovereign Wealth Funds: A Practitioner's View," Sovereign Investment Lab Annual Report. Milan, Italy: University of Bocconi.

Thatcher, M. 2013. "National Policies Towards Sovereign Wealth Funds in Europe: A Comparison of France, Germany and Italy," Kuwait Programme on Development, Governance and Globalisation in the Gulf States, Policy Brief No. 2. London: London School of Economics.

CHAPTER 5

Playthings and Parallel Budgets

THE ECONOMIC AND GOVERNANCE PERFORMANCE OF SOVEREIGN WEALTH FUNDS

Andrew Bauer

Natural Resources Governance Institute

Sovereign wealth funds (SWFs) have helped a number of countries improve public financial management.[1] In Chile, they have been used to save for pensions and to cover budget deficits when copper revenues have declined. The Norwegian and Saudi Arabian funds have protected their economies from oil price shocks and sterilized capital inflows, helping to mitigate Dutch disease effects. Some Persian Gulf countries and U.S states, including Oman and North Dakota, have used them to save revenues from nonrenewable resources so that future generations may benefit from today's exploration, development and production. Still others, like Texas, have used them as an endowment to finance specific public services, such as higher education.

However, a survey of fund performance makes apparent that these "good news" stories are the exception rather than the rule (Bauer, Rietveld, and Toledano 2014). Poor SWF governance has often undermined public financial management systems. Moreover, some funds have been used as sources of patronage and corruption, with dramatic results. For example, the Libyan and Kuwaiti funds have incurred billions of dollars in avoidable losses owing to financial transactions that benefited friends of the regime or investment managers (Saigol and O'Murchu 2011; Bazoobandi 2012). And in Nigeria, billions of dollars of public money were withdrawn from the Excess Crude Account without plan or justification (Ndagi 2013).

Ostensibly designed to steady macroeconomic management or set aside savings for the future, many funds have lacked clear goals or rules and thus have complicated public finance. In Azerbaijan, for example, billions of dollars' worth of strategic government projects are financed directly out of the State Oil Fund of the Republic of Azerbaijan (SOFAZ), including a railway across Azerbaijan, Georgia, and Turkey. These expenditure items are not subject to the same reporting or public procurement requirements as those financed out of the normal budget process. And in some countries (e.g., Angola and Russia), SWFs have been used to avoid public scrutiny, facilitating the wasteful spending of billions of dollars (Bauer, Rietveld, and Toledano 2014).

Fund operations are often opaque and not subject to independent oversight. The Algerian, Bruneian, Omani, and Turkmen funds are some of the most extreme examples of weak transparency; the Brunei Investment Agency website provides a statement of values and not much else. Even some governments, such as those of Equatorial Guinea, Iran, Kuwait, and Qatar, that are signatories to the Santiago Principles, which commit them to a basic standard of disclosure vis-à-vis their funds, fail to publish detailed information on investments or activities (International Working Group of Sovereign Wealth Funds 2008). This opacity and a lack of independent oversight raise questions around how these funds are being used and whom they are benefiting.

In many cases, SWFs have simply been ineffective. While funds in Chile, Norway, Peru, and Saudi Arabia have helped smooth government spending despite having to deal with volatile oil or mineral revenues, self-declared stabilization funds in Kazakhstan, Trinidad and Tobago, and Venezuela have failed to stabilize the budget. And some savings funds have failed to save as their mandate requires. For example, one of the objectives of the Alberta Heritage Savings Trust Fund in Canada is to save oil revenues for future generations. Yet, despite sky-high production and historically high prices at times from 1987 to 2013, only two relatively small deposits were made into the Fund over this period (see chapter 13).

In this chapter, I describe what good macroeconomic or fund performance means. I then attempt to explain why most funds have performed poorly from a macroeconomic and governance perspective and provide recommendations on how SWFs can avoid these pitfalls. I draw heavily on case studies and research conducted by the Natural Resource Governance Institute and the Columbia Center on Sustainable Investment on natural resource funds; that is, SWFs in natural resource–rich settings.

WHAT CONSTITUTES GOOD MACROECONOMIC OR GOVERNANCE PERFORMANCE?

Any extrabudgetary fund ought to serve either a macroeconomic or governance objective, preferably both. Legitimate reasons for their establishment include managing fiscal surpluses; securing sources of funding for chronically underfunded expenditure items, like pensions or environmental protection; and depoliticizing certain budget allocations and preventing budget cuts (Allen and Radev 2010). However, more often than not, such funds are established for other reasons, such as avoiding public scrutiny over public expenditure decisions or circumventing parliamentary oversight. Sovereign wealth funds can be deemed to be performing well if they achieve at least one of five possible objectives:

- **Smoothing expenditures:** Governments can save a portion of fiscal revenues in funds (sometimes formally called "stabilization funds") when revenues are high and draw down on these funds when revenues decline in order to prevent "boom–bust" spending cycles. For example, the American state of Wyoming has been able to grow through periods of temporary oil and mineral price declines due in part to the availability of a pool of funds to draw on during downturns (as also discussed in chapter 13).
- **Sterilizing capital inflows:** Sovereign wealth funds can help mitigate "Dutch disease" by sterilizing large capital inflows, in this case, foreign exchange inflows associated with large remittances; foreign aid; or oil, gas, or mineral sales. Countries or regions with relatively small economies that receive large unexpected inflows—for instance, from scaling up oil, gas, or mineral production quickly—may find that these inflows can lead to exchange rate appreciation or inflation. This can cause local businesses to become less competitive internationally and harm the nonresource economy. Governments can help mitigate Dutch disease by saving a portion of their fiscal revenues in foreign assets. This is called "fiscal sterilization." Countries such as Norway and Saudi Arabia have kept their exchange rates under control or inflation lower than it would have been otherwise by saving resource revenues in foreign assets rather than spending them domestically.
- **Saving fiscal surpluses:** Governments may wish to run a fiscal surplus over the long term in order to create an endowment for future generations for at least three reasons. First, large oil or mineral producers may wish to prevent a recession once these resources are depleted.

Second, there is an ethical case to be made for intergenerational equity; some believe that our children should receive the same share of financial benefits as the current generation. Third, some governments may find it difficult to spend all resource revenues as they are collected without generating significant waste because they do not possess the managerial systems, technology, labor, or skills to spend vast sums effectively (also described as a lack of "absorptive capacity"). In response, some governments save a portion of fiscal revenues; investing them in productive assets and living off the investment returns can extend the financial benefits of extraction beyond the life of the oil field or mine, perhaps even indefinitely. With small populations, high personal incomes, and vast oil wealth, many Persian Gulf countries, including Kuwait, Oman, Qatar, and the United Arab Emirates, as well as Norway, have chosen to save for these reasons. In low-income settings, some governments have elected to "park" some revenues in foreign assets until they develop enough capacity to spend the money well or until the economy grows enough to absorb the revenues, as in the cases of Timor-Leste and the oil-rich Bojonegoro Regency in Indonesia, which is currently establishing a subnational SWF.[2]

- **Earmarking revenues for public investments:** SWFs can be used to limit the discretion of politicians in making spending decisions by earmarking revenues for specific public investments like roads, water systems, hospital equipment, or education programs. Importantly, *earmarking* does not refer to making public spending decisions through the fund's choices of asset holdings, bypassing the formal budget process. Doing so could damage the integrity of the public financial management system, possibly circumventing accountability mechanisms such as parliamentary oversight and audits, and could lead to the use of resource revenues for patronage. Examples of earmarking include Ghana's rule that oil revenues must fund "development-related expenditures" and Alabama's earmarking of some oil and gas revenues for land conservation, municipal capital expenditures, and senior services.
- **Ring-fencing natural resource revenues:** Sovereign wealth funds can help protect public funds from corruption or mismanagement, especially in natural resource–rich settings. Given the size and complex nature of revenue streams (e.g., royalties, profit taxes, bonuses, license fees) entering government coffers from extractive companies, natural resource revenues are often a target of misappropriation. Separating resource revenues can help reduce the risk of corruption and mismanagement,

but only where there are strict and comprehensive disclosure requirements for fund operations and where there is a formal and effective
oversight mechanism to monitor these operations. For example, the São
Tomé and Príncipe National Oil Account is subject to rigorous transparency provisions that ensure that oil revenues are well accounted for,
and fund operations are open to public scrutiny.

Another common reason for establishing SWFs is to gain political and
financial autonomy. In low- and middle-income countries, governments
can draw upon precautionary savings in cases of financial crisis instead
of borrowing from private banks or international financial institutions,
both of which can impose burdensome conditions on a government.
Sovereign wealth funds can be a powerful source of protection against
foreign influence and market forces. The same logic applies within countries, as subnational governments seek autonomy from national authorities. Legislators in the Northwest Territories in Canada, for instance, have
stated that their newly established Heritage Fund, financed by mineral
revenues, will give the territorial government greater political autonomy
from the Canadian federal government. That said, an SWF cannot be
deemed to be well performing simply if it achieves this political objective.

HOW WELL DO SOVEREIGN WEALTH FUNDS PERFORM BASED ON THESE CRITERIA?

There are very few funds in the world that fully achieve their intended
objectives. Based on the CCSI–NRGI study (Bauer, Rietveld, and
Toledano 2014), the SWF Scoreboard (Truman 2010), and observations
of macroeconomic performance in countries with SWFs, we can draw
some conclusions.

First, only a handful of funds help smooth budget expenditures.
Among the few governments that effectively mitigate revenue volatility
are those of Chile, Norway, Peru, Qatar, Saudi Arabia, and the American
state of Wyoming. Most other self-declared stabilization funds have failed
to achieve these objectives, including those of Azerbaijan, Ghana, Iran,
Kazakhstan, Mexico, Mongolia, Nigeria, and Venezuela. Figure 5.1 illustrates the public finances of four of these countries. Two governments,
those of Chile and Saudi Arabia, have used their funds to enact "countercyclical" fiscal policy. Iran and Venezuela, meanwhile, engage in "procyclical" fiscal policy, despite the presence of a stabilization fund in each.

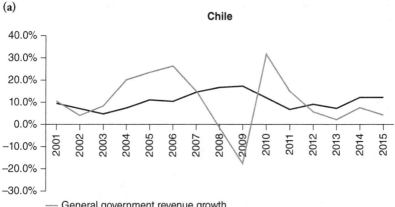

(a)

Chile

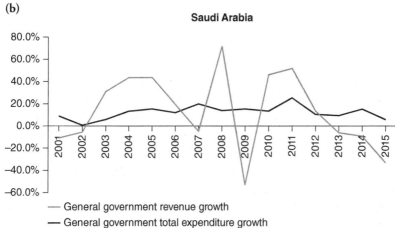

(b)

Saudi Arabia

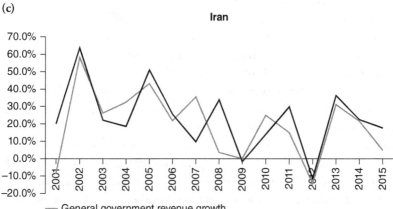

(c)

Iran

Figure 5.1   Public finances in four countries with stabilization funds: (a) Chile; (b) Saudi Arabia; (c) Iran; (d) Venezuela.

(d)

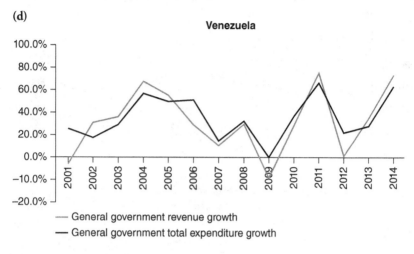

Figure 5.1 (*continued*)

Second, the evidence on the sterilization of large capital inflows is mixed. For instance, although oil-dependent Timor-Leste has accumulated $16.9 billion in its Petroleum Fund (as of June 2015), inflation ran above 10 percent while oil prices where high from 2011 to 2013. Similarly, inflation in oil-dependent Algeria and natural gas–dependent Trinidad and Tobago topped out at about 9 percent in 2012 due to high petroleum revenues. In all three countries, inflation dropped once oil prices began to fall. In contrast, Brunei, Norway, Oman, Qatar, and Saudi Arabia kept inflation below 4 percent over the same period, in part by using their SWFs to sterilize oil revenue inflows.[3]

The main reason for the failure of some SWFs to effectively sterilize capital inflows has been a lack of "fiscal rules" governing budget allocations (or compliance with these rules) and, relatedly, an absence of operational rules governing deposits and withdrawals from SWFs (Bauer 2014). Of the eighteen jurisdictions surveyed by the CCSI and NRGI, 25 percent did not have rules governing deposits and withdrawals (Bauer, Rietveld, and Toledano 2014). However, these results are biased since half the world's SWFs in resource-rich settings were too opaque to study. Middle Eastern and Central Asian countries were least likely to legislate operational rules for their funds.

The third conclusion we can draw is that there is no doubt that a number of countries, mainly those in the Middle East, have accumulated vast reserves in their SWFs. For example, Abu Dhabi has accumulated about $773 billion since 1976 in the Abu Dhabi Investment Authority

(ADIA), just one of its SWFs. Norway has accumulated $877 billion in its SWF since 1996. And Kuwait holds about $592 billion in the Kuwait Investment Authority. These savings implicitly shift the benefits of present-day economic activity to future generations. Yet, the international record on meeting the savings objective is not spotless. In Azerbaijan, for instance, the lack of a withdrawal rule has led to discretionary withdrawals that have enabled the government to spend lavishly when oil prices are high and to make cuts when oil prices have declined (Aslanli 2015). In Canada, the Alberta Heritage Savings Trust Fund was established as a savings fund in 1976, although deposits were halted in 1987. As a result of a lack of a deposit rule, the fund saved less than CDN$4 billion in oil revenues over 25 years, despite hundreds of billions of dollars in oil revenues entering government coffers over the same period. In 2013, the Alberta government finally instituted a set of fiscal rules with long-term savings and fiscal stabilization objectives in mind (see chapter 13).

Fourth, and perhaps most alarmingly, SWFs have often become channels of patronage and corruption, rather than the mechanisms for protecting public finances that they were intended to be. There are two common ways that SWFs have been mismanaged: through illegal or unjustified withdrawals and through asset allocations that serve private or political interests. Both are enabled by fund opacity and, especially, lack of oversight.

In a prime example of how pools of money can become tempting targets, the Russian government arbitrarily suspended its fiscal rules in 2010. Since then, it has raided the National Wealth Fund of tens of billions of dollars, which had been intended to finance future Russian pension liabilities, and nearly emptied the Reserve Fund, even before oil prices began to fall (Kryukov, Tokarev, and Yenikeyeff 2011). In another example, the Timor-Leste appeals court found that a $290.7 million withdrawal from the Petroleum Fund in 2008 was illegal. The government was subsequently forced to return the money to the budget (La'o Hamutuk 2008).

Mismanagement via asset allocation is perhaps more common, though data are lacking owing to fund opacity. According to the SWF Scoreboard, only 53 percent of SWFs published full annual reports in 2012 (Bagnall and Truman 2013). That said, there are a few well-known examples of corruption and patronage that can be cited. The Kuwait Investment Authority, for instance, lost approximately $5 billion from poor investments in Spanish companies in the early 1990s owing to a combination of lack of oversight and a lack of rules limiting investment risk (Bazoobandi 2012).

A better publicized case is that of the Libyan Investment Authority (LIA), which invested in opaque hedge funds run by friends of the Gaddafi regime in the late 2000s. The LIA made a $300 million investment in Palladyne International Asset Management, a previously unheard-of fund with links to the former chairman of Libya's National Oil Corporation. Despite investing slightly more than half of these funds, Palladyne recorded more than $50 million in losses from 2008 to mid-2010.

What's more, the LIA did not carry out its due diligence when taking on risky structured financial products sold by investment banks and hedge funds such as Goldman Sachs, Permal, and Millennium Global (a case also mentioned in chapter 4). As a result, it took excessive risk and overpaid for financial management services. For example, it invested $1.2 billion in equity and currency derivatives managed by Goldman Sachs, an investment that lost 98.5 percent of its value by June 2010 because of the global financial crisis. Also, Permal was paid $27 million in fees for managing $300 million in investments. Rarely do management, transaction, or expense fees combined exceed more than a few percentage points, much less reach the 9 percent paid to Permal. In a 2010 internal review, LIA management wrote, "High fees have been directly responsible for the poor results" (Saigol and O'Murchu 2011).

THREE RECOMMENDATIONS FOR IMPROVING SWF PERFORMANCE

The CCSI–NRGI report "Managing the Public Trust: How to Make Natural Resource Funds Work for Citizens" (Bauer, Rietveld, and Toledano 2014) outlines the full range of government policies necessary for making SWFs effective. Here, I will highlight three recommendations that may do the most to improve fund performance. In order, they are (1) clarifying and aligning operational rules—namely deposit, withdrawal, and investment rules—with the fund's objectives; (2) ensuring independent oversight; and (3) prohibiting home investments.

RECOMMENDATION 1: CLARIFYING AND ALIGNING OPERATIONAL RULES WITH FUND OBJECTIVES

As stated, many funds either have unclear deposit, withdrawal, and investment rules or lack them altogether. In Kazakhstan, for example, the government sets the list of companies whose payments make their way into the National Fund. By changing the list every year, it can determine how much revenue is placed in the budget and how much is deposited into the fund. In addition, publicly owned companies may be treated differently from private companies. Payments from national oil companies or state-owned mining companies are usually deposited directly into the fund but may be subject to special rules allowing them to retain certain profits (Bauer 2014). In all cases, which revenue streams are to be deposited into the fund and the timing of deposits should be clarified in law, which is currently not the case.

While deposit rules are generally clear and adhered to, withdrawal rules—those that specify how often withdrawals can be made, where they must go, the amount of any transfer, and whether they need to be approved by Parliament—are more often absent. Funds in Abu Dhabi, Azerbaijan, Botswana, Iran, Kuwait, and Oman are just some that do not have explicit withdrawal rules. The result is usually "procyclical" fiscal policy, whereby the government spends more when the economy is growing and cuts spending when fiscal revenues decline, exacerbating natural boom–bust cycles. In the best cases, amounts permitted for withdrawal are determined by fiscal rules, which, where they exist, are more often than not legislated. In countries with expenditure or balanced budget rules (e.g., Chile, Norway, Peru), withdrawals must not exceed the maximum budget deficit or minimum surplus.

Explicit limitations on investment risk are also often absent. In the CCSI–NRGI survey (Bauer, Rietveld, and Toledano 2014) of eighteen jurisdictions, 35 percent did not have any rules limiting investment risk. Even where excessive risk taking is limited, rules can be drafted in a way that allows for excessive risk taking. In Uganda, for example, the Public Finance Bill lists qualifying instruments that the newly established Petroleum Revenue Investment Reserve can invest in. It then states that the fund may invest in "any other qualifying instrument prescribed by the Minister."

As discussed in chapters 4, 8, and 11, a fund's investment risk profile should be a function of its policy objectives (e.g., stabilization fund assets should be more liquid than savings fund assets), the strength of the systems set up to prevent mismanagement, and the capacity to manage complex investments (or at least the capacity to manage the managers). No matter what risk profile is chosen, it should be well defined and enforced through explicit rules that limit exposure. Certain investments should be prohibited outright; for example, those in high-risk financial instruments, risky alternative assets, or volatile currencies.

RECOMMENDATION 2: ENSURING INDEPENDENT OVERSIGHT

It bears repeating that SWFs store public money. As such, their managers have an obligation to serve the public interest. This means that funds should be subject to strong conflict-of-interest standards, publish comprehensive information on their activities, and allow independent bodies—such as an independent auditor or civil society group like Ghana's Public Interest and Accountability Committee—to oversee performance.

Independent oversight bodies can encourage good financial management by praising compliance with the rules and good fund governance. In some cases, they can also discourage poor behavior by imposing punitive measures ranging from naming and shaming to fines, imprisonment, or international sanctions. For example, the Canadian province of Alberta requires that its legislature conduct annual reviews of fund performance, ensuring compliance with regulations, and hold annual public meetings on fund activities. These requirements are in addition to periodic reviews of investment methodology and regular external audits that are publicly available (World Bank Institute 2010).

However, independent oversight bodies can do their jobs only if they have access to good-quality information. This means that funds must regularly publish accurate and data-disaggregated reports on their activities in a format that is fully accessible to lay readers. All regulations, policy documents, quarterly financial statements, and annual internal and independent external audits should be released publicly and be required to meet international standards. Reports should not only be backward looking; they should also clarify what will be achieved in the future to set benchmarks for performance and set public expectations (Bauer, Rietveld, and Toledano 2014).

RECOMMENDATION 3: PROHIBITING HOME INVESTMENTS

In spite of the challenges mentioned, perhaps the most significant cause of poor operational performance is an unclear mandate. While some funds have well-defined mandates—in Ghana, the Petroleum Holding Fund ring-fences all oil revenues, the Heritage Fund saves revenues for the benefit of future generations, and the Stabilization Fund helps to mitigate budget volatility—in most cases, funds are established without a well-defined mandate, making it difficult for policymakers to decide on operational rules or manage the fund's investments.

For example, in Azerbaijan, SOFAZ's three objectives are to accumulate and preserve revenues for future generations, finance major government projects, and "preserve macroeconomic stability by decreasing dependence on oil revenues and stimulate the development of the non-oil sector." It is unclear what proportion of the fund is designated for each objective and what operational rules, if any, help the fund achieve them. Multiple objectives in and of themselves are not necessarily problematic, but the lack of operational rules to help funds meet their objectives and lack of clarity around those objectives are.

These problems usually manifest themselves in the transformation of an SWF into a parallel—and often unaccountable—budget. In response to an acute need for domestic investment in many developing countries, some countries have used their SWFs to invest directly at home. This trend has been encouraged by some researchers who have suggested that, although domestic investment by SWFs involves risk, there are also opportunities associated with this policy option (Gelb et al. 2014; see also chapters 7, 8, and 11). Already, governments in Angola, Azerbaijan, Iran, Nigeria, and Russia, for example, are using their SWFs to channel money to special domestic projects (see also chapter 10, which focuses on Nigeria's SWF).

While the idea of using an SWF to invest domestically may resonate with government officials and politicians in low-income, resource-rich countries—particularly at this time of low commodity prices and surging fiscal deficits among oil and mineral exporters—there are strong arguments against using SWFs for this purpose. Governments can establish safeguards to limit SWF mismanagement and corruption, namely conflict-of-interest standards combined with legislative approval and strong fund transparency and oversight. However, the challenges associated with creating a parallel budget or multiple mandates may not be so easy to overcome. A single SWF may not be well placed to be a checking account, a savings account, an education or health financing vehicle, and a development bank all at once.

There are at least six reasons why it is generally inadvisable to use an SWF for domestic spending or investment:

1. **Domestic spending or investment through SWFs can undermine macroeconomic objectives.** The very reason governments usually

create these funds is to address the macroeconomic challenges associated with natural resource revenue inflows. In Norway and Timor-Leste, for example, funds work in tandem with fiscal rules that require governments to save a portion of their resource revenues to help mitigate Dutch disease. If governments transfer money to a fund, then transfer money back into the economy through domestic spending, the fund's macroeconomic objective of sterilizing capital inflows could be undermined.

2. **Domestic spending or investment through SWFs can undermine public financial management systems.** In many countries, the budget process—including project appraisal, public procurement, and project monitoring—does not adequately deliver needed social programs and physical infrastructure. Governments sometimes respond by creating new institutions to bypass budget systems that do not work, such as an SWF that invests at home as well as abroad. This can lead to the establishment of uncoordinated *parallel budgets*—each with its own appraisal, procurement, and monitoring system. While budget processes may well be flawed in many countries, the best approach is usually not to create new institutions with unintended consequences, but rather to repair what is broken.

3. **Domestic spending or investment through SWFs can undermine public accountability.** Bypassing normal budgetary systems can also undermine legislative oversight and democracy. Budget allocations are usually examined and approved by legislatures. This is rarely the case for specific SWF investments. In Azerbaijan and Iran, for instance, governments have used SWFs to finance politically motivated projects without submission to parliamentary scrutiny. Given the private interests that politicians and SWF investment managers often have in their own countries, lack of accountability can lead to politically motivated investments or investments for personal gain. The risk is even higher where most SWF activities are not publicly disclosed, as is the case in most countries with funds.

4. **Financial and development mandates require different expertise.** Financial managers specializing in maximizing financial returns are usually not trained in identifying or managing infrastructure projects (as also discussed in chapter 4). A single institution may not be well placed to achieve both financial returns and domestic development, unless there are strict firewalls between the two portfolios.

5. **Multiple mandates can lead to inconsistent and confused decision making.** A fund with multiple objectives—say, promoting domestic economic development and generating returns on savings for the benefit of future generations—can become difficult for officials to manage and may lead to poor investment decisions. What percentage of the fund should be allocated to which objective? Can the ratio change, and if so, with whose approval? If one portfolio grows faster than another, is there a need for rebalancing? Is fund liquidity or investment in local businesses for the long term more important? In theory, strict guidelines can help address these challenges, but in practice, where funds are allowed to make home investments, such guidelines are rarely drafted or enforced, allowing fund managers excessive discretion to make politically or privately motivated investments.

6. **There is no opportunity cost to banning domestic spending or investment through SWFs in most developing countries.** If we construe SWFs as *government savings* mechanisms (rather than as extrabudgetary *spending* funds), they should be managed in much the same way a family or institutional trust fund is managed—meaning maximizing returns for future use given a particular risk appetite. Sovereign wealth fund managers generally set an investment target (e.g., 4–6 percent annually), which is an implicit declaration of risk appetite. In order to achieve this objective, fund managers will choose financial instruments that are likely to generate the target financial return while minimizing the risk of loss. In most developing countries, the chance is quite low that any single domestic asset can satisfy the fund managers' criteria for maximizing return and minimizing risk (this would not necessarily be the case in China, western Europe, or the United States, for instance, owing to the size of their economies and the sophistication of their financial markets). Therefore, in developing countries, the opportunity cost of prohibiting domestic investment in order to maximize financial returns is near zero.

Evidence on SWF treatment of home spending and investment already exists. Countries and subnational jurisdictions whose funds cannot invest domestically include Abu Dhabi (ADIA), Botswana, Chile, Ghana, Kazakhstan, Norway, and Timor-Leste. While each country may be faced with challenges, these funds generally achieve their objectives. On the other hand, there are countries where funds can invest or spend at home:

Angola, Azerbaijan, Equatorial Guinea, Iran, Kuwait, Libya, Nigeria, and Russia. Many of these funds have become conduits for corruption, patronage, and financial mismanagement, as described. Moreover, very few have achieved their stated objectives.

This is not to say that governments should never establish extrabudgetary funds designed to channel money domestically. The American state of Alabama's Forever Wild Land Trust Fund, which earmarks resource revenues for roads and environmental protection, Liberia's aid-funded Health Sector Pool Fund, and Timor-Leste's multiyear Infrastructure and Human Capacity Development Fund are all well-functioning special funds. However, these are all essentially accounts, rather than institutions with their own organizational structures, staff, and buildings. They should not be confused with SWFs, which are designed as savings mechanisms and invest at least partly in foreign assets.

What is important for good governance in these cases is that all spending be approved by the legislature and be subject to project appraisal, procurement, and monitoring systems that are the same as or stronger than those for other government spending. In the case of Ghana, for example, 70 percent of resource revenues spent out of its SWF is earmarked for domestic investment. However, the government channels this money back through the budget rather than spending or investing it outside the budget process.

Similarly, many governments establish development banks or state-owned holding companies to invest in commercially viable domestic investments that have trouble attracting capital. Examples include the Brazilian Development Bank, the Qatar Development Bank, France's Agence des participations de l'État, and Kazakhstan's Samruk-Kazyna (which is a holding company despite calling itself an SWF). As with any state-owned company, investment decisions ought to be free from political interference, be it through independent boards or other oversight mechanisms, and have clear administrative or developmental mandates.

In short, SWFs, as savings mechanisms for macroeconomic management, should not be the vehicles of such direct spending. If there is underinvestment in the domestic economy, a far better approach to remedy the situation is to enact fiscal rules that allocate fiscal revenues more appropriately between the budget and an SWF. Different vehicles may be required to achieve domestic investment goals *and* manage the macroeconomic challenges associated with large and volatile fiscal revenue inflows. One tool cannot fix every problem.

NOTES

1. In this chapter, a sovereign wealth fund is defined as a special-purpose investment vehicle owned by a government that invests at least in part in foreign financial assets and holds no explicit liabilities. This definition draws on a number of sources, namely the International Working Group on Sovereign Wealth Funds (IWG) which defines sovereign wealth funds as

> special purpose investment funds or arrangements, owned by the general government. Created by the general government for macroeconomic purposes, SWFs hold, manage, or administer assets to achieve financial objectives, and employ a set of investment strategies which include investing in foreign financial assets. The SWFs are commonly established out of balance of payments surpluses, official foreign currency operations, the proceeds of privatizations, fiscal surpluses, and/or receipts resulting from commodity exports. (IWG 2008)

Edwin Truman (2010) defines sovereign wealth funds as "large pools of government-owned funds that are invested in whole or in part outside their home country." Truman includes subnational funds. Similarly, Castelli and Scacciavillani (2012) define them as "publicly owned investment vehicles with a mandate to transfer wealth to future generations by investing in an international portfolio of securities and assets, including companies." They specifically exclude investment vehicles primarily geared toward domestic development, such as state-owned enterprises or national development banks and entities financed primarily through transfers of central bank reserves. The challenge to agree on a single definition is highlighted in the introduction of this volume.

2. In low-income, capital-scarce economies such as that of Timor-Leste, spending needs are immediate, so fiscal space must be provided to allow the government to build the "absorptive capacity" to transform resource revenues into long-lasting assets such as infrastructure and human resources.

3. According to the International Monetary Fund World Economic Outlook as of October 2016, http://www.imf.org/external/pubs/ft/weo/2016/02/.

REFERENCES

Allen, R., and D. Radev. 2010. "Extrabudgetary Funds." Washington, DC: International Monetary Fund. www.imf.org/external/pubs/ft/tnm/2010/tnm1009.pdf.

Aslanli, K. 2015. "Fiscal Sustainability and the State Oil Fund in Azerbaijan," *Journal of Eurasian Studies* 6, no. 2: 114–121.

Bagnall, A. F., and E. M. Truman. 2013. "Progress on Sovereign Wealth Fund Transparency and Accountability: An Updated SWF Scoreboard," Policy Brief 13–19. Washington, DC: Peterson Institute for International Economics.

Bauer, A. 2014. "Fiscal Rules for Natural Resource Funds: How to Develop and Operationalize an Appropriate Rule." In "Managing the Public Trust: How to Make Natural Resource Funds Work for Citizens," edited by A. Bauer. New York: Columbia Center on Sustainable Investment and Natural Resource Governance Institute. www.resourcegovernance.org/natural-resource-funds.

Bauer, A., M. Rietveld, and P. Toledano. 2014. "Managing the Public Trust: How to Make Natural Resource Funds Work for Citizens," edited by A. Bauer. New York: Columbia Center on Sustainable Investment and Natural Resource Governance Institute. http://ccsi.columbia.edu/files/2014/09/NRF_Complete_Report_EN.pdf.

Bazoobandi, S. 2012. *Political Economy of the Gulf Sovereign Wealth Funds: A Case Study of Iran, Kuwait, Saudi Arabia and the United Arab Emirates.* New York: Routledge.

Castelli, M., and F. Scacciavillani. 2012. *The New Economics of Sovereign Wealth Funds.* West Sussex, UK: Wiley.

Gelb, A., S. Tordo, H. Halland, N. Arfaa, and G. Smith. 2014. "Sovereign Wealth Funds and Long-Term Development," World Bank Policy Research Working Paper 6776. Washington, DC: World Bank.

International Working Group of Sovereign Wealth Funds. 2008. "Sovereign Wealth Funds: Generally Accepted Principles and Practices ('Santiago Principles')," www.iwg-swf.org/pubs/eng/santiagoprinciples.pdf.

Kryukov, V., A. Tokarev, and S. Yenikeyeff. 2011. "The Contest for Control: Oil and Gas Management in Russia." In *Plundered Nations? Successes and Failures in Natural Resource Extraction,* edited by P. Collier and A. J. Venables, 262–303. New York: Palgrave Macmillan.

La'o Hamutuk. 2008. "Timor-Leste Appeals Court Invalidates 2008 State Budget," www.laohamutuk.org/econ/MYBU08/BudgetRuledUnconstitutional08.htm.

Ndagi, M. U. 2013. "Nigeria: Devouring Excess Crude Account." *Daily Trust,* September 7. http://allafrica.com/stories/201309090256.html.

Saigol, L., and C. O'Murchu. 2011. "After Gaddafi: A Spent Force," *Financial Times,* September 8. www.ft.com/intl/cms/s/0/1b5e11b6-d4cb-11e0-a7ac-00144feab49a. html#axzz2PclPUcQK.

Truman, E. 2010. *Sovereign Wealth Funds: Threat or Salvation?* Washington, DC: Peterson Institute for International Economics.

World Bank Institute. 2010. "Parliamentary Oversight of the Extractive Industries Sector," http://www.agora-parl.org/sites/default/files/parliamentary_oversight_and _the_extractive_industries.pdf.

PART II

The Rise of Sovereign Development Funds
Debates and Policy Implementation

CHAPTER 6

A Simple Typology of Sovereign Development Funds

Adam D. Dixon and Ashby H. B. Monk
University of Bristol and Stanford University

INTRODUCTION

The substantial collapse of crude oil prices in the last quarter of 2014 was a stark reminder of the volatility of commodity prices generally (Deaton 1999). For consumers, the collapse of oil prices was welcome. For producers, particularly governments dependent on oil revenues for the majority of their spending, the collapse has far-reaching economic, social, and political consequences. The ramifications for developing countries with undiversified economies are especially severe. In recent years, however, many natural resource–producing countries have stashed away some of their revenues in stabilization funds or more financially sophisticated sovereign wealth funds (SWFs) (e.g., Balding 2012; Clark, Dixon, and Monk 2013). With reserves in the bank, countries should be able to weather the collapse in natural resource revenues, at least in the short term. For those that did not put aside resource revenues during periods of high commodity prices, or for those that overcommitted current and future government spending on high commodity prices, the surplus savings that do exist may not be enough. If they had thought that global commodity markets had re-entered a period of stability at high prices following the last collapse in 2008 during the global financial crisis, they were wrong.

The recent collapse in oil prices thus provides for a constructive moment to re-evaluate resource revenue savings and the form and function of the institutions that are charged with managing and employing those savings to productive purposes. For countries with significant natural resource endowments, chiefly those with undiversified and underdeveloped economies, there are conflicting demands on how to spend and save the revenues that come from them. On the one hand, resource revenues provide for an important budgetary resource where the ability to raise funds through taxation is limited. In funding the budget, resource revenues can be used, in theory, for any number of objectives that support long-term economic growth and diversification of the economy, from health care and education to building infrastructure. So long as resource revenues are stable and increasing, this model would seem to work (Karl 1997; Ross 2012). But, commodity prices are prone to collapse and to periods of instability. Couple price uncertainty with uncertainty on the production side, and there is a robust argument for saving resource revenues and spending them slowly over time, or during periods when resource revenues are low (Eifert, Gelb, and Borje Tallroth 2003).

In the latter model, resource revenues flow to the budget and to a stabilization fund, which generally holds highly liquid assets, such as U.S. dollars or U.S. Treasuries. Stabilization funds are often simply accounts at the government treasury or the central bank. The other rationale for an approach based on measured spending and savings of resource revenues is to limit or prevent the so-called "Dutch disease," which occurs when production in the extractive sector pushes up the value of the national currency, therefore reducing the competitiveness and development of other tradable sectors (Corden and Neary 1982). But, there are opportunity costs and sterilization costs to holding such low-yielding assets. For example, Rodrik's (2006) estimate of the cost of holding excess reserves in developing countries was nearly 1 percent of gross domestic product. Accordingly, a number of commodity-producing countries have funneled resource revenues into more financially advanced SWFs capable of investing additionally or delegating investment into higher-yielding assets and securities, generally outside the country in international capital markets.

Notwithstanding the need to mitigate Dutch disease by holding assets offshore, there is still a reason to contest investing all savings internationally, especially in less-developed economies where local capital is scarce and the developmental demands of the population are great (Collier et al. 2011). The argument for holding U.S. Treasuries or those of other advanced economies is that they are a store of value and they are highly liquid. This is correct, but it also results in providing an economic resource to these advanced economies for the purposes of their own economic and social development: It is a flow of economic resources from a poor country to a rich country. Hence, there is an argument for investing resource revenues locally through a state-sponsored investment fund, acting separately from and in addition to the spending of resource revenues through the government budget, a consideration underlined by several chapters of this volume (chapters 2, 8, and 12). An SWF in this form could be called a sovereign development fund (SDF), as its mandate is to actively invest in sectors and projects that catalyze further economic growth and development.

Investing locally is not, however, without significant risks and complications (Dixon and Monk 2014a). Investing locally may face, in certain cases, political opposition, as resources are channeled to specific sectors or regions. There may be insufficient local expertise to execute and monitor investments. There may be insufficient competition from comparable investment entities to allow for price discovery and performance benchmarking. And, the local opportunities and capital needs may be inappropriate for a boutique private equity–like investment fund, but rather more appropriate for an institution comparable to a development bank, or simply more appropriate for direct government outlays (as also discussed in chapter 8). The former is focused on equity investment and venture financing with ownership rights, whereas the latter focuses on debt financing.

If active investment is inappropriate or constrained, however, the possibility of employing an internationally oriented SWF in local micro-level development is not precluded. Here, the investment income from the international portfolio could be distributed as a cash dividend to all citizens or funneled into services (e.g., health, education) that support and facilitate social and economic development. In this manner, the internationally oriented SWF is rendered an SDF, but of a different form.

In this chapter, we unpack the possibilities and constraints facing SDFs. Our focus and logic are primarily conceptual and deductive, rather than directly empirical and inductive. In the next section, we consider how and in what ways sovereign wealth can be employed for the purpose of economic development. We present two types of SDF, while also considering various constraints in establishing an SDF in relation to political authority, financial capability, and development-related investment opportunities.

DEVELOPMENT AND SOVEREIGN WEALTH

It is crucial to note that a sovereign fund of any form and function is not a replacement for conventional government functions and spending through the budget. Sovereign funds are first and foremost financial institutions that may provide some sort of support function to such traditional government obligations and policy agendas, but financial institutions of any type are limited in their function. No advanced economy developed on the basis of a single financial institution. Development of the financial sector and the capabilities of financial institutions were arguably important for the development of modern high-income economies (Gerschenkron 1962), facilitating the flow of capital across space to growing sectors and regions, but such development occurred in conjunction with broader institutional development and generally significant state support (Acemoglu and Robinson 2012). Put simply, the capabilities of a sovereign fund, no matter its size, must not be overstated (as also highlighted in chapter 2). Expectations must be tempered. However, this does not preclude the possibility of a sovereign fund supporting economic growth and development in certain ways. There are, in that case, three broad policy areas to which a sovereign fund could contribute: macroeconomic policy, microeconomic policy, and social policy (see Rodrik 2007 for further specification of these three policy domains).

MACROECONOMIC POLICY

In relation to macroeconomic policy, a sovereign fund could play a role in fiscal policy, facilitating the smoothing of resource revenue spending over time, and in monetary policy by limiting the appreciation of the exchange rate. It could also play a role in supplying liquidity in the event of severe macroeconomic shocks and crises. The potential organizational and institutional form of the sovereign fund or funds that provide these functions is not restricted to any one particular configuration. However, many of these functions demand a short time horizon of the investment portfolio and a high degree of liquidity. Limiting appreciation of the exchange rate requires that the assets be held offshore.

In the event of a macroeconomic shock or the collapse of government revenues, ready access to the resources of the fund is required. This means that the fund cannot be tied up in long-term, illiquid assets. The fund could be invested in a broad range of financial assets, such as equities, but there is a risk that the performance of such assets would be correlated to the events or circumstances to which the government requires access to the fund. Put simply, taking greater risk with the investment portfolio may limit the ability of the fund to provide precautionary savings or a smoothing function for government spending. Hence, provision of these functions could come from a simple stabilization fund invested in low-risk assets. Often, these funds are merely separate accounts at the central bank or treasury. Yet, there is no reason why a more sophisticated and independent sovereign fund could not be employed as a lender of last resort or to smooth government spending. The asset allocation of the fund could include a proportion devoted to lower-risk securities, as do many cognate large-asset owners (e.g., public pension funds).

SOCIAL POLICY

In facilitating macroeconomic policy in these ways, the sovereign fund (or stabilization fund) is a passive agent supporting economic growth and development. The fund does not replace the functions of budgetary spending in the economy, nor does it take a role in deciding where capital flows in the economy. In supporting the budget in this fashion, the fund is also passively supporting social policy, assuming the government invests in health care and education as a means of raising the capabilities of the workforce and that the budget is used in poverty mitigation efforts. It would likewise be supporting government spending on old-age benefits.

Here, however, a separate pension reserve fund could be established that invests over the long term to match long-term pension obligations, which are increasing across many parts of the world due to demographic aging (Palacios 2003). For most low-income economies, however, demographic structures are still young. Current pension obligations are generally a very small proportion of government obligations, and they are unlikely to grow significantly over the medium term as continued underdevelopment limits life expectancy (Holzmann and Hinz 2005). Where pension reserve funds have been established, they are usually in middle- to high-income economies where there are greater short- and medium-terms costs associated with demographic aging.

There is no reason why a stabilization fund or a similar account held at the treasury or central bank holding low-risk assets could not fulfill this function as well. But as the liabilities associated with old-age pension obligations are long term, there is a greater argument for matching such liabilities with an investment strategy that is likewise longer term in focus. In effect, there is less of a need to hold highly liquid low-risk assets. There is a greater capacity to take increased investment risk (e.g., investing in equities), where performance is likely to be more volatile in the short run but where the risk-adjusted returns over the long term are greater (Dimson, Marsh, and Staunton 2002). Yet, taking on greater risk would require a sovereign fund with an institutional and organizational form that is more sophisticated and purpose built.

MICROECONOMIC POLICY

Microeconomic policy broadly refers to how productive efficiency of the economy is underwritten. This includes institutions such as property rights and the rule of law. But it also includes how and to what degree the state intervenes in the market. By this logic, a sovereign fund can be another mechanism through which the state participates in fomenting the productive capabilities of the market economy. This type of sovereign fund could be classified as an SDF. In this capacity, the fund could, in theory, catalyze economic activity and greater diversification of the economy by investing in particular sectors or infrastructural assets. The latter should not, however, be a replacement for or a direct competitor of government provision and maintenance of infrastructure. The SDF in our model operates as a market-based entity where there is likely to be external participation, whether local or foreign. But if local and foreign private investment is already forthcoming, this function is unnecessary and potentially distortive. The SDF helps crowd in investment where it may not be forthcoming or is insufficient. It could also help attract foreign firms through strategic alliances that have the purpose of facilitating technology and knowledge transfer (Haberly 2011). But, the success of any of this over the long term also assumes that it coincides with the broader institutional development that underwrites and incentivizes productive efficiency and productive capabilities.

But supporting microeconomic policy does not necessarily have to come in the form of an SDF acting as strategic investment fund. Some have argued that development can be supported by transferring cash dividends from natural resource production directly to the poor (Gillies 2011; Moss 2011). In addition to increasing purchasing power, increasing the incomes of those most in need could decrease long-term poverty by improving human capital. In short, limiting social deprivation creates the time and possibility for developing human capital and therefore productive efficiency. Again, this is not an argument for reducing the role or obligations of the state in ensuring adequate provision of basic services (e.g., health, education).

A system of cash transfers does not require a sovereign fund to administer them. They could be disbursed from current revenues. Or, the investment income from a long-term savings fund could be distributed directly to the citizenry in the form of a citizens' dividend. In effect, the fund is managed as a long-term concern but with recurring benefits in the short term, subject to financial performance and contingent on the capacity of the economy to absorb the dividend. This provides a long-term intergenerational savings mechanism while also helping current generations emerge from poverty. Helping the current generation emerge from poverty, and therefore creating a more capable and resilient economy and society, is ostensibly better for future generations than simply leaving future generations with a trust fund.

A SIMPLE TYPOLOGY

Sovereign funds come in a variety of different forms and have a variety of functions to serve different policy outcomes and concerns. However, it is important to stress that mission clarity is crucial to the success of any sovereign fund. Sovereign funds cannot be all things to all people (Bauer, Rietveld, and Toledano 2014). Stabilization funds, for example, should be invested offshore in highly liquid low-risk assets. Stabilizations funds are therefore inappropriate for making direct high-risk investments in the local economy. Doing so may compromise their mission of stabilizing the government budget and serving as a source of precautionary savings, which indirectly supports economic growth and development. A long-term savings fund focused on portfolio investing and generating long-term risk-adjusted returns from global financial markets again may not be the most appropriate vehicle for catalyzing domestic industry. Sovereign funds can be designed to fulfill multiple functions (e.g., a savings fund can serve a stabilization function through an aligned strategic asset allocation or separate portfolios), but there are limits. Establishing separate funds may be a more effective means of aligning form and function.

We are interested in developing an understanding of sovereign funds focused on furthering domestic economic growth and development, particularly in low- to middle-income resource-rich countries. The following discussion is not meant to be prescriptive, nor should it be interpreted restrictively. We define two "ideal typical" development funds. The first type, Type I, is a development fund that is actively managed in a similar fashion to a private equity or venture capital fund, making investments in sectors and projects that are deemed strategic to encouraging economic growth, development, and diversification. This could include investments in public companies inasmuch as there is a developed local (or regional) equities market, where there is also developed regulatory oversight. Investing through public markets may not provide sufficient monitoring and control opportunities.

The second type of development fund, Type II, is a fund that is invested internationally—in part to mitigate Dutch disease—and returns a cash dividend to all citizens. Although targeting the most in need is a possibility, this strategy would likely face opposition from those who do not receive the benefit. In a context where cash dividends are difficult to administer, or are deemed to be of insufficient priority, a Type II dividend-focused development fund could likewise be earmarked to support other development needs, such as helping to finance education and health care investments. The Type II fund is, in effect, geared toward ensuring distributive justice, while supporting productive efficiency and productive capabilities in relation to human capital development.

A Type I fund would not be appropriate for regular dividend distribution, as the assumption is that its investments would be less liquid or illiquid over the short to medium term. In short, the Type II fund is designed to preserve wealth over the long term, while returning regular dividends contingent with financial market performance. This orientation is comparable to the Alaska Permanent Fund, which distributes a dividend to all state residents annually (Widerquist and Howard 2012). The Type I fund, in contrast, is oriented toward developing and holding productive assets over the long term, but without the need or goal of returning cash in the short to medium term. This model mirrors that adopted by Malaysia's Khazanah, Singapore's Temasek, and Bahrain's Mumtalakat.

We next consider the constraints and opportunities SDFs face as financial institutions employing a particular investment strategy and style. The intent is to understand the viability and potential constraints different types of funds may confront and therefore their suitability as a policy tool in different contexts. We delineate three areas: (i) the structure of political authority; (ii) local financial capabilities; and (iii) catalytic opportunities.

THE STRUCTURE OF POLITICAL AUTHORITY

Sovereign funds of any kind are inherently state entities (Balding 2012; Hatton and Pistor 2012). No matter the degree of autonomy afforded a sovereign fund, its independence is relative. A sovereign fund is never absolutely independent; a sovereign fund serves the objectives of the sponsor. Consequently, the sovereign fund is subject to the prevailing structure of the political authority of the state. That prevailing structure may constrain different investment strategies (as also highlighted in chapter 4). In a representative democracy, where authority is distributed across society, reaching consensus on allowable investment objectives may be difficult to obtain. Or, the targeting of particular sectors or even individual firms may be contested. Targeting may appear to favor particular interest groups over others, even if the rationale for such investments has firm commercial bases. In countries where political authority is concentrated, such as in a single-party state or an absolute monarchy, such challenges to the legitimacy of particular investment strategies, particularly those targeted at specific sectors or firms, may not be contested. Even if such grievances did arise, there would be limited opportunity to exercise voice and demand accountability.

Where political authority is distributed, it is arguably more difficult to rationalize and maintain a targeted investment portfolio than it is to rationalize and maintain a diversified investment portfolio. Diversification, following conventional financial theory, namely modern portfolio theory, is effectively a depoliticized form of investing. Diversifying across asset classes and geographies strips away any appearance of impropriety or the potential thereof. A targeted investment portfolio may not have any political basis to it, but it is more difficult to strip away the appearance of politics with such a portfolio. Where political authority is concentrated, the legitimacy of the investment, at least in the local context, is not subject to significant contestation. Hence, the investment portfolio could be either diversified or targeted, or a combination thereof. In figure 6.1 we visualize this relationship. The x-axis shows the investment portfolio along a spectrum from diversified to targeted. The y-axis shows political authority along a spectrum from distributed to concentrated. The relationship shown by the black line suggests that the more distributed political authority is, the greater the demands for a diversified portfolio, whereas greater concentration of authority allows for either complete diversification or increasing targeting.

By this logic, a Type II fund may not be as appropriate as a Type I fund in a political environment characterized by distributed authority. Consider, for example, the ongoing political contestation surrounding the establishment and legitimacy of Nigeria's new Sovereign Investment

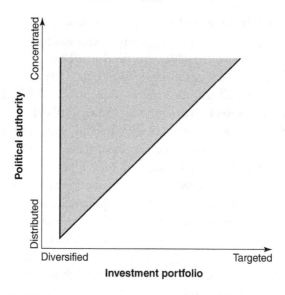

Figure 6.1 **Political authority and the scope of investment.**

Authority, which aims to be a strategic investor in the country's economy and infrastructure alongside foreign partners (Ezeani 2012). In a political environment characterized by concentrated political authority, both Type I and Type II funds would, in contrast, be feasible. Yet, the relationship portrayed in figure 6.1 should not be read restrictively. While there is logic behind this relationship, it does not mean that countries with distributed political authority could not likewise design and employ a fund that makes targeted and strategic investments. Exercising the latter requires greater attention to and precision regarding how the fund is governed and how it communicates what it does and why. Governance and communication still matter for a Type II fund in the context of distributed political authority, but governing and explaining a diversified portfolio is comparatively simpler.

LOCAL FINANCIAL CAPABILITIES

It may appear that an environment characterized by concentrated authority has better prospects and greater options in the design of an SDF. Unfortunately, the facets of SDF design are more complicated than this. Financial services is a knowledge-intensive industry. Finance relies on the skills and expertise of people. These people may be in supply in some places, namely larger international and regional financial centers, but they are often in short supply elsewhere. Or, where financial capabilities and other indispensable professional capabilities (e.g., law, accountancy) do exist, they may be insufficiently diverse in their range. For a government trying to establish a sovereign fund, such limitations pose significant challenges (Dixon and Monk 2014b). On the one hand, available talent may simply be in insufficient supply. On the other hand, where talent and expertise do exist locally, the government may struggle to attract people away from other firms, particularly if it is unwilling to match private-sector compensation rates (as also underscored in chapter 4).

If financial capabilities are limited or underdeveloped, the investment approach of the fund will be constrained. In figure 6.2, we visualize this relationship. The y-axis shows financial capabilities on a spectrum from undeveloped to developed. We take a broad view of financial capabilities here. This view includes the various types of individuals that take part in investment management and deal execution, from asset managers to legal advisers and accountants. We also include the range of these individuals' expertise, from sector-specific to geographical expertise. The x-axis shows investment approach on a spectrum from passive investment (e.g., indexing) to active investment, which includes more complex investment strategies and direct investing. The solid line represents

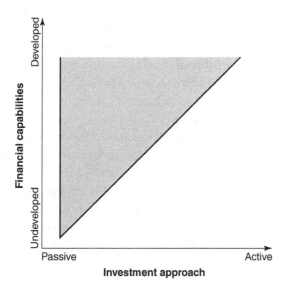

Figure 6.2　Financial capabilities and the scope of investment.

the relationship between financial capabilities and investment approach. Those places with greater financial capabilities (e.g., London, New York) are able to execute passive and/or active investment approaches. Those places with less developed capabilities are likely to be limited to more passive investment strategies.

By this logic, it is much simpler to implement a Type II fund that follows a more passive investment strategy and where asset management is delegated to external managers. Even though asset management is outsourced, this does not mean that local capabilities and expertise are of lesser significance. Insourced asset management poses major challenges and is usually limited only to relatively large asset owners (Clark and Monk 2013). Outsourcing investment functions solves the problem of insufficient local capabilities, but managing and monitoring the investment contracts and deciding on asset allocation still requires some sophistication, particularly when greater risks are taken with the investment portfolio. Following the logic illustrated in figure 6.2, a Type II fund with limited local financial capabilities would struggle (or be at significant risk) when delegating investment management to anything more sophisticated than basic index trackers. Put another way, the state sponsor and the fund's board must have a basic modicum of understanding of what external asset managers are doing, the risks they are taking, and the fees they are charging.

The logic of figure 6.2 has more significant implications for the employment of a Type I fund. The availability of local talent and expertise is mission critical. Outsourcing is not out of the question, but the issue of local supply and the quality of that local supply again surfaces. Buying in outside talent and expertise is expensive, and such individuals are unlikely to have the necessary local knowledge. As we have indicated, the figures and two "ideal types" we are presenting are not meant to be overly prescriptive. Indeed, a Type I fund facing limited local capabilities could buy in outside talent (while also training local talent), it could outsource some mandates, and it could partner with other foreign investors that bring greater expertise and potentially more credibility. Notwithstanding such possibilities, the logic presented in figure 6.2 has important implications. For a sovereign fund to operate as a financial institution in local and international markets, it should have an appropriate and adequate governance structure that shapes investment decision making coupled with the necessary expertise. Figure 6.2 simply highlights the likely constraints facing many governments around the world.

CATALYTIC OPPORTUNITIES

The fundamental difference of catalytic opportunities in the investment styles of Type I and Type II funds raises another critical issue that requires consideration: whether finance leads to or follows development (Patrick 1966). For some, finance and financial intermediaries lead to development. In this perspective, there is, in effect, a large role for financial intermediaries in identifying and financing entrepreneurs and technological changes that lead to economic growth and development (Schumpeter 1934). They catalyze opportunities. Accordingly, the sophistication and quality of financial institutions and the financial services industry are critical. Financial intermediaries emerge in advance of the demand for their services, assets, and liabilities. Individual financial institutions and the industry as a whole play an active role in economic growth and change, identifying, researching, and financing the most promising sectors, firms, corporate managers, and entrepreneurs. This perspective underpins the rationale of a Type I fund.

For others, finance and financial intermediaries follow development. From this perspective, the financial system and the financial intermediaries therein simply follow in the wake of enterprising firms and entrepreneurs, facilitating the flow of capital between savers and borrowers, between high-growth regions and low-growth regions, and from slow-growth sectors to high-growth sectors (Robinson 1952). Put simply, financial intermediaries respond to the demand for their services. When an entrepreneur has a new idea or when a firm sees growth opportunities that it cannot finance with internal resources, financial intermediaries respond. In contrast to the previous orientation, the catalytic agent is less the financial intermediary than it is the entrepreneur or the enterprising firm. Financial intermediaries and the quality of the services rendered still matter, but they are passive actors in the growth and development process.

Although either extreme may not reflect reality, the implications are still worth considering in the context of SDF design. If one subscribes to the former view—the catalytic view—then there is a reason to be confident in the potential of a Type I fund. However, this view is still contingent on the quality of the services rendered by the fund. As highlighted in the previous section, talent and organizational design matter. To reiterate, without sufficient local talent, employing a Type I fund may be a futile exercise. Assuming such conditions, one may have greater confidence in a Type II fund, whose underlying design logic reflects the demand-following, or passive, perspective on the role of finance in growth and development.

If, however, local talent is sufficient, or buying in talent and partnering with foreign investors can solve the problem of insufficient local talent and expertise, there is still the question of whether there are sufficient catalytic opportunities. Consider, for example, that in advanced economies, many new technologies have emerged from universities and government- or military-funded research (Mazzucato 2011). Likewise, the private market for greenfield infrastructure investment has been historically small. Most private infrastructure investment is in brownfield sites (O'Neill 2009). In short, advanced economies have benefited from cumulative public investment that provides the economic and social basis that facilitates higher-yielding investment opportunities for the private sector. By this logic, a Type I fund may not be effective without a sufficient level of economic development that is financed through more conventional channels (e.g., public investment). As emphasized earlier, a Type I fund, or any government-sponsored institutional investor, is not a replacement for conventional government functions and public investment.

As we have stressed, over the long term, sovereign funds are only successful inasmuch as they are part of wider institutional development. For some countries, catalytic opportunities may not be readily available, or they may be inappropriate for a Type I fund. Catalytic opportunities may develop over time, along with broader institutional development. But until such time, a passive Type II fund may be more appropriate. Adding the problem of sourcing talent and expertise further reinforces the Type II option. This logic is visualized in figure 6.3, where the x-axis represents local catalytic opportunities, and the y-axis represents local financial capabilities. The quadrants of the graph suggest the possible fund configuration given local conditions. Where, for example, local catalytic opportunities are great (i.e., where a targeted investment approach is appropriate) but where local financial capabilities are underdeveloped, a Type I fund that co-invests with outside partners would be possible. If local financial capabilities are also developed, co-investment (or buying in talent) would not be essential, but it is also possible. Where local catalytic opportunities and local financial capabilities are limited, an outsourced Type II fund would be the most appropriate. If local financial capabilities were developed, then insourcing of some asset management functions would be a possibility. Insourcing, however, is generally limited to funds with enough assets under management that allow for economies of scale. This is not typical of most funds, particularly in low-income economies.

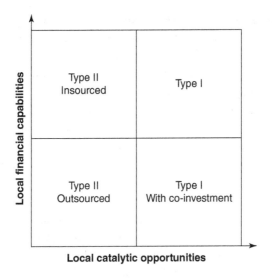

Figure 6.3 Local financial capabilities and local catalytic opportunities.

CONCLUSION

We began this chapter by noting the recent collapse in global crude oil prices, which will invariably wreak havoc to those dependent government budgets and economies. This recent collapse is not special, nor is it uncommon. Commodity production can bring vast wealth to a country, but it has not been the development cure one would hope for. Although the creation of sovereign funds as a means of managing resource revenues and putting them to different uses are not a panacea to the developmental challenges facing resource-rich countries, particularly low-income countries, they may at least be a useful tool to support broad-based development while moving the country beyond resource dependency. Yet, there are various exogenous conditions that may limit the design scope and operational capacity of such a fund.

In that respect, we outlined three design constraints that require reflection for a government considering establishing a sovereign fund to facilitate development: (i) the structure of political authority; (ii) the available financial capabilities; and (iii) the availability and appropriateness of opportunities to catalyze economic growth and development through targeted investment. In some political contexts, certain investment strategies may not be accepted as legitimate, although they may be made legitimate through a robust governance architecture, public engagement and communication, and transparency. An investment strategy may be unfeasible because there are insufficient human resources available to execute it. But this problem could be solved, potentially, through collaboration with external partners and service providers. And, a targeted local investment may be inappropriate because the private sector is already making such investments or the investments are unlikely to derive extra-financial benefits that underwrite economic and social development. It may be more appropriate, in contrast, to funnel the returns from a passive portfolio to support human capital development or even distribute as a cash dividend.

Making use of the tools of finance to spur development means that a sovereign fund must be even more savvy and rigorous than the average investor. At the same time, this means that the sponsoring government must understand the strengths and weaknesses of various forms and functions a sovereign fund could assume. The simple typology presented, in that vain, is about signaling the likely constraints and why they exist such that they are either avoided or accounted for through appropriate organizational design and governance. This chapter is ultimately meant as a nonexhaustive contribution to the understanding of the sovereign fund–finance–development nexus. With the introduction of new sovereign funds devoted to development and the aging of others, there should be greater empirical evidence to refine and test our assumptions of what works and what does not.

REFERENCES

Acemoglu, D., and J. A. Robinson. 2012. *Why Nations Fail: The Origins of Power, Prosperity and Poverty.* New York: Crown.
Balding, C. 2012. *Sovereign Wealth Funds: The New Intersection of Money and Politics.* New York: Oxford University Press.
Bauer, A., M. Rietveld, and P. Toledano. 2014. "Managing the Public Trust: How to Make Natural Resource Funds Work for Citizens," edited by A. Bauer. New York: Columbia Center on Sustainable Investment and Natural Resource Governance Institute. http://ccsi.columbia.edu/files/2014/09/NRF_Complete_Report_EN.pdf.
Clark, G. L., A. D. Dixon, and A. H. B. Monk. 2013. *Sovereign Wealth Funds: Legitimacy, Governance, and Global Power.* Princeton, NJ: Princeton University Press.
Clark, G. L., and A. H. B. Monk. 2013. "The Scope of Financial Institutions: Insourcing, Outsourcing and Off-shoring," *Journal of Economic Geography* 13, no. 2: 279–298.
Collier, P., R. van der Ploeg, M. Spence, and A. J. Venables. 2011. "Managing Resource Revenues in Developing Economies," *IMF Staff Papers* 57, no. 1: 84–118.

Corden, W., and J. Neary. 1982. "Booming Sector and De-industrialisation in a Small Open Economy," *The Economic Journal* 92, no. 368: 825–848.

Deaton, A. 1999. "Commodity Prices and Growth in Africa," *The Journal of Economic Perspectives* 13, no. 3: 23–40.

Dimson, E., P. Marsh, and M. Staunton. 2002. *Triumph of the Optimists: 111 Years of Global Investment Returns*. Princeton, NJ: Princeton University Press.

Dixon, A. D., and A. H. B. Monk. 2014a. "Financializing Development: Toward a Sympathetic Critique of Sovereign Development Funds," *Journal of Sustainable Finance & Investment* 4, no. 4: 357–371.

———. 2014b. "Frontier Finance," *Annals of the Association of American Geographers* 114, no. 4: 852–868.

Eifert, B., A. Gelb, and N. Borje Tallroth. 2003. "The Political Economy of Fiscal Policy and Economic Management in Oil-Exporting Countries." In *Fiscal Policy Formulation and Implementation in Oil-Producing Countries*, edited by J. M. Davis, R. Ossowski, and A. Fedelino, 82–122. Washington, DC: International Monetary Fund.

Ezeani, J. 2012. "An Overview of the Nigerian Sovereign Investment Authority." Boston: SovereigNET, Fletcher School, Tufts University, http://fletcher.tufts .edu/~/media/Fletcher/Microsites/swfi/pdfs/2012/NigeriaSWFFinal.pdf.

Gerschenkron, A. 1962. *Economic Backwardness in Historical Perspective: A Book of Essays*. Cambridge, MA: Belknap.

Gillies, A. 2011. "Giving Money Away? The Politics of Direct Distribution in Resource-Rich States," Working Paper 231. Washington, DC: Center for Global Development.

Haberly, D. 2011. "Strategic Sovereign Wealth Fund Investment and the New Alliance Capitalism: A Network Mapping Investigation," *Environment and Planning A* 43, no. 8: 1833–1852.

Hatton, K. J., and K. Pistor. 2012. "Maximizing Autonomy in the Shadow of Great Powers: The Political Economy of Sovereign Wealth Funds," *Columbia Journal of Transnational Law* 50, no. 1: 1–81.

Holzmann, R., and R. P. Hinz. 2005. *Old-Age Income Support in the 21st Century: An International Perspective on Pension Systems and Reform*. Washington, DC: World Bank.

Karl, T. L. 1997. *The Paradox of Plenty: Oil Booms and Petro-states*. Berkeley: University of California Press.

Mazzucato, M. 2011. *The Entrepreneurial State*. London: Demos.

Moss, T. 2011. "Oil to Cash: Fighting the Resource Curse through Cash Transfers," Working Paper 237. Washington, DC: Center for Global Development.

O'Neill, P. 2009. "Infrastructure Investment and the Management of Risk." In *Managing Financial Risks: From Global to Local*, edited by G. L. Clark, A. D. Dixon, and A. H. B. Monk, 163–188. Oxford: Oxford University Press.

Palacios, R. 2003. "Securing Public Pension Promises Through Funding." In *The Pension Challenge: Risk Transfers and Retirement Income Security*, edited by O. S. Mitchell and K. A. Smetters, 116–158. Oxford: Oxford University Press.

Patrick, H. 1966. "Financial Development and Economic Growth in Underdeveloped Countries," *Economic Development and Cultural Change* 14, no. 2: 174–189.

Robinson, J. 1952. *The Rate of Interest, and Other Essays*. London: Macmillan.

Rodrik, D. 2006. "The Social Cost of Foreign Exchange Reserves," *International Economic Journal* 20, no. 3: 253–266.

——. 2007. *One Economics, Many Recipes: Globalization, Institutions, and Economic Growth*. Princeton, NJ: Princeton University Press.

Ross, M. L. 2012. *The Oil Curse: How Petroleum Wealth Shapes the Development of Nations*. Princeton, NJ: Princeton University Press.

Schumpeter, J. 1934. *The Theory of Economic Development: An Inquiry into Profits, Capital, Credit, Interest, and the Business Cycle*. Cambridge, MA: Harvard University Press.

Widerquist, K., and M. Howard, eds. 2012. *Exporting the Alaska Model: Adapting the Permanent Fund Dividend for Reform Around the World*. New York: Palgrave Macmillan.

CHAPTER 7

Domestic Investment Practices of Sovereign Wealth Funds

EMPIRICAL EVIDENCE TO INFORM POLICY DEBATES

Ekaterina Gratcheva and Nikoloz Anasashvili
The World Bank Treasury

The design and implementation of policies and governance arrangements around domestic investment mandates have become a matter of increasing importance for sovereign wealth funds (SWFs) and other large public investors. However, the quality of analysis of this important topic has been hampered by a lack of clear and consistent data on domestic investment practices by SWFs. In this chapter, we aim to contribute to the documentation of the existing practices of these institutions by drawing on the results of the global survey conducted by the World Bank Treasury's Reserves Advisory and Management Program (RAMP) in 2015 with support from the International Forum of Sovereign Wealth Funds.

We report the findings of the survey and provide an interpretation of the results. It is important to acknowledge the significant diversity among SWFs in terms of the domestic market context and fund design, which play a substantive role in shaping investment practices for domestic investments. Nevertheless, given the lack of domestic investment survey data, this chapter provides some helpful insights into the current domestic investment practices of SWFs.

THE RISE OF DOMESTIC INVESTMENT MANDATES

By 2015, a significant number of countries had established various forms of institutions to manage their sovereign assets, ranging from more traditional stabilization funds and funds for future generations, both of which invest in foreign assets, to funds focusing on economic development within the country or the neighboring region. More recently, funds have been established that integrate several of these objectives (e.g., those of

Nigeria and Angola). Recent discoveries of new natural resource deposits, oil and gas in particular, primarily in developing countries, and the commodity price boom cycle over the last decade have influenced public debate on the most effective way to manage these resources in order to contribute to national development and prosperity. Thus, it is unsurprising that the debate has shifted to the most effective ways to channel increased natural resource revenue to fund domestic development objectives from a more traditional approach of mitigating the negative impacts of resource abundance that, in many countries, led to the accumulation of substantial foreign assets in national SWFs.

Until the early 2000s, most SWFs were established with stabilization and intergenerational transfer objectives and were designed to invest all or almost all of their assets abroad. Historically, SWFs avoided significant domestic investments, primarily in order to avoid Dutch disease and increased inflationary pressure on the domestic currency. Many SWFs continue to invest their assets exclusively in foreign assets. An extensive track record of designing and managing such funds over the last seventy years (and even longer in the case of some American state permanent funds) has produced a significant body of practical knowledge and tools that provide policy makers with blueprints for how to implement such funds for a given country. Further, the peer community of existing SWFs has developed a set of principles and best practices, in the form of the Santiago Principles, that combine the voices of a diverse set of SWFs across countries of all income levels.

However, an increasing number of funds, especially those created in the past decade in developing economies, are eager to invest domestically in order to galvanize local economies and help finance domestic infrastructure. With a particular emphasis on African countries that are experiencing significant natural resource discoveries, more recent studies have called for rethinking conventional policy advice on this matter. Today, there appears to be a growing recognition that for resource-rich developing countries, the optimal allocation of SWF assets is likely to include a significant domestic investment component (see chapter 2 for an exposition of the International Monetary Fund's latest analysis of this issue).

Those advocating for domestic investment by SWFs cite multiple potential benefits. Such advantages include tax benefits, informational advantages associated with proximity to local economies, and denomination in local currency. There are, however, disadvantages associated with a concentration of assets in domestic economies that lead to significant idiosyncratic risks: a limited set of local investment opportunities; absorptive, institutional, and technical capacity constraints; and a greater potential for conflicts of interest and political interference in investment decision making that could steer significant investment into politically driven projects. These challenges are substantial and vary significantly from country to country. Therefore, clear governance frameworks and investment management guidelines are critical for public funds that invest or plan to invest a significant proportion of their assets domestically (as also explained in chapters 5 and 8).

THE CONTRASTING ORIGINS OF DOMESTIC INVESTMENTS BY PUBLIC ASSET MANAGERS

Public pension funds have a longer track record of investing in domestic markets. In fact, until relatively recently, public pension funds had been managing mostly domestic portfolios and had been typically restricted from investing in foreign assets. The economic reasons for such restrictions included the objective to deepen domestic capital markets and to avoid exchange rate risks owing to having assets denominated in a currency other than that of the pension fund's liabilities (World Bank 2000). In the early 1990s, however, public pension funds started gradually relaxing limits on foreign investments as policy makers recognized the benefits of global diversification (Reisen 1997). However, the assets of most public pension funds are still predominantly invested in domestic economies.

In contrast to public pension funds, the evolution of domestic investment by SWFs is less linear. Established SWFs with domestic investment mandates were typically founded for different reasons and took different evolutionary paths to their current status as important investors in their domestic economies, with three basic paradigms evident. One paradigm in this evolution is exemplified by funds such as Singapore's Temasek Holdings and Malaysia's Khazanah Nasional Berhad. At present, both institutions are recognized as SWFs with well-established domestic investment portfolios. Both institutions were established as holding companies to improve the management of government shares in domestic firms, rather than as managers of capital funded from the country's fiscal surpluses or the excess of foreign exchange reserves. They are, in many respects, comparable to the private equity funds that assume an active role in reforming and managing domestic companies.

Another model is illustrated by funds including Australia's Future Fund and New Zealand's Superannuation Fund (see chapter 3), which were created with the purposes of defraying their respective governments' future pension liabilities. Both funds were funded primarily from fiscal surpluses, and their investment mandates excluded the consideration of domestic economic development criteria. These funds are explicitly prohibited by legislation from holding or taking substantial controlling interests in any operating entity, including takeovers of listed companies and acquisitions of majority interests in unlisted entities. Both funds have, however, invested in their respective domestic asset classes, both public and private, on the basis of the assets' risk–return characteristics and the total portfolio return maximization within certain risk parameters around their investment objective. The investment portfolios of these funds are highly diversified across global asset classes, and the proportion of domestic assets is much smaller than that of Temasek or Khazanah.

Finally, in a third evolutionary category are funds that were originally created at times of fiscal surplus with an objective of managing portfolios of foreign assets and that were later transformed into funds with domestic mandates at times of fiscal pressure and scarce capital owing to the lingering impact of the global financial crisis on public and private finances. Examples include Ireland, Kazakhstan, and Russia, whose funds have either been fully transformed to invest exclusively domestically (Ireland) or, through a gradual evolution of the investment portfolio, have come to include investments in strategic domestic investments (Kazakhstan, Russia).

While taking distinct evolutionary paths, these institutions are now facing similar challenges and share an objective of developing themselves into world-class investment institutions that demonstrate a measurable impact on their domestic economies and generate investment returns. These and newly established funds have been joining relevant international organizations and fora, such as the International Forum of Sovereign Wealth Funds, to share their experiences and contribute to the development of best investment practices within the current economic and political environments. This chapter contributes to the debate by providing an overview of the existing practices of several institutions with domestic mandates and highlighting the common challenges faced by these institutions and the impact of distinct contexts on the institutional practices. In the next several sections, we present the results of the RAMP survey in the following areas: a general overview of the funds that undertake domestic investment, the governance arrangements of these funds, their investment objectives, and their investment operations. We also share insights into various partnerships that these funds undertake to execute specific investments, how they view domestic infrastructure investments, and their current concerns and expectations for the medium-term future.

STUDY OBJECTIVES AND DESIGN

We define a sovereign wealth fund as a long-term investment fund owned by a sovereign nation, distinct from investments by national pension funds with explicit pension liabilities, state-owned enterprises, development banks, and development funds, and distinct from central bank management of official foreign exchange reserves. Based on this definition, there are a significant number of SWFs managing foreign assets and many with a long track record.

There are many fewer sovereign funds that invest most of their portfolios domestically as part of managing a country's sovereign wealth. There are some notable institutions, such as Temasek in Singapore and Khazanah in Malaysia, that are currently classified by some definitions as an SWF with significant domestic investments. However, such funds have evolved as public companies to manage government holdings and improve the return on government assets. New institutions that target domestic assets have recently been established, but these institutions are still in the early stages of institutional and operational development. In addition to their scarcity and novelty, sovereign funds that invest domestically are less open and less transparent than their peers who invest in foreign assets. Further, when information is publicly available, it is not easily comparable across institutions, as reports reflect unique domestic realities.

To bridge this information gap, the objective of the RAMP survey was to obtain an in-depth view of current policies and practices across existing institutions. The survey included detailed questions on all aspects of investment management, from governance and investment policies to investment operations and human resources matters. The results of this analysis should contribute to the ongoing debate about key principles and best practices for sovereign institutions with large domestic portfolios, similar to the Santiago Principles, which were developed by and for funds managing foreign assets.

Table 7.1   Distribution of survey respondents by continent

Continent	Number of funds
Africa	4
Americas	11
Asia	3
Europe	6
Oceania	2
Total	**26**

In order to increase the sample size, the survey also includes public pension funds with both domestic and foreign investment mandates. We excluded public pension funds with solely domestic investments in order to facilitate comparison between SWFs (which very rarely invest exclusively domestically) and public pension funds. The questionnaire was sent directly to senior fund officers. Twenty-six funds (ten SWFs and sixteen public pension funds) participated in the survey, with total assets under management exceeding $1.8 trillion in the aggregate; 90 percent of survey completions were submitted by chief investment officers or other senior managers. The funds surveyed represent sixteen countries, nine of which are advanced economies and seven of which are emerging-market and developing economies (based on classification by the International Monetary Fund). While the SWFs represented in the survey are equally split between advanced and developing economies, most of the participating public pension funds are from advanced economies. The funds represent all continents, as summarized in table 7.1. Twenty-five of the twenty-six funds are authorized to invest both domestically and abroad through national, state, or other regulations.

Although neither the names of these funds nor the details of their responses can be disclosed, we present selected findings and aggregated

Table 7.2   Distribution of survey respondents by vintage

Vintage	Percent	Count
0 ≤ 5 years	15.4%	4
5 ≤ 10 years	7.7%	2
10 ≤ 15 years	11.5%	3
15 ≤ 20 years	3.9%	1
> 20 years	61.5%	16
Total		**26**

Table 7.3 Distribution of survey respondents by assets under management

Assets under management ($ billion)	Percent	Count
0 ≤ 5	11.5%	3
5 ≤ 10	7.7%	2
10 ≤ 50	46.2%	12
50 ≤ 250	26.9%	7
> 250	7.7%	2
Total		**26**

information that should be of particular interest to policymakers searching for effective mechanisms to govern domestic investments.

WHO INVESTS IN DOMESTIC ASSETS?

Most of the SWFs in the sample have been established within the past fifteen years, with several notable new funds having been created in the last three to five years; most of the public pension funds that participated in the survey have been operating for more than fifteen years, as shown in table 7.2. Half of the SWFs in the sample manage assets less than or equal to $10 billion; by contrast, almost all of the public pension funds in the sample manage more than $10 billion in assets, as presented in table 7.3. For SWFs, the primary source of assets is evenly split between natural resources and fiscal surpluses, whereas, for all but one of the public pension funds, the primary source is pension contributions, as shown in table 7.4.

Table 7.4 Distribution of survey respondents by primary source of funding

Source of funding	Percent	Count
Currency reserves	0.0%	0
Natural resources	19.2%	5
Fiscal surpluses (other than natural resources)	19.2%	5
Pension contributions	57.7%	15
Other	3.9%	1
Total		**26**

GOVERNANCE ISSUES

Governance plays a critical role in sound asset management practices and ensuring the long-term sustainability of an investment institution. Sound governance is of even greater importance in the domestic investment context, given the higher likelihood of political interference with the investment process and the potential for greater conflicts of interest for governing bodies when channeling capital into the domestic economy (as discussed in chapters 2, 4, and 5). A fund's public ownership and its mandate to invest domestically create an opportunity and often incentives for governments to direct funds in a politically motivated way, which could lead to explicit or implicit pressure on fund managers to undertake financially suboptimal investments (see also chapter 8). In our analysis of the RAMP survey, we focused on four specific aspects of fund governance: (1) the government approval required in operations and the government's role in the selection of individual investments; (2) the governing system and board composition; (3) remuneration policy; and (4) policy for seeking representation on investee company boards.

With regard to government involvement in the investment process, survey responses indicate that only a few SWFs and even fewer public pension funds require government approval for specific investments. However, based on the survey responses, it appears that public funds require government approval for a range of important decisions, as described in table 7.5. It is unsurprising that the sample's public pension funds report being more insulated from government involvement in their investment operations: 50 percent of public pension funds reported not requiring government approval for any of the listed fund management decisions, whereas only 10 percent of SWFs reported being similarly isolated. This difference is likely a reflection of the different ownership structure of the assets of SWFs versus public pension funds. In the case of SWFs, the central government, typically through the ministry of finance, is entrusted with the formal ownership of sovereign assets. Pension fund members and beneficiaries, on the other hand, own public pension fund assets. In the study's sample, reflecting the trend in the broader universe of funds, central or local governments are owners of 70 percent of the SWFs, whereas pension fund members and beneficiaries own 75 percent of the public pension funds.

There are two main governance systems governing an institution or corporation: a unitary board or a two-tier board. Under a unitary board,

Table 7.5   Answers to survey question "Which of the following aspects of fund management require government approval?"

Aspect of fund management	Percent	Count	% of SWFs	% of PPFs
Selection of domestic investments	12%	3	10%	13%
Particularly large-ticket-size investments (domestic or foreign)	12%	3	20%	6%
Determining the fund's annual budget and expenses	32%	8	40%	25%
Appointment of the fund's CEO, executive director, or equivalent	32%	8	50%	19%
Appointment of the fund's CIO	12%	3	20%	6%
Hiring and dismissing of other senior staff	0%	0	0%	0%
Determining salaries and benefits structure of staff	24%	6	20%	25%
Other	4%	1	10%	0%
None of the above	36%	9	10%	50%
Total		**25**		

Abbreviations: CEO, chief executive officer; CIO, chief investment officer; PPF, public pension fund; SWF, sovereign wealth fund.

there is a single board of directors, comprising executive and nonexecutive directors. The two-tier structure comprises two separate boards: the management board responsible for day-to-day management, consisting of executives and led by the chief executive; and the supervisory, or corporate, board, which has a wider membership and is responsible for the strategic oversight of the institution and is led by the chairperson. Unitary boards are common in both SWFs and public pension funds. In the RAMP survey, eight out of ten SWFs and eleven out of sixteen public pension funds reported having unitary boards. The remaining funds in the sample, both SWFs and public pension funds, reported having a two-tier governing system.

One governance mechanism to mitigate direct or indirect government involvement in investment management decisions is to ensure the independence and competence of a fund's governing board. A typical practice to ensure a board's independence is to select board members who are not affiliated with the government. Ensuring board members' competence necessitates having specific education, experience, and/or certification requirements in place. About a third of the SWFs in the survey sample have no government-affiliated members on their board. For the remaining funds, at least 40 percent and at most 100 percent of their board members are government affiliated. Having board members with financial or banking experience and/or relevant financial certification or education can contribute to a professional asset management practice that prioritizes financial risk-adjusted return. In the RAMP study, 30 percent of the SWFs reported either financial certification or minimum banking or financial experience as a qualification requirement for board members.

A further key aspect of governance is the remuneration policy of public asset managers. Portfolio performance–linked compensation is a common practice in the asset management industry, where market-based salaries and bonuses linked to the financial performance of investment portfolios are seen as incentives for staff to generate superior investment returns. In contrast, many SWFs, which are public investment institutions, are subject to public sector human resources policies and, as such, are constrained by public sector remuneration standards. In the RAMP sample, 60 percent of SWF investment managers reported being subject to general public sector remuneration policies, whereas less than 40 percent of public pension funds reported being subject to such policies, as summarized in table 7.6.

The fourth aspect of governance we examine here is a fund's policy regarding representation on investee company boards. With an increasing focus on environmental, social, and governance (ESG) investments by institutional investors, more and more SWFs are seeking representation on boards of investee companies. In the RAMP sample, 60 percent of SWFs reported seeking representation on the boards of their investee companies, although some only in "exceptional circumstances." Examples of such exceptional circumstances included "if the fund [owns] more than

Table 7.6   Answers to survey question "Is your investment team subject to general public sector remuneration policies?"

Response	Percent	Count	% of SWFs	% of PPFs
Yes	50%	12	60%	38%
No	50%	12	30%	56%
Total		**24**	**9**	**15**

Abbreviations: PPF, public pension fund; SWF, sovereign wealth fund.

Table 7.7   Answers to survey question "Does your fund seek representation on the boards of investee companies?"

Response	Percent	Count	% of SWFs	% of PPFs
Yes	28%	7	40%	19%
No	56%	14	30%	69%
Only in exceptional circumstances	16%	4	20%	13%
Total		**25**		

Abbreviations: PPF, public pension fund; SWF, sovereign wealth fund.

10 percent of issued equity of the company," the management of "some real assets," or "shareholder votes resulting from direct holdings in assets and [trust] unit-holder votes from the fund's interests in pooled vehicles when assets are managed directly" by the fund's team. In the case of public pension funds, 70 percent of survey respondents reported not seeking representation on investee boards, and 13 percent reported seeking representation "only in exceptional circumstances." Table 7.7 presents the responses to this question.

In the context of domestic investments, seeking representation on the boards of investee companies could lead to potential conflicts of interest and, as such, this practice should be specifically accounted for in the fund's conflict-of-interest policies. The RAMP survey results indicate that even though most public pension funds and SWFs have written conflict-of-interest policies, only 10 percent of SWFs (and 13 percent of public pension funds) have conflict-of-interest policies that specifically cover representation on investee company boards.

INVESTMENT OBJECTIVES

The inherent differences between SWFs and public pension funds are further illustrated by the institutional mandates and investment objectives of these funds. The RAMP survey results reaffirmed that countries appear to establish SWFs for a variety of strategic and investment objectives, which results in institutional diversity. In contrast, public pension fund assets are managed to meet contractual pension liabilities, and, as a result, public pension funds are more homogeneous in their investment design. Table 7.8 compares the full range of objectives of SWFs to those of public pension funds.

Table 7.8 Distribution of the investment objectives of survey respondents by fund objective

Fund objective	Percent	Count	% of PPFs	% of SWFs
Directly pay pension and other social security benefits	53.9%	14	87.5%	0%
Generate wealth for future generations	26.9%	7	0.0%	70%
Make strategic investments in local companies	7.7%	2	0.0%	20%
Make transfers to the national budget to fund future superannuation costs	7.7%	2	0.0%	20%
Make transfers to the national budget for stabilization purposes	7.7%	2	0.0%	20%
Manage domestic state-owned enterprises	3.9%	1	0.0%	10%
Generate higher earnings for foreign reserves	3.9%	1	0.0%	10%
Contribute directly to the diversification and sustainable growth of the local economy	15.4%	4	12.5%	20%
Strengthen the government's long-term financial position by making provision for unfunded future pension liabilities	30.8%	8	37.5%	20%
Co-invest in local economy with international investors and attract foreign direct investment	7.7%	2	0.0%	20%
Engage in and promote foreign investments in domestic infrastructure	7.7%	2	0.0%	20%
Other	3.9%	1	0.0%	10%

Abbreviations: PPF, public pension fund; SWF, sovereign wealth fund.

Based on the collective responses to four survey questions, most funds appear not to distinguish between domestic and foreign investments in terms of investment management practices. The majority of funds in the sample reported not having different financial return targets or a different risk tolerance for domestic investments versus foreign investments. Further, whereas most funds reported not having different investment horizons for domestic versus foreign investments, all of those that reported having longer investment horizons for domestic investments than for foreign portfolios are funds in developing countries.

The majority of the surveyed funds (60 percent of SWFs and nearly 70 percent of public pension funds) reported not having an explicit return target for domestic investments, as presented in tables 7.9, 7.10, and 7.11.

Table 7.9   Answers to survey question "Do you have explicit return targets for domestic investment?"

Response	Percent	Count	% of SWFs	% of PPFs
No explicit targets	65.4%	17	60%	69%
Yes, specific financial return	23.1%	6	20%	25%
Yes, specific nonfinancial return	7.7%	2	10%	6%
Yes, specific financial and nonfinancial return	0.0%	0	0%	0%
Other	3.9%	1	10%	0%
Total		**26**	**10**	**16**

Abbreviations: PPF, public pension fund; SWF, sovereign wealth fund.

Among those funds that did report having a return target, two-thirds have a specific financial return target, such as a hurdle nominal or real rate of return (e.g., "CPI + 4 percent", "real 4–5 percent," or "exceeding the rolling cost of domestic government bonds"), whereas the remaining funds reported having a nonfinancial return target. Examples of specific nonfinancial return targets include ESG considerations and supporting local infrastructure development.

When selecting individual domestic investments, almost half of all respondent funds take into account nonfinancial returns, such as economic, social, or strategic considerations. In this regard, there are no significant differences in survey results between SWFs and public pension funds or between funds in advanced versus developing economies.

Table 7.10   Answers to survey question "Do you quantify and assign weights to nonfinancial return criteria?"

Response	Percent	Count	% of SWFs	% of PPFs
Yes, we quantify and fully weigh economic return	9.5%	2	20%	0%
Yes, we quantify and fully weigh social return	4.8%	1	10%	0%
Yes, we quantify and fully weigh other nonfinancial return	0.0%	0	0%	0%
No, we do not quantify or weigh nonfinancial return	85.7%	18	40%	88%
Total		**21**		

Abbreviations: PPF, public pension fund; SWF, sovereign wealth fund.

Table 7.11   Answers to survey question "In selecting individual domestic investments, do you take into account the following criteria?"

Criterion	Percent	Count	% of SWFs	% of PPFs
Financial return	100%	25	90%	100%
Economic return (i.e., return not accruing directly to the investor but to the economy/government at large)	36%	9	40%	31%
Social return	20%	5	20%	19%
Strategic economic considerations	28%	7	40%	19%
Other strategic considerations (e.g., national security)	4%	1	10%	0%
Other	12%	3	20%	6%
Total		**25**		

Abbreviations: PPF, public pension fund; SWF, sovereign wealth fund.

While 30 percent of the surveyed funds reported taking into account economic, social, or strategic returns in selecting individual domestic investments, these funds do not quantify such return. These results suggest that even though these funds are established to contribute to the country's economic development, they undertake their investment based on commercial consideration and do not engage in a "trade-off" between financial and nonfinancial returns. Thus, these funds consider a nonfinancial return as an ancillary benefit to investments that are expected to deliver maximum risk-adjusted financial return for the overall portfolio. Further, nonfinancial returns are challenging to measure, and it is particularly difficult for funds to identify specific benchmarks for assessing the nonfinancial performance of fund managers.

Of the surveyed funds, those with lower financial return targets for domestic investments are public pension funds in advanced economies. Two of these funds reported expecting higher volatility (risk) abroad compared to well-developed domestic markets and, correspondingly, lower financial return on domestic assets. All but one of the funds with a higher risk tolerance for domestic investments are in developing countries. The reasons for higher domestic risk tolerance may include higher expected volatility in domestic markets and/or acceptance of higher risk in order to pursue nonfinancial returns (e.g., economic, social) accruing to the domestic economy at large.

HOW PUBLIC ASSET MANAGERS INVEST

Most of the surveyed public asset managers invest in a broad range of domestic asset classes and do not have legislated restrictions on specific asset classes. About one-third of the twenty-six funds surveyed (three SWFs and six public pension funds) have at least 30 percent of their assets invested in domestic public equities. The biggest difference between SWFs and public pension funds in terms of the proportion of investment in different domestic asset classes is manifested in the proportion of investments in domestic government bonds: all funds that invest more than 20 percent of their assets in domestic government bonds are public pension funds. Only 60 percent of respondent SWFs invest in domestic government bonds, and 50 percent invest less than or equal to 10 percent of their assets in such instruments. All respondent public pension funds invest in domestic government bonds. Alternative asset classes, such as private equity and real estate, are popular among the surveyed funds (as also discussed in chapter 4), with 80 percent of funds reporting that they invest in various forms of domestic private equity and real estate. Table 7.12 presents the details of the domestic portfolios of the surveyed funds.

Even though most surveyed funds do not have specific domestic asset class restrictions, some of the funds (located in advanced economies) have other general restrictions that apply to domestic investments. Such restrictions include prohibitions to borrow money (in most circumstances), bans on direct investment in nonfinancial assets (while allowing investment in real assets indirectly through trusts and private or listed companies), and restrictions on acquiring a majority stake in any entity.

About half of all surveyed funds invest in domestic private equity exclusively through privately managed funds. In many cases, this restriction is due to legislation explicitly requiring that private equity must be invested exclusively through external fund managers. In other cases, where both SWFs and public pension funds are allowed to invest in private equity themselves, management has decided to outsource the implementation of domestic private equity investment owing to the cost of building a dedicated team for a specific market, as well as challenges in attracting and retaining qualified in-house staff (as also underscored in chapter 4). About a quarter of the surveyed funds also use external fund managers to insulate investment management from political interference. Table 7.13 presents the reasons for outsourcing private equity and real asset investment execution reported by the surveyed funds.

Table 7.12 Answers to survey request "Please select the ranges, by asset class, of domestic assets as a percentage of assets"

Asset class	0% ≤ 10%	10% ≤ 20%	20% ≤ 30%	30% ≤ 40%	40% ≤ 50%	50% ≤ 60%	60% ≤ 70%	70% ≤ 80%	80% ≤ 90%	≤ 90%	Count
Government-issued bonds	11 50%	6 27%	2 9%	1 4%	2 9%	0 0%	0 0%	0 0%	0 0%	0 0%	22
% of SWFs	50%	10%		0%	0%	0%	0%	0%	0%	0%	6
% of PPFs	38%	31%	13%	6%	13%	0%	0%	0%	0%	0%	16
Corporate bonds	15 65%	6 26%	2 9%	0 0%	0 0%	0 0%	0 0%	0 0%	0 0%	0 0%	23
% of SWFs	60%	10%		0%	0%	0%	0%	0%	0%	0%	7
% of PPFs	56%	31%	13%	0%	0%	0%	0%	0%	0%	0%	16
Publicly traded equities	9 38%	5 21%	1 4%	1 4%	2 8%	5 21%	1 4%	0 0%	0 0%	0 0%	24
% of SWFs	40%	10%	0%	10%	0%	20%	0%	0%	0%	0%	8
% of PPFs	31%	25%	6%	0%	13%	19%	6%	0%	0%	0%	16
Private equity	22 88%	2 8%	0 0%	0 0%	0 0%	0 0%	1 4%	0 0%	0 0%	0 0%	25
% of SWFs	80%	0%	0%	0%	0%	0%	10%	0%	0%	0%	9
% of PPFs	88%	13%	0%	0%	0%	0%	0%	0%	0%	0%	16
Real assets (e.g., infrastructure, property, timber)	20 80%	4 16%	0 0%	0 0%	1 4%	0 0%	0 0%	0 0%	0 0%	0 0%	25
% of SWFs	70%	10%	0%	0%	10%	0%	0%	0%	0%	0%	9
% of PPFs	81%	19%	0%	0%	0%	0%	0%	0%	0%	0%	16

Abbreviations: PPF, public pension fund; SWF, sovereign wealth fund.

Table 7.13   Answers to survey request "If you hire external managers, select all the important reasons for outsourcing the management of all or some domestic private equity and real asset investments"

Reason for outsourcing management	Private equity Count	Private equity Percent	% of SWFs	% of PPFs	Real Assets	% of SWFs	% of PPFs
Challenges in attracting the right talent in house	14	56%	40%	63%	13	50%	50%
Difficulty of retaining qualified staff in house owing to public salary scale limitations	11	44%	20%	56%	12	40%	50%
Isolation of asset management from political interference	6	24%	0%	38%	4	0%	25%
Cost of building a dedicated team for a specific market	17	68%	60%	69%	14	60%	50%
Other	3	12%	10%	13%	3	10%	12.5%
Not applicable	3	12%	10%	13%	6	10%	31.2%
Total	**25**		**9**	**16**	**24**	**8**	**16**

Abbreviations: PPF, public pension fund; SWF, sovereign wealth fund.

For almost all of the funds surveyed, domestic portfolios are less than or equal to 20 percent of domestic capital markets or gross domestic product, as shown in table 7.14. Therefore, from a macroeconomic perspective, it appears that the surveyed funds do not have an overly large influence on domestic markets. This observation is further corroborated by responses from the fund managers who assess the impact of their domestic portfolios on domestic economies. Most respondents indicated that they do not "significantly impact" prices in domestic markets through their investments or domestic currency hedging.

Surveyed SWFs report co-investing with a broader range of investment partners than public pension funds. As presented in table 7.15, a much larger proportion of SWFs than public pension funds partner with foreign institutional investors and international financial institutions for co-investments in domestic real assets. These results are consistent with the emerging trend of SWFs self-organizing in various fora for the benefit of seeking investment partnerships and sourcing co-investment deals (a development also discussed in chapter 13).

Table 7.16 presents various reasons cited by the surveyed funds for maintaining investment partnerships. The two most common reasons for partnering with other investors in domestic real and private equity

Table 7.14 Answers to survey request "Indicate the size of your domestic investment portfolio relative to the size of your economy"

Feature of domestic market	0% ≤ 20%		20% ≤ 40%		40% ≤ 60%		60% ≤ 80%		80% ≤ 100%		Count
Domestic capital markets (listed markets)	23	95.8%	1	4.2%	0	0.0%	0	0.0%	0	0.0%	24
% of SWFs	80%		0.0%		0.0%		0.0%		0.0%		8
% of PPFs	93.8%		6.3%		0.0%		0.0%		0.0%		16
GDP	24	96.0%	1	4.0%	0	0.0%	0	0.0%	0	0.0%	25
% of SWFs	100%		0.0%		0.0%		0.0%		0.0%		10
% of PPFs	87.5%		6.3%		0.0%		0.0%		0.0%		15

Abbreviations: GDP, gross domestic product; PPF, public pension fund; SWF, sovereign wealth fund.

investments are to benefit from co-investors' skills and experience and to share financial risk. Other considerations include the size of the deal and the transaction costs. The track record of co-investors was also reported as being important to nearly half of the surveyed funds.

FOCUS ON DOMESTIC INFRASTRUCTURE

As presented in table 7.17, investing in alternative asset classes is common among the surveyed SWFs. Whereas 80 percent of surveyed SWFs

Table 7.15 Answers to survey question "If you co-invest domestically in real assets, what type of partners do you use?"

Partner	Percent	Count	% of SWFs	% of PPFs
Private asset managers	85.7%	18	80%	63%
Domestic banks	19.1%	4	30%	6%
International financial institutions (IFIs)	19.1%	4	30%	6%
Development banks	14.3%	3	20%	6%
Foreign governments	9.5%	2	10%	6%
Foreign institutional investors	28.6%	6	50%	6%
Local government	4.8%	1	10%	0%
Other	28.6%	6	20%	25%
Total		**21**		

Abbreviations: PPF, public pension fund; SWF, sovereign wealth fund.

Table 7.16 Answer to survey question "What are the most important reasons for partnering with other investors for domestic investments in real assets or private equity?"

Reason for partnering	Real assets		% of SWFs	% of PPFs	Private Equity		% of SWFs	% of PPFs
Sharing financial risk	15	68.2%	60%	56%	15	75%	50%	63%
Sharing political risk	5	22.7%	10%	25%	4	20%	0%	25%
Benefiting from co-investors' skills and experience	18	81.8%	80%	63%	17	85%	70%	63%
Benefiting from co-investors' successful track record	13	59.1%	40%	56%	14	70%	40%	63%
Participating in large-ticket-size deals	13	59.1%	50%	50%	12	60%	30%	56%
Cost considerations	10	45.5%	30%	44%	8	40%	20%	38%
Other	2	9.1%	20%	0%	2	10%	20%	0%
Total	22				20			

Abbreviations: PPF, public pension fund; SWF, sovereign wealth fund.

report investing in either greenfield or brownfield domestic infrastructure, most funds avoid taking on construction risk in domestic infrastructure projects.

Direct investments in domestic infrastructure are still limited among most funds, including those in advanced economies, as presented in table 7.18. The most common reason reported for outsourcing domestic infrastructure investments, for both SWFs and public pension funds, is the cost of building a dedicated team for a specific market. Other reasons

Table 7.17 Answers to survey request "Select all subcategories of private equity and real assets that you invest in domestically"

Subcategory of private equity and real assets	Percent	Count	% of SWFs	% of PPFs
Real estate/properties (e.g., commercial, residential)	100.0%	24	90%	94%
Timber and/or timberland	33.3%	8	40%	25%
Greenfield infrastructure (taking on construction risk)	25.0%	6	30%	19%
Brownfield infrastructure (not taking construction risk)	54.2%	13	70%	38%
Total		24		

Abbreviations: PPF, public pension fund; SWF, sovereign wealth fund.

Table 7.18   Answers to survey question "If you invest in domestic private equity and/or infrastructure, how do you invest?"

Value		Directly		Through privately managed funds		Listed		Other	Responses
Private Equity	9	41%	21	95.5%	2	9%	1	4.5%	**22**
% of SWFs		30%		70%		10%		10%	7
% of PPFs		38%		88%		6%		0%	15
Infrastructure	6	37.5%	10	62.5%	4	25%	2	12.5%	**16**
% of SWFs		30%		60%		30%		10%	6
% of PPFs		19%		25%		6%		6%	10

Abbreviations: PPF, public pension fund; SWF, sovereign wealth fund.

for outsourcing infrastructure investments are similar to the reasons discussed in the private equity investment section: complying with legislative requirements, hiring the best available talent in each market, and diversifying the portfolio and origination of deals. Attracting and keeping competent staff remains a challenge for funds, especially in advanced economies, as most of these funds reported being constrained by public sector salary limitations.

Sovereign wealth funds invest in domestic infrastructure through various financial instruments. The two most common are through equity in a project and project finance loans, as shown in table 7.19. Other means of

Table 7.19   Answers to survey question "How do you invest domestically in infrastructure?"

Investment method	Percent	Count	% of SWFs	% of PPFs
Equity in a project	58.3%	14	50%	56%
Project finance loans	20.8%	5	30%	13%
Infrastructure bonds issued by a special purpose vehicle	12.5%	3	0%	19%
Government bonds earmarked for infrastructure	0.0%	0	0%	0%
Subsovereign bonds earmarked for infrastructure	0.0%	0	0%	0%
With risk guarantees	0.0%	0	0%	0%
Other	16.7%	4	30%	6%
Not applicable	25.0%	6	10%	31%
Total		**24**		

Abbreviations: PPF, public pension fund; SWF, sovereign wealth fund.

investing in domestic infrastructure include master limited partnerships and private equity funds.

EXPECTATIONS AND CONCERNS

The RAMP survey also sought to understand the perspective of funds regarding the challenges they expect to face when investing domestically within the next five to seven years, as shown in table 7.20. Both SWFs and public pension funds reported that they are interested in increasing their exposure to and diversity of domestic assets and complying with domestic investment quotas or other government regulations. Increasing the diversity of domestic investments in the next five to seven years was

Table 7.20 Answers to survey question "With regard to domestic investments, what are the most important challenges for your fund within the next five to seven years?"

Challenge	Percent	Count	% of SWFs	% of PPFs
Finding reputable international partners for co-investment in domestic assets	16%	4	30%	6%
Efficiently increasing the fund's exposure to domestic assets	32%	8	30%	31%
Increasing the diversity of domestic investments	48%	12	60%	38%
Finding enough domestic deals (that are commercially on par with the fund's other investments) to comply with domestic investment quotas or other government regulations	20%	5	30%	13%
Dealing with lower rates of return on domestic bonds	60%	15	30%	75%
Improving corporate governance and transparency of domestic investments	28%	7	30%	25%
Dealing with political interference in fund management and/or investments	16%	4	20%	13%
Coordinating with the government on the overall size of domestic investments	0%	0	0%	0%
Delineating the role of the government and the role of the fund in domestic investments	4%	1	10%	0%
Other	4%	1	0%	6%
Total		**25**		

Abbreviations: PPF, public pension fund; SWF, sovereign wealth fund.

reported as being the most common interest for SWFs given the ongoing expectations (and sometimes pressure) on SWFs to serve as a development tool for domestic economies.

In contrast, public pension funds are mostly concerned with dealing with the lower rates of return on domestic bonds within the next five to seven years, given the market expectation of the reversal of the historically low interest rates over the last several years and the impact it will have on the ability of public pension funds to manage their pension liabilities.

CONCLUSION

The implementation of policies and governance arrangements around domestic investment mandates has become a matter of increasing importance for SWFs and other large public investors. There is a growing expectation—and often rising political pressure—to invest at least part of SWF portfolios in domestic assets in order to serve a variety of developmental purposes, including developing and deepening local capital markets, supporting domestic debt issuance, and investing in domestic infrastructure and growth sectors. While there are some exceptions—and, as we highlighted at the beginning of the chapter, different historical origins and contexts for the development of existing domestic investment mandates among the limited number of established SWFs with significant domestic investments—this is a relatively recent development in the evolution of SWFs, but one that is unlikely to be reversed in the foreseeable future. To a large extent, the rise of the domestic investment question for SWFs reflects the growing popularity of these funds in developing countries with massive domestic investment needs.

However, the analysis of this important topic has been hampered by the lack of clear and consistent data on domestic investment practices by SWFs. In this chapter, we have attempted to contribute to the documentation of the existing practices of these institutions by drawing on the results of the global survey conducted by the World Bank Treasury's Reserves Advisory and Management Program in 2015 with support from the International Forum of Sovereign Wealth Funds. In order to increase the sample size, and provide a comparative perspective with an investor class that has a longer track record in domestic investment, we also included a number of public pension funds in the survey.

The most important contribution of the survey, and this chapter's analysis of its findings, is to add to the public and comparative information available on the domestic investment policies, practices, and governance arrangements of SWFs. The survey findings have been organized across a number of categories: which funds invest in domestic assets, the governance arrangements around the execution of domestic investment mandates, the articulation of domestic investment objectives (including financial versus nonfinancial criteria), the operational models for (i.e., co-investment models and different financial instruments) and magnitude of (the size of domestic investments relative to the overall portfolio, capital markets, and local economy) domestic mandates, and funds' expectations and concerns about the execution of domestic investments in the future.

By including and contrasting survey results from public pension funds with those of SWFs, policymakers can gain a comparative perspective on the practices of a related investor class. There are important and understandable differences between SWFs and public pension funds with respect to domestic investments, not least owing to their contrasting histories and mandates. However, it is insightful to see how these differences impact the respective policy and governance arrangements for domestic investments. Finally, policymakers can use the design of the survey, the nature of the questions asked, and the aggregated results to think through key aspects of their own policy and governance frameworks around the increasingly important issue of domestic investments.

REFERENCES

Reisen, H. 1997. "Liberalizing Foreign Investments by Pension Funds: Positive and Normative Aspects," *World Development* 25, no. 7: 1173–1182.

World Bank. 2000. "Portfolio Limits: Pension Investment Restrictions Compromise Fund Performance," World Bank Pension Reform Primer Series. Washington, DC: World Bank.

CHAPTER 8

Sovereign Wealth Fund Investments in the Home Economy

Alan Gelb, Silvana Tordo, and Håvard Halland[1]
The World Bank

Sovereign wealth funds (SWFs) represent a large and growing pool of savings. Many are owned by natural resource–exporting countries and have long-term objectives, including intergenerational wealth transfer. For a number of reasons, including the need to sterilize foreign exchange inflows to avoid exchange rate appreciation (Dutch disease[2]) and a lack of domestic investment opportunities, these funds have traditionally invested in external assets, especially securities traded in major markets.

Over time, and in part reflecting the low returns in high-income countries following the global financial crisis, the investment holdings of SWFs have broadened to include real property and investments in developing economies. Potentially competitive returns in developing economies and sharp reductions in traditional sources of long-term financing following the global financial crisis have contributed to a growing interest among national authorities in permitting, and even encouraging, the national SWF to invest domestically, in particular to finance long-term infrastructure investments. Such pressure is inevitable, considering the fact that many countries with substantial savings, several of them recent resource exporters, also have urgent needs. A number of existing SWFs now invest a portion of their portfolios domestically, and more are being created to play this role.

Is it appropriate to use SWFs to finance long-term development needs? Does it matter whether these investments are domestic or foreign? In this chapter, we consider these issues, in particular the controversial question of using SWFs to finance domestic projects motivated, in part, by the perceived importance of these projects to development. We focus on direct commercial or quasi-commercial domestic market investments by

SWFs in resource-driven countries and explore the conditions that affect an SWF's ability to invest efficiently and prudently while fostering local economic diversification and mobilization of private capital. Financing funds, whose disbursements to the domestic economy go through the government budget, have been less controversial and are not discussed here. These institutions, which include large and well-known funds such as Norway's Government Pension Fund Global, have been amply analyzed elsewhere.

At first glance, the long-term goals of an SWF and the long-term investment needs of developing countries appear to be aligning. As a specialized investor, a high-capacity SWF might also be able to bring appraisal skills to the table to help improve the efficiency of the investment program. However, domestic investment by an SWF risks destabilizing macroeconomic management and undermining both the quality of public investments and the wealth objectives of the fund. The source of these risks is essentially that the SWF is owned by the same entity—the government—that seeks to promote domestic public investments. These risks may be mitigated, but not eliminated.

Naturally, no approach is risk free. For example, the level of fiscal spending can be benchmarked by fiscal rules that emphasize sustainability, but may not be contained; spending may also be of low quality, especially if dependence on rents weakens the incentives for taxpayers to scrutinize expenditure. Building up large external savings funds runs the risk of their being raided by future governments, either directly (as when funds are used for purposes other than those originally intended or when planned contributions are not paid) or indirectly (through unsustainable accumulation of public debt). On the other hand, in some views, the risks of using SWFs to finance domestic public investments are so serious as to recommend that SWF portfolios be confined to foreign assets, with all public investment funding appropriated through the budget.

The first priority is to ensure that domestic investments made by the SWF are considered in the context of the public investment plan and phased to ensure a sustainable flow of investment spending rather than destructive and costly boom–bust macroeconomic cycles. The second priority is to create a clear separation between the government as promoter of investments and as owner of the SWF: domestic investment by the SWF should not be used to finance public expenditure, bypassing budgetary controls. At the same time, it is necessary to build capacity for the SWF to operate as an expert professional investor that can contribute positively to the quality of the public investment program. Possible approaches include (i) screening investments for commercial or near-commercial financial return; (ii) investor partnerships, possibly including other SWFs and development lenders, as well as private investors, to diversify risk and increase implementation capacity; (iii) institutional design of SWF governance to credibly insulate it from political pressure, strengthen accountability, ensure oversight, and bring technical skills to bear on investment decisions; and (iv) full transparency, in particular of individual domestic investments and their financial performance.

Although in this chapter we use the generic term *sovereign wealth fund*, our focus is on resource funds. From a risk perspective, it is useful to consider resource funds separately, as a subclass of SWFs. Two aspects set resource funds apart from other SWFs, and from public pension funds. First, since resource funds are capitalized by proceeds from oil, gas, and mineral exports, the inflow of large amounts of foreign currency can lead to destabilization and appreciation of the exchange rate and inflation of asset bubbles. Second, the political economy of resource funds differs from that of other SWFs, and from development banks, since resource funds do not need to raise capital in financial markets and do not rely on pension contributions, fiscal surpluses, or taxes that affect a significant share of the electorate. The lack of a strong constituency, such as pension contributors or lenders, combined with the conflict of interests arising from the government's combined role as owner of the fund and promoter of its investments, makes resource funds highly vulnerable to political interference. Political meddling can in turn put the wealth objectives of the funds, as well as the quality of domestic investments, at risk. Funds may be captured by political factions and used to avoid parliamentary scrutiny of spending on politically motivated projects.

THE DIVERSIFICATION OF SOVEREIGN
WEALTH FUND INVESTMENTS

Rich natural resource reserves, primarily hydrocarbons and minerals, offer great development opportunities but also expose producing countries to difficult policy questions: How much should be saved for the long term, and how should savings be invested? How much should be set aside in precautionary reserves to cushion the potentially damaging impact of volatile resource markets? How should large investment programs be phased in to avoid hasty and wasteful spending in the face of

Table 8.1   Functions of sovereign wealth funds

Function	Investment objective	Strategic asset allocation
Savings	Provide for intergenerational equity, national endowments, or the meeting of particular long-term or contingent liabilities (pensions)	Long-term investment horizon, diversification with moderate to high risk tolerance, and low-liquidity requirement in the short to medium term
Precautionary	Stabilize spending in the face of short- and medium-term volatility in resource income	Liquidity, safety (capital preservation), short- to medium-term investment horizon
"Buffer"	Hold committed funds in order to pace disbursements with the capacity of the economy to absorb large foreign exchange inflows and the capacity to absorb investments without significant loss in the productivity of these investments	Safety (capital preservation), liquidity, short- to medium-term investment horizon

absorptive constraints? Sovereign wealth funds can be set up to play a number of roles (table 8.1), but it is important to stress that they are only a mechanism to help address such questions; their establishment is no substitute for strengthening fiscal management or improving governance (Dixon and Monk 2011). Unfortunately, many countries have created funds only to undermine them or render them irrelevant through poor or inconsistent policy (an issue also highlighted in chapters 2 and 5).

Multiple objectives can be achieved through appropriate strategic asset allocation within one fund, or assets can be separated into separate funds with distinct portfolio characteristics. For example, if the long-term portfolio has adequate liquidity, a savings fund can do double duty as a precautionary fund (van den Bremer and van der Ploeg 2012).

Some SWFs with a primary mandate of investing abroad have a long record of domestic activities (table 8.2). Truman (2011) estimated that domestic holdings constituted 16 percent of total investments using a sample of sixty SWFs, although these included some pension funds. Infrastructure investments are also not uncommon in SWF portfolios. As of 2012, at least 56 percent of all SWFs held investments in the infrastructure asset class; of these, approximately 36 percent included investments in social infrastructure such as hospitals and schools (Preqin 2012).

The motivation for the vast bulk of these investments has been commercial. These investments have typically been focused on bankable

Table 8.2 Sovereign wealth funds with domestic investment mandates

Country	Fund	Year established	Objectives	Asset value ($ billion)[a]	Domestic portfolio (%)	Funding source
Abu Dhabi	Abu Dhabi Investment Council	2007	To assist the government of Abu Dhabi in achieving continuous financial success and wealth protection, while sustaining prosperity for the future; to increasingly participate in and support the sustainable growth of the Abu Dhabi economy	627.0	N/A	H
Angola[b]	Fundo Soberano de Angola	2012	To generate sustainable financial returns that benefit Angola's people, economy, and industries	5	N/A	H
Australia	Future Fund	2005	To strengthen the Australian government's long-term financial position by making provision for unfunded Commonwealth superannuation liabilities	75	30	NC
Bahrain	Mumtalakat	2006	To create a thriving economy diversified from oil and gas, focused on securing sustainable returns and generating wealth for future generations	13.5	N/A	H
France	Strategic Investment Fund	2008	To make strategic investments in French firms to prevent them from being bought at discounted prices by foreign investors through participation and investment in innovative enterprises with a long-term investment horizon	25.1	100	NC
Kazakhstan	Samruk-Kazyna	2008	To develop and ensure implementation of regional, national, and international investment projects; to support and modernize existing assets of the Samruk-Kazyna Group of Companies; to support regional development and implementation of social projects; to support national producers	47.4	N/A	H

Table 8.2 (continued)

Country	Fund	Year established	Objectives	Asset value ($ billion)[a]	Domestic portfolio (%)	Funding source
Malaysia	Khazanah Nasional Berhad	2003	To promote economic growth and make strategic investments on behalf of the government, contributing to nation building; to nurture the development of selected strategic industries in Malaysia with the aim of pursuing the nation's long-term economic interests	34.4	N/A	NC
Nigeria	Nigeria Infrastructure Fund[c]	2011	To invest in projects that contribute to the development of essential infrastructure in Nigeria	1	100	H
Palestine	Palestine Investment Fund	2003	To strengthen the local economy through strategic investments while maximizing long-term returns for the fund's ultimate shareholder—the people of Palestine	0.9	80	NC
Russia	Russian Direct Investment Fund	2011	To make equity investments in strategic sectors within the Russian economy on a commercial basis by co-investing with large international investors in an effort to attract long-term direct investment capital	10.0	N/A	H
South Africa	Public Investment Corporation	1911	To deliver investment returns in line with client mandates; to contribute positively to South Africa's development	114.6	N/A	H
Taiwan, China	National Development Fund, Executive Yuan	1973	To serve as a catalyst for the economic development of Taiwan, China, and to accomplish a multiplier effect in the courses of its investment process	16.1	N/A	NC
United Arab Emirates	Mubadala Development Company	2002	To facilitate the diversification of Abu Dhabi's economy, focusing on managing long-term, capital-intensive investments that deliver strong financial returns and tangible social benefits for the Emirate	641.0	N/A	H

Abbreviations: H, hydrocarbons; NC, noncommodities; N/A, not applicable.

[a] The 2012 Preqin Sovereign Wealth Fund Review.
[b] From the Fundo Soberano de Angola website (www.fundosoberano.ao/language/en): "While the Fund considers investments across Africa and globally, it has a strong focus on investing in the domestic market, building Angola's infrastructure and creating opportunities for the people of Angola. By taking a long-term view with our investments, we aim to achieve sustainable and stable returns."
[c] The Nigeria Infrastructure Fund is one of three funds managed by the Nigeria Sovereign Investment Authority and absorbs between 20 and 60 percent of the authority's funding.

Source: World Bank data, based on publicly available information and disclosures from the relevant funds.

infrastructure projects, especially high-return existing infrastructure, rather than greenfield investments, and the vast majority of investment flows have focused on nondomestic assets, mostly in Europe and Asia, although a portion have benefited domestic infrastructure projects. While this aspect of their portfolios may suggest that SWFs have the potential to be partners for development finance institutions as well as for private investors, SWF decision making has largely been driven by portfolio optimization strategies that emphasize return and risk diversification, even though the funds may have investments in developing countries (Balding 2008).

DOMESTIC INVESTMENTS IN RESOURCE-EXPORTING COUNTRIES

The long-term fiscal sustainability of resource-rich countries may be benchmarked against some version of permanent income (PI). In earlier formulations, this benchmark was used for the primary fiscal deficit, excluding resource revenues and comparing it with the permanent income flow expected from the resource sector (box 8.1). This practice has been called into question. To the extent that a part of fiscal spending is for productive investment, that part should be counted as savings rather than consumption. This opens up greater fiscal space for domestic investment spending, but only if the investment is effective in building up national wealth (see also chapter 2).

Following this argument, it has been shown that not every country finds it optimal to build up a savings fund that invests abroad. If the domestic, risk-adjusted rate of return on investment is higher than that on foreign assets, the optimal strategy might involve boosting domestic investment rather than accumulating long-term foreign assets (Berg et al. 2012; Collier et al. 2009; van der Ploeg and Venables 2010). For countries capable of effectively using funds for productive purposes, domestic investments—including some naturally within the scope of the public sector—can potentially help the economy to grow and diversify away from risky dependence on a dominant resource.

In practice, even if these conditions are satisfied, macroeconomic and institutional absorptive capacity constraints will require that a portion of the revenue be invested in liquid financial assets outside the domestic economy, possibly for a number of years. There will also still be a need to hold precautionary reserves, sometimes for quite extended periods, because of the nature of commodity cycles. If the sole objective of

Box 8.1: Domestic Investments and Fiscal Benchmarks

The long-run fiscal sustainability of resource-rich countries is sometimes benchmarked against a version of permanent income (PI). The present value of the discounted stream of the nonresource primary balance (NRPB; the difference between total spending and nonresource fiscal revenue) should equal the present value of resource wealth (W; the assets in the SWF plus the discounted present value of all future resource revenue). Under simplifying assumptions, this relationship can be expressed as NRPB = rW, where r is the real return on the wealth portfolio. The rule will not provide an unchanging benchmark, since markets, reserves, and wealth projections will evolve over time, but at any moment, it provides a conditional benchmark, given future expectations.

The PI approach has been criticized for providing a fiscal benchmark that is too tight (Baunsgaard et al. 2012; Ossowski 2012). A poor, resource-constrained country that invests more resource revenues domestically (e.g., on infrastructure) could boost nonresource growth and create a virtuous cycle of increased fiscal space. Capital scarcity should also mean that domestic investments can have higher financial returns than those available on foreign assets in a traditional SWF, again increasing fiscal space through increasing r.

The PI approach can be modified to reflect country-specific conditions and yet still provide a useful benchmark for fiscal policy. One approach is to treat all public investment as adding to national wealth and redefine the rule to reflect only the nonresource current balance. However, this strategy eliminates the role of the approach as a fiscal anchor and also opens the door to creative accounting, as there is a strong incentive to redefine current spending items as capital investments. Not all investments will be productive. Even if productive in the very long run, some might incur recurrent costs that will be difficult to cover for many years.

A balanced approach is to screen proposed investments by their economic and financial returns according to their impact on the real return on wealth, rW. Following this reasoning, domestic investments with high returns are the most appropriate for an SWF because of the emphasis on managing them as elements of a portfolio of national assets. Even if they open up fiscal space, the domestic investments of an SWF need to be coordinated by strong, integrated expenditure management because of absorptive capacity constraints and the risk of inducing damaging boom–bust cycles.

accumulating funds in an SWF is stabilization, no domestic investment within that fund is advisable.

Effective public investment management arrangements are essential to growth (Gupta et al. 2011). However, the link between investment and growth is neither automatic nor guaranteed. Public investment poses significant management and governance challenges, including low capacity, weak governance and regulatory frameworks, and lack of coordination among public entities. Many resource-exporting countries have launched massive investment programs to little effect (Gelb 1988). Poor and badly managed public investment often results in wasted resources and corruption, particularly where macroeconomic and institutional absorption constraints exist (Berg et al. 2012). Efficient management is a critical factor for the success of public investment programs (Rajaram et al. 2010). An index of the quality of public investment management shows that such management tends to be markedly weaker in resource-exporting developing countries than in other countries (Dabla-Norris et al. 2011). On average, countries tend to be relatively stronger in the early stages of strategic guidance and appraisal and weaker in the later stages of project implementation, especially project audit and evaluation.

The variable performance of countries in managing their public investment programs points to the fact that not all have strong central management at the level and quality of public spending, properly integrated into the budget, and subject to oversight by Parliament. In addition, few resource exporters have managed to sustain countercyclical fiscal policy in the face of large swings in resource markets. This leaves their economies vulnerable to destructive boom–bust cycles, which have a direct impact on investment quality and returns.

Opening up a separate window for domestic investment by a country's SWF has the potential to exacerbate these risks. It can further fragment the public investment program and may even provide an avenue to bypass parliamentary scrutiny of spending. With its resources provided by resource rents and not from the capital market, the SWF is not subject to oversight by market actors and institutions. Further, even if the fund is restricted to commercial investments or investments with near-commercial returns, it could exacerbate macroeconomic and asset-price cycles by investing heavily when resource prices are booming. Therefore, the fund can offer potential benefits relative to alternative approaches only if, as a high-capacity expert investor, it operates in coordination with the government's macro-fiscal policy.

INVESTMENT RULES AND INSTITUTIONAL
MODELS TO MITIGATE RISK

While it is not possible to eliminate all of the risks of an SWF investing in the domestic economy, it may be possible to mitigate some of them and at the same time ensure that the SWF's engagement helps strengthen the quality of public investments by acting as a high-quality, commercially driven investor. This requires (i) ensuring that its investments are not destabilizing to the macro-economy; (ii) limiting the scope of domestic SWF investments to those appropriate for a wealth fund; (iii) investing through partnerships with entities that bring credible standards for project quality and governance; (iv) establishing credible governance arrangements to ensure that the SWF operates with independence, professionalism, and clear accountability mechanisms; and (v) mandating full transparency, particularly of each domestic investment and its performance.

COORDINATE INVESTMENTS WITH MACROECONOMIC POLICY

Especially if large, the domestic spending of an SWF needs to be considered within the overall macroeconomic framework. Otherwise, there is a risk that it will rapidly scale up investments when resource prices and revenues are high, undermining efforts at countercyclical fiscal policy and imposing costs on other investors. This consideration is also important for the quality and cost of the SWF's investments themselves, to limit the adverse impact of stop-and-go cycles.

In addition, SWFs usually receive their funding from the budget, as a one-time endowment, or as discretionary transfers or the earmarking of specific sources of revenue. During market downturns, the government would normally ring-fence public sector expenditure, curtailing or halting transfers to the SWF. Therefore, the SWF's investment program needs to be carefully crafted to limit the risk of sudden and costly financing shortages.

INVEST IN COMMERCIAL OR NEAR-COMMERCIAL PROJECTS

Public investments can be evaluated from two perspectives: (i) their financial or private returns, and (ii) their broader economic and social returns. The latter include, in addition to the financial return, positive or negative externalities for the wider economy and society that can cause the social rate of return to be higher or lower than the financial rate of return. For example, an infrastructure project might have positive economic externalities that are not fully captured by its financial return. A toll road, while paying for itself, can also alleviate congestion on alternative routes. This would bring down business costs beyond the cost of the toll, attracting job-creating private investment and cutting unemployment. It could also improve public health by improving access to medical facilities. On the other hand, if undertaken at the height of a resource-led spending boom, its construction could increase congestion and lead to higher costs and delays for others, leading to negative externalities. It is not always easy to estimate financial returns or to quantify economic and social returns. This difficulty reinforces the importance of the independent assessment and vetting of project proposals. Some worthy investments may have no direct financial returns at all and may instead require years of recurrent spending to realize a value for the country. A possible example is investments in early childhood development that boosts the cognitive skills and earning capacity of a future workforce.

As a wealth fund, an SWF should not invest in projects that are justified primarily by their economic or social externalities. Such investments should be funded through the normal budget process, which should also provide for the future recurrent costs necessary for operations and maintenance. By preserving the value of its assets over time through commercial or quasi-commercial investments, the SWF would perform an intergenerational wealth transfer function, compatible with the modified PI approach discussed in box 8.1. Moreover, SWF investment that is not warranted on commercial grounds greatly complicates the accountability of the fund as its management can no longer be benchmarked on financial returns. The fund may also not be accountable for the wider social and economic impacts of investments, which may depend on factors outside its control. For example, a sector ministry may choose not to provide the recurrent inputs to operate the assets (e.g., schools) built by the fund. This dilution of accountability leaves the fund vulnerable to political manipulation.

An SWF should therefore screen domestic investment proposals primarily according to their financial return, seeking development opportunities with market or close-to-market financial returns—and where it can crowd in, rather than displace, private investors. Taking advantage of its long-term horizon, the fund could provide financing to extend the term of available private credit; it could offer a range of instruments to share risk and make commercially attractive projects viable for the market. In some circumstances, the fund may accept a somewhat below-market return on domestic investments with large economic benefits. This home bias should be clearly stipulated. For example, instead of an external rate of return of, say, 4 percent in real terms over an investment horizon of ten years, it could stipulate a real return of 2 percent over a horizon of twenty years.

For investments that are not fully justified on commercial grounds, it is essential to have a clear and transparent process for benchmarking financial return and for balancing financial and nonfinancial goals. The risk is that any such formulation may reduce public accountability, because estimates of economic benefits are more ambiguous than those of financial benefits. Identifying the size of the home bias is a challenging endeavor, owing to country- and project-specific considerations. An alternative approach could be for the government to set the overall target return on investment for the SWF's portfolio and the threshold minimum rate of return for all investments (e.g., the government's average long-term real borrowing rate on commercial loans). The SWF would then be free to decide the composition of its investment portfolio so as to maximize the overall rate of return, while guarding against investing in projects with expected negative returns. For clear accountability, it is also important to separate out the below-market portion of the portfolio from the rest when reporting on investments and their returns.

Seeking domestic investment opportunities with market or close-to-market financial returns—and where private investors can be crowded in by the assurance of some public financial support—implies that the domestic investment program of an SWF cannot be driven by quantity mandates (e.g., to hold a particular percentage of its portfolio in domestic investments). The SWF needs to be able to shape the rhythm of domestic investment according to the opportunities available and consistent with macroeconomic policy trade-offs. In the upswing of the resource cycle, the fund may see relatively few domestic opportunities relative to its rapidly growing resources. In this case, it should not be forced to invest domestically in low-quality projects. The SWF should be free to plan its portfolio with a long-term perspective, including by investing domestically only as good opportunities emerge. Further, potentially attractive domestic investments should be allowed to compete with foreign assets for investable funds based on expected returns and sound investment management principles.

INVEST THROUGH PARTNERSHIPS

Sovereign wealth funds are usually permitted by their charters to invest in traded securities only as minority shareholders. A similar principle should apply to domestic investments, whether portfolio or direct. This opens up the investment decision to external evaluation, adds to the expertise at the disposal of the fund, and also creates a more credible investor body to monitor the implementation of the investment and the policy framework that affects its financial performance. Sovereign wealth funds that make equity investments may be passive, long-term investors with no desire to impact company decision making by actively using their voting rights, or they may have a more active ownership policy. Explicit limitations may also be imposed by the establishment law.

Funds can actively seek to create investor pools with one another and with other sources of institutional capital, as well as with private investors. Partnership agreements at the project or portfolio level may be crafted to strengthen an SWF's investment efficiency and investment selection process in order to mirror that used by private equity investors. Sovereign wealth funds may also seek to leverage the investments of the multilateral development banks.

Sovereign wealth funds should not seek to duplicate the roles of existing institutions. If a well-managed and skillful national development bank already exists, there is no need to further fragment domestic investment by adding an SWF, at least with regard to domestic investment with a commercial or quasi-commercial return. Table 8.3 outlines alternative institutional solutions. It is worth noting that when an SWF invests at a commercial or quasi-commercial return, its mandate does not overlap with that of the domestic development bank.

INSTITUTIONAL MODELS FOR RISK MITIGATION

Establishing rules for the type (e.g., commercial or quasi-commercial investment) and modalities (e.g., no controlling stakes, leveraging private investment) of investment that an SWF is permitted is one way to ensure separation between the activities of the SWF and those of other government institutions with investment mandates (e.g., the budget, the national development bank, the investment authority, state-owned enterprises). But, good corporate governance is a prerequisite for effective and

Table 8.3 Domestic investment mandates: sovereign wealth funds and development banks

	Investment parameters of the sovereign wealth fund	
	Return is below quasi-commercial	Commercial and quasi-commercial return
Development bank with a strong track record	Domestic investment is implemented by the development bank.	Domestic investment by the SWF competes on equal terms with returns on foreign assets.
Development bank with a poor track record	The development bank is restructured.	There is no minimum or maximum domestic investment target.
No development bank or not possible to restructure	The domestic investment function of the SWF is subject to parliamentary scrutiny. Parliamentary approval of maximum envelope for domestic investment and home bias parameters are part of the budget process and compensated through the budget. Investment partnerships and fund pooling are undertaken to leverage private sector investment and reduce risk. The mandates of the SWF and the unrestructured development bank are clearly separated.	The SWF invests only as a minority shareholder. Resource allocation is based on market principles. Investment partnerships and fund pooling are undertaken to leverage private sector investment and reduce risk. The methodology to assess quasi-commercial returns is clearly defined and based on measurable criteria. Quasi-commercial investments are disclosed separately.

Abbreviation: SWF, sovereign wealth fund.

sustainable performance. Sound corporate governance arrangements provide incentives for the board and management to pursue shareholders' objectives and facilitate the monitoring of performance by shareholders and owners. This is particularly important for SWFs and other state-owned institutions, especially those with complex mandates that may include supporting green investments, "ethical" investments, or other national policies.

Sovereign wealth funds are normally established as separate legal entities with statutory responsibility for managing investments at arm's length from the government. In some countries, international and domestic investments are channeled through dedicated SWFs; in others, the SWFs invest domestically through a separate, wholly owned subsidiary.

The objectives and mandate of the fund, the organization of the ownership function of the state, and the institutional arrangements that govern an SWF's internal management bodies and processes are usually specified in a purpose-designed law, as well as company law, financial sector regulations, and the SWF's statutes. The Santiago Principles for the operations of SWFs (International Working Group of Sovereign Wealth Funds 2008); the "Revised Guidelines for Foreign Exchange Reserve Management" (International Monetary Fund 2013); existing literature on good corporate governance practice, including the "OECD Principles of Corporate Governance" (Organisation for Economic Co-operation and Development [OECD] 2004); and the "OECD Guidelines on Corporate Governance of State-Owned Enterprises" (OECD 2005) provide a detailed framework for effective corporate governance. The following is an outline of the external and internal corporate governance issues that are of particular relevance to SWFs permitted to make domestic investments.

External governance is associated with the relationship between the SWF and the state as its owner. Ownership provides certain rights and obligations, including voting on matters defined by law and by the SWF's statutes; electing, appointing, and removing board members; and obtaining information on the performance of the SWF, its board, and its management. For SWFs, the minister of finance usually acts as owner on behalf of the state. However, dual responsibility is possible, for example where the fund is given public policy objectives in specific sectors or spending is earmarked for specific uses. Table 8.4 contains examples of ownership arrangements for SWFs permitted to make domestic investments.

Particularly where several representatives act as owner, competing interests may dilute accountability and weaken the incentives for the performance of the board. Therefore, clarity of roles and responsibility, transparency, as well as separation between ownership and regulatory/ supervisory functions are important to prevent conflicts of interest, and to ensure accountability and operational independence in the management of the SWF. Having an explicit ownership policy can reinforce the authority and responsibility of the owner and provide guidance to the board (OECD 2005).

The objectives and mandate of the SWF provide the framework for the fund's management to define investment strategies and measure performance. It is therefore important that the objectives and

Table 8.4 Examples of sovereign wealth fund ownership arrangements

Fund	Country	Method of establishment	Type of organization	Ownership function
Public Investment Corporation	South Africa	*Public Investment Corporation Act*, 2004	Corporation	Minister of finance
Investment Authority	Kuwait	Law 47/1982	Independent legal entity	Minister of finance
Samruk-Kazyna	Kazakhstan	Presidential decree nos. 669 and 962	Joint stock company	The president of the republic
Khazanah Nasional Berhad	Malaysia	*Companies Act*, 1965	Public limited company/investment holding company	Minister of Finance Incorporated, a corporate body incorporated pursuant to the *Minister of Finance (Incorporation) Act*, 1957

mandates be clear. Translating objectives into performance targets is among the tasks of the shareholder representative. Such objectives should include overall financial performance targets, operational targets to guide business practice and monitor efficiency, and clear public policy targets to measure the fund's contribution to local economic development whenever a home bias exists. Targets should be clear, and a methodology for measuring them should be made explicit in the shareholder compact or similar agreement between the owner and the board of the fund.

INTERNAL GOVERNANCE

Internal governance encompasses institutional arrangements—such as the composition, structure, functioning, and authority of the board of directors or trustees—and the SWF's management processes, including recruitment, decision making, raising capital, investment autonomy, risk management, asset classes, audit, and public disclosures. Many general corporate governance principles apply here equally, including professionalism, distinguishing ownership from supervision, independence (including, as far as possible, from government), and the appropriate use of specialized committees. Table 8.5 summarizes the internal governance arrangements for a small sample of SWFs with domestic investment authority.

Table 8.5 Examples of sovereign wealth fund internal governance arrangements

Fund	Country	Number of directors on board	Number of independent directors	Structure	Appointment authority and process	Duties	Board committees	Term of service
Khazanah Nasional Berhad	Malaysia	9	5 (with expertise in audit, economics, and finance)	Chaired by the prime minister; includes the special economic advisor to the prime minister, the deputy minister of finance, and the managing director	Minister of Finance Incorporated	The board of directors has all powers necessary to direct and supervise the management of the business and affairs of the company subject to any articles of association.	Audit, Executive	N/A
Kuwait Investment Authority	Kuwait	9	3	Chaired by the minister of finance; includes the energy minister, governor of the central bank, and undersecretary		The goals of the board are to formulate the general policy of the authority and supervise implementation, monitor investment programs, adopt financial and administrative regulations, approve investments and transaction, and approve budget and annual financial accounts.	Audit, Executive	4-year term, renewable if at least 3 board members do not hold any public office
Samruk-Kazyna	Kazakhstan	10	3 (of which 2 are foreign nationals; expertise in law, business, and economics)	Chaired by the prime minister; includes the deputy prime minister, minister of oil and gas, minister of finance, and assistant to the president	The Council of Ministers through an Amiri Decree	The goals of the board are to approve the investment plan and budget; approve investment, monitor execution, and approve disclosures; and identify key performance indicators within the framework of the development plan of the fund.	Nomination, Remuneration, Audit, Control and Analysis	At the discretion of the "sole shareholder"

Public Investment Corporation (PIC)	South Africa	10	7 (with expertise in business, finance, economics, and accounting)	Chaired by the deputy minister of finance (nonexecutive director); includes the CEO and CIO	Minister of finance, after consulting the Council of Ministers	The board is responsible for overall strategy and approval of capital expenditure.	Director's Affairs, Investment, PIC Properties, Human Resources and Remuneration, Audit and Risk, Social Responsibility and Ethics	No fixed term for nonexecutive directors, but one-third of the board are to retire from office at each annual meeting
Temasek Holdings	Singapore	9	8 (including heads of corporations, former government officials, and representatives of national trade union; chair previously held several cabinet-level positions in the Singapore government)	The majority of board members are nonexecutive, independent, private sector business leaders.	Minister of finance, subject to the president's concurrence	The goals of the board are to define long-term strategic objectives, approve annual budget and annual audited statutory accounts, approve major investment and divestment proposals, approve major funding proposals, appoint the CEO, and establish succession plans.	Executive, Audit, Leadership Development, Compensation	No fixed term
Future fund	Australia	7	7 (with a legislated requirement of substantial expertise in investing or managing financial assets or in corporate governance)	Independent board of guardians drawn from outside government	Treasurer and minister for finance and deregulation	Accountable to the government for the safekeeping and performance of fund assets	Audit, Risk, Remuneration, Governance, Conflict	N/A

Abbreviations: CEO, chief executive officer; CIO, chief investment officer; N/A, not applicable.

The domestic investment models for SWFs can be broadly grouped into two categories:

- *Traditional:* SWFs that invest in equity and debts of domestic companies, preferably quoted on the domestic stock exchange. This model requires the existence of a local equity market and is therefore of limited applicability in developing countries.
- *Frontier:* SWFs that invest in real assets directly or through the creation of special-purpose vehicles to leverage funding from private investors or other sources. These funds have many features in common with development banks and investment banks.

An SWF may use both investment models as necessary to fulfill its mandate and comply with risk criteria set by the owner and/or the board. However, the implementation of these investment models requires different skills and expertise and entails the use of different financial instruments with different risk levels, with implications for the internal governance processes of the SWF. As noted previously, it also entails different risks for fiscal policy management. This subsection will focus on two critical processes of internal governance: (i) investment decisions and risk management, and (ii) audit and disclosures.

INVESTMENT DECISIONS AND RISK MANAGEMENT

The implementation of the investment mandate involves several steps that are common to all SWFs, whether they can invest domestically or not. These include the setting of specific investment targets and benchmarks; the identification of investment opportunities and their assessment, ranking, and selection; the definition of investment strategies; the due diligence of selected alternatives; the investment itself; and the monitoring of results. The policy objectives of the owner and the flexibility of the investment mandate, together with the level of sophistication of the domestic financial and capital markets, affect the *operational skills* required to implement the mandate and the *internal processes* to ensure compliance and efficiency in the execution of the mandate. A discretionary portfolio mandate could provide a wide range of autonomy and flexibility to select investments that respond to the general investment criteria set by the owner (e.g., asset classes or subclasses, with a target return or a benchmark, and a degree of risk tolerance). On the other hand, an SWF mandated to support domestic companies considered strategic by the government would require a project-specific mandate and the identification of qualifying investments by the owner. The SWF investment policy should be clearly defined and consistent with its defined objectives and risk tolerance, as set out in the investment mandate, and should be publicly disclosed.

Sovereign wealth funds usually have a long-term investment horizon, but the liquidity of their domestic portfolio largely depends on the level of sophistication of the domestic financial and capital markets, as well as the owner's investment objectives. Funds that invest in companies listed on the domestic stock exchange require skills and internal management processes similar to those of SWFs with international portfolios and asset managers. Those that invest mainly in real assets require competences and internal management processes comparable to those of development banks and private sector investment banks. The absence of a functional domestic stock exchange in many resource-rich, developing countries necessarily impedes the use of the traditional investment model.

To a certain extent, an SWF's competence gaps can be addressed by the use of external managers. However, this approach may be more suited to the implementation of traditional investment models with a discretionary portfolio mandate. For frontier investment models, and in the absence of suitable domestic investment institutions (e.g., domestic development banks), co-investing (including through public–private partnerships) may be of help to address concerns about the quality of an SWF's due diligence process as well as to defray risks—but only provided that the investment partners' interests are well aligned and the SWF has an adequate level of project selection and assessment capacity. Frontier investments open the door to flexible tools of project financing; on the other hand, marking to market and benchmarking to reference classes are challenging for this type of investment.

Risk management refers to the process of *managing uncertainty*. Standard risk metrics can be used to manage the risk of simple reference portfolios of standard asset classes, but managing the risk of direct investments and private equity is more complex and labor intensive. Direct investment is less liquid and requires a clear appreciation of the trade-off between potential returns (financial, economic, and social) and illiquidity, as well as resources for monitoring sustainable performance. Investment partners can help manage exposure to risk and may provide a buffer against political capture of and interference in the investment process. An effective *risk management process* should include a risk management policy, to be established by the SWF's board and identifying risks, tolerance levels, and permitted instruments (e.g., hedging and derivatives); systems and procedures for risk identification, measurement, monitoring, and control; institutional oversight and responsibilities (a board, a risk management committee, and senior management); procedures to deal with problem investments; and a risk management review mechanism.

AUDIT AND DISCLOSURES

Rigorous internal audit procedures and standards, and independent external audits, are critical to good corporate governance and accountability. To ensure independence from the owner, the internal audit function should report directly to the board. Many SWFs have audit committees; these should be chaired by an independent, nonexecutive board member to ensure the integrity of the oversight process and to shelter the audit function from political interference. This is particularly relevant when board members are also government officials.

External audit should be conducted according to international standards by a reputable international audit firm that is independent of management and the owner. External financial audit provides the board with an independent assessment of the accuracy of reporting by management and the quality and integrity of financial and operational controls. Audit conducted by the state supreme audit institution normally focuses on the use of public funds and budget resources and is not a substitute for external audit (Scott 2007).

Legislation usually provides for the board's accountability arrangements, including tabling the annual report and audited financial statements in Parliament and presenting interim reports on the SWF's performance to the owner representative. In addition, the SWF may be subject to the oversight of the relevant capital and financial market regulator. In addition to audited financial statements, SWFs whose mandate includes a home bias should publicly disclose investment mandates; investment policy; risk management policy; asset allocation; and targets, benchmarks, and results for asset classes and direct investment to strengthen external accountability and credibility as investment partners.

CONCLUSION

The emergence of SWFs with domestic investment mandates represents a shift of emphasis as domestic investments are increasingly prioritized among the funds' uses of natural resource rents. About twenty sovereign funds now have a specific mandate in this area, including some that traditionally have invested abroad. Following recent resource discoveries, more domestic investment mandates are being established.

While information available on the policies and performance of domestic portfolios is incomplete, experience indicates that an SWF that is permitted or mandated to invest domestically, like a development bank, risks being influenced by the political economy of the country. The risks are large, and in some views prohibitive. Many resource-rich countries, flush with funds, have invested but seen little payoff. Sometimes, this has been a result of accelerating investment beyond the limits of macroeconomic or management capacity. Investment programs have also often been politically captured, used to distribute patronage, and undermined by corruption.

The experiences of similar institutions suggest a number of considerations for a country contemplating allowing an SWF to invest domestically. The overall objective is to create a system of checks and balances to help ensure that the SWF does not undermine macroeconomic management or become a vehicle for politically driven "investments" that add nothing to national wealth. The difficult environments in which some SWFs are being established suggest that such concerns will often be relevant. The main priorities concern consistency with macroeconomic policy, the criteria for selecting investments, partnerships, external and internal governance arrangements, and transparency and reporting.

MACROECONOMIC INTEGRATION

Experiences in resource-rich countries indicate that private and public sector investments tend to be correlated with fluctuations in the prices of the country's major commodity exports. This creates damaging boom–bust cycles. To avoid exacerbating asset-price and macroeconomic cycles, as well as running into absorption constraints, if the SWF's domestic portfolio is large relative to the size of the economy, its domestic investments must be considered in the context of overall private and public sector investment.

APPROPRIATE INVESTMENTS

Sovereign wealth fund investments need to be screened for financial return (e.g., to maintain capital value in real terms), as well as adequate economic justification. If the SWF is to function as a quality domestic investor, it cannot be subject to investment quotas but must be able to adjust its spending to demand and absorption constraints. Most SWFs that permit domestic investment therefore also manage a holding portfolio of undisbursed funds.

PARTNERSHIPS

Sovereign wealth funds will benefit from investing in partnership with others. This could involve collaborating with private investors, pooling with other SWFs, and co-financing with international financial institutions. Confining investments to minority stakes can reduce risk, bring in additional expertise, and enhance the credibility of the investment decision. Especially for frontier investment models, co-investing may help defray project risk and address concerns about the quality of an SWF's due diligence process. But there will still need to be an adequate level of operational skills within the SWF.

EXTERNAL GOVERNANCE

The ownership function of an SWF normally rests with a central ministry (e.g., finance) or, in some cases, with the head of state. The objectives and mandate of the SWF must be set out in a clear and unambiguous manner. The mandate should be translated into performance targets, clearly and transparently, as in a shareholder compact between owner and board. Supervisory and oversight functions should be separated from ownership, for example, by placing them with the auditor general. It is advisable to separate regulation from ownership, for example, by placing regulation with the regulatory body for financial and capital markets.

INTERNAL GOVERNANCE

To ensure an adequate level of expertise and independence, all board members should meet skills and experience requirements. For a politically independent selection process, candidates should be nominated by an independent election committee, supported by an internationally recognized professional executive search firm. The presence of public officials on the board weakens the separation of responsibility within government for exercising ownership, on the one hand, and exercising supervisory responsibilities, on the other (an accepted principle for state-owned enterprises). The large majority of board members should thus be independent directors from outside government. Independence can be further strengthened by appointing foreign nationals, less likely to be amenable to political pressure with regard to the fund's domestic investment priorities, and establishing an external advisory board of independent experts.

Since the domestic frontier model for an SWF's investment function resembles that of investment banks and, to some extent, development banks, guidelines on staffing and investment policies can draw on best-practice examples. These guidelines should include a clear and transparent methodology for evaluating trade-offs between financial returns and economic and social returns (home bias). However, when a development bank exists, care should be exercised to clearly separate its functions from those of the SWF and to refrain from using the SWF as an alternative to restructuring an inefficient development bank. Public–private partnerships can help screen project proposals but require due diligence to ensure that the balance between risk and return does not unduly favor the private partners. Internal auditors should report directly to the board, and external audit should be undertaken by an internationally reputable firm that is independent of the owner.

TRANSPARENCY AND REPORTING

Consistent with good practice, SWFs permitted or mandated to invest domestically should issue accessible public reports covering their activities, assets, and returns. Where part of the portfolio is market based and part invested in projects with below-market returns, these should be reported separately.

SUGGESTED NEXT STEPS

Although not entirely novel, SWFs that are permitted or mandated to invest domestically are emerging on a wider scale. They have not been systematically surveyed, leaving much to be understood about their processes and activities. As they combine features of traditional SWFs and development banks, they can draw on good-practice examples from both types of institutions, as well as from one another. More research is needed to better understand their operations and potential role for financing in developing countries.

NOTES

1. This chapter was adapted from Gelb, Tordo, and Halland. 2014.

2. Dutch Disease characterizes an economy suffering from a negative impact of a sharp inflow of foreign currency, such as the discovery of large oil reserves or mining deposits. The foreign currency inflows lead to local currency appreciation, which makes the country's export products less price competitive and increases imports.

REFERENCES

Balding, C. 2008. "A Portfolio Analysis of Sovereign Wealth Funds," HSBC School of Business, ESADE University Faculties—ESADEgeo. http://ssrn.com/abstract=1141531.

Baunsgaard, T., M. Villafuerte, M. Poplawski-Ribeiro, and C. Richmond. 2012. "Fiscal Frameworks for Resource-Rich Developing Countries," IMF Staff Discussion Note SDN/12/04. Washington, DC: International Monetary Fund.

Berg, A., R. Portillo, S. S. Yang, and L. Zanna. 2012. "Public Investment in Resource-Abundant Developing Countries," IMF Working Paper 12/274. Washington, DC: International Monetary Fund.

Collier, P., F. van der Ploeg, M. Spence, and A. J. Venables. 2009. "Managing Resource Revenues in Developing Economies," OxCarre Research Paper 15. Oxford: Oxford Centre for the Analysis of Resource-Rich Economies, University of Oxford.

Dabla-Norris, E., J. Brumby, A. Kyobe, Z. Mills, and C. Papageorgiou. 2011. "Investing in Public Investment: An Index of Public Investment Efficiency," IMF Working Paper 11/37. Washington, DC: International Monetary Fund.

Dixon, A. D., and A. H. B. Monk. 2011. "What Role for Sovereign Wealth Funds in Africa's Development?" Oil-to-Cash Initiative Background Paper. Washington, DC: Center for Global Development.

Gelb, A. 1988. Oil Windfalls: Blessing or Curse? Oxford: Oxford University Press.

Gelb, A., S. Tordo, and H. Halland. 2014. "Sovereign Wealth Funds and Long-Term Development Finance," Policy Research Working Paper 6776. Washington, DC: World Bank.

Gupta, S., A. Kangur, C. Papageorgiou, and A. Wane. 2011. "Efficiency-Adjusted Public Capital and Growth," IMF Working Paper 11/217. Washington, DC: International Monetary Fund. www.imf.org/external/pubs/ft/wp/2011/wp11217.pdf.

International Monetary Fund. 2013. "Revised Guidelines for Foreign Exchange Reserve Management," www.imf.org/external/np/pp/eng/2013/020113.pdf.

International Working Group of Sovereign Wealth Funds. 2008. "Sovereign Wealth Funds: Generally Accepted Principles and Practices ('Santiago Principles')," www.iwg-swf.org/pubs/eng/santiagoprinciples.pdf.

Organisation for Economic Co-operation and Development. 2004. "OECD Principles of Corporate Governance." Paris: Organisation for Economic Co-operation and Development. www.oecd.org/daf/ca/corporategovernanceprinciples/31557724.pdf.

——. 2005. "OECD Guidelines on Corporate Governance of State-Owned Enterprises." Paris: Organisation for Economic Co-operation and Development, updated 2015. http://www.oecd.org/corporate/guidelines-corporate-governance-SOEs.htm.

Ossowski, R. 2012. "Macro-fiscal Management in Resource-Rich Countries," Draft, December 9. Washington, DC: World Bank.

Preqin. 2012. "2012 Preqin Sovereign Wealth Fund Review." New York: Preqin Ltd.

Rajaram, A., T. M. Le, N. Biletska, and J. Brumby. 2010. "A Diagnostic Framework for Assessing Public Investment Management," Policy Research Working Paper 5397. Washington, DC: World Bank. https://openknowledge.worldbank.com /handle/10986/3881.

Scott, D. 2007. "Strengthening the Governance and Performance of State-Owned Financial Institutions," Policy Research Working Paper 4321. Washington, DC: World Bank.

Truman, E. M. 2011. "Sovereign Wealth Funds: Is Asia Different?" Working Paper 11–12. Washington, DC: Peterson Institute.

Van den Bremer, T., and F. van der Ploeg. 2012. "How to Spend a Windfall: Dealing with Volatility and Capital Scarcity," OxCarre Research Paper 85. Oxford: Oxford Centre for the Analysis of Resource-Rich Economies, University of Oxford.

Van der Ploeg, F., and A. J. Venables. 2010. "Absorbing a Windfall of Foreign Exchange: Dutch Disease Dynamics," OxCarre Research Paper 52. Oxford: Oxford Centre for the Analysis of Resource-Rich Economies, University of Oxford.

CHAPTER 9

Sovereign Wealth Funds in the Context of Macro-Fiscal Frameworks for Resource-Rich Developing Countries[1]

Corinne Deléchat, Mauricio Villafuerte, and Shu-Chun S. Yang
Institute of Economics, National Sun Yat-Sen University,
Taiwan; International Monetary Fund

For developing countries, natural resources represent a unique opportunity to close their large infrastructure gaps and improve social outcomes.[2] However, preventing volatile natural resources to have adverse impacts on macroeconomic stability is perhaps a bigger challenge than in more advanced economies, owing to institutional weaknesses and capacity constraints. Taking chapter 2 (" 'Best-Practice' Sovereign Wealth Funds for Sound Fiscal Management") as a starting point, we first review fiscal frameworks and fiscal rules that are particularly relevant for resource-rich developing countries (RRDCs) and, in this context, present key considerations for the management of resource funds. Later, we present an analytical tool—a dynamic general equilibrium model with a sovereign wealth fund (SWF)—suitable for RRDCs. Using Liberia and Kazakhstan as examples, model simulations demonstrate how an SWF can serve as a saving tool and fiscal buffer to help smooth government spending given volatile revenue flows.

MACRO-FISCAL FRAMEWORKS FOR RESOURCE-RICH DEVELOPING COUNTRIES: A BRIEF LITERATURE REVIEW

Until recently, the conventional policy advice for resource-rich countries to manage their resource wealth has been mostly guided by the permanent income hypothesis (PIH) (e.g., Barnett and Ossowski 2003; Davis et al. 2001). Under the PIH, countries should aim to limit spending out of resource revenue flows to amounts equivalent to the interest earning on the present value of the estimated resource wealth, while saving the rest of the windfall in financial assets in SWFs to guarantee intergenerational consumption and fiscal sustainability. Norway and Timor-Leste prior to 2011 are examples of countries following a PIH approach.[3] Both have SWFs that have accumulated large amounts of savings out of oil revenue.

Recent work, however, has questioned the relevance of the PIH for RRDCs where poverty is high, capital scarce, and access to international capital markets limited. In such circumstances, some frontloading of consumption toward poorer current generations is desirable, whereas the bulk of resource revenue ought to be used either for investment or saving for future generations (e.g., Collier et al. 2010; van der Ploeg and Venables 2011; International Monetary Fund 2012a; van den Bremer and van der Ploeg 2013). In particular, these authors argue that in the case of capital-scarce developing countries, the PIH ought to be modified to favor a frontloading of domestic public investment in assets with a high social return (e.g., education, health, infrastructure), rather than investing in foreign financial assets. This is because current generations are poorer than future generations, so that the marginal social value of an incremental dollar of consumption is higher now than in the future; the PIH is more appropriate for economies already on a sustained growth path that wish to permanently raise their consumption and place higher weights on the welfare of future generations (Collier et al. 2010).

However, since resource revenue is volatile and there may be bottlenecks in ramping up public investment (van der Ploeg 2012), a gradual investment strategy is recommended, with excess resource revenue being saved in an SWF. This approach is in line with the "fiscal sustainability approach" (Baunsgaard et al. 2012) and the "sustainable investment" strategy recommended by Berg et al. (2013), who show how combining public investment with a resource fund can help address the macroeconomic problems associated with both the exhaustibility and volatility of natural resources revenue. The model they propose explicitly incorporates public investment inefficiencies and absorptive capacity constraints. Although empirical evidence is scarce, existing studies suggest that an increase in public investment spending raises the public capital stock by only about half that increase (Arestoff and Hurlin 2006), with the cost of public investment rising as spending increases. Similarly, Collier et al. (2010) note that developing countries are more susceptible to management and implementation bottlenecks and thus should first invest in their capacity to make investments and manage projects efficiently (the idea of "investing in investment" advocated by Collier [2009]; see also Collier et al. 2010; van der Ploeg 2012; Buffie et al. 2012). In these models, resource funds can help address various objectives: stabilization—to address volatility, "parking"—to allow sufficient time for governments to address supply-side constraints and, in particular, inefficiencies in public investment,[4] and saving for future generations—to address the exhaustibility of natural resources (van den Bremer and van der Ploeg 2013).

OPERATIONAL FISCAL ANCHORS FOR RESOURCE-RICH DEVELOPING COUNTRIES

In the case of RRDCs that are about to start or scale up natural resource exploitation (e.g., Mongolia, Mozambique, Tanzania), the efficient use of resource revenue to boost long-term growth is predicated on their ability to overcome two main challenges. First, governments need to be able to capture their fair share of resource revenue. Sound fiscal regimes that combine a royalty, corporate income tax, and resource rent tax with effective and transparent resource revenue administration are essential for maximizing government revenue over project life (International Monetary Fund 2012b). The urgent need for revenues may also influence the terms of contracts negotiated by governments with foreign mining companies, where the initial contracts may provide generous returns to the foreign investors (and in some cases to domestic elites) who are prepared to invest in such uncertain environments but provide little benefit to the governments.

Second, RRDCs need to manage their resource revenue wisely by (i) deciding how much of the resource revenue to consume or invest in the short term and how much to save, given that natural resources are exhaustible but the production horizon is uncertain, and (ii) finding ways to delink spending from volatile revenue to avoid boom–bust cycles.[5] Overcoming these challenges may unlock success in harnessing natural resource revenue for sustainable development.

Indeed, many developing countries, including RRDCs, have prepared ambitious development strategies aiming at reaching emerging market or middle-income status in a number of years, mostly through implementing large-scale public infrastructure projects (e.g., Côte d'Ivoire, Liberia). The historical record on the success of public investment surges in delivering sustained higher growth, however, is not very encouraging, as described most recently by Warner (2014). The poor track record of RRDCs in escaping the resource curse and delivering faster growth is also well documented in the literature (Gelb 1988; Sachs and Warner 1999,

2001; Bhattacharyya and Collier 2011; van der Ploeg 2011). In effect, most RRDCs have been unable to save the higher resource revenue and smooth the volatility of resource flows, thus experiencing boom–bust cycles that have been detrimental to growth.

To help address these challenges, Baunsgaard et al. (2012) and the International Monetary Fund (2012a) have proposed a set of fiscal rules tailored to the various circumstances of RRDCs (table 9.1).

• For countries *with long reserve horizons* (i.e., where the key issue is to avoid boom–bust cycles), a structural primary balance (SPB)[6] anchor based on a natural resource price rule (or smoothing formula) may be appropriate. Price rules are particularly helpful *when the country derives a relatively large share of its revenue from natural resources* in order to smooth the domestic transmission of fluctuations in the price of natural resources. Chile is a good example of a country using an SPB rule, with a financing SWF subordinated to the fiscal framework. Excess copper revenue that does not contribute to annual budgets is saved in two SWFs: the Economic and Social Stabilization Fund and the Pension Reserve Fund. However, the calculation of a full-fledged SPB can pose challenges for fragile countries where economic cycles are erratic and therefore should be limited to adjustments to natural resource–related revenue (as in Mongolia).

• In cases where the *resource production horizon is long* but the main source of uncertainty or volatility lies with *production volumes* rather than commodity prices and *resource revenue doesn't represent a large share of total revenues*, Deléchat et al. (2017) show that a simple nonresource balance (NRB) target rule can be effectively used as a fiscal anchor to avoid boom–bust cycles in the short term while maintaining fiscal sustainability. They show that this is preferable to a rule based on the nonresource primary balance (NRPB) such as the PIH, which places more emphasis on long-term fiscal sustainability. Although the NRB target is de-linked from the natural resource revenue flow, it can be calibrated to deliver a stable and sustainable path of public investment while avoiding unsustainable debt accumulation (see the Liberia application of the DIGNAR model shown later in the chapter). Such a rule is also simple to understand and implement, which is important in low-income countries with weaker institutions and governance and poor-quality data. The sustainable NRB target rule is akin to Botswana's Sustainable Budget Index.[7] Under the proposed rule, total expenditure is capped by a sustainable NRB deficit target, where the deficit target is a function of projected resource revenue and is consistent with

Table 9.1 Fiscal frameworks for resource-rich countries

Fiscal policy indications		
Fiscal balance concepts	**Overall fiscal balance:** total revenue minus total expenditure; indicator of long-run fiscal sustainability **Nonresource balance:** overall balance excluding resource revenue and spending associated with the resource sector **Nonresource primary balance:** Nonresource balance excluding interest payments; indicator of fiscal policy stance	
Fiscal sustainability benchmarks		
Long-term fiscal sustainability benchmark	**PIH annuity or modified PIH:** allows some frontloading of spending but then requires downward spending adjustment to be consistent with the PIH annuity value of resource wealth **Fiscal sustainability approach:** based on debt sustainability framework; allows scaling up of spending while stabilizing long-run net resource wealth below PIH annuity	
Fiscal policy anchor/rule (short to medium term)		
	Capital-scarce	No scarcity of capital
Long-lasting resources	Flexible nonresource primary balance rule plus expenditure growth cap Price-based rule (overall balance) plus expenditure growth cap Nonresource balance rule with or without expenditure growth cap	Nonresource primary balance rule Price-based rule (overall balance) plus expenditure growth cap
Short-lasting resources	Flexible nonresource primary balance rule plus expenditure growth cap Modified PIH-based framework (nonresource primary balance)	PIH-based framework (nonresource primary balance)

Source: Adapted from Baunsgaard et al. 2012.

medium-term debt sustainability, with current spending fully financed by nonresource revenue. In this context, resource revenue is allocated to infrastructure and, possibly, human capital spending, with any surplus being accumulated in a natural resource fund to smooth investment over time.

• When available information suggests that the *resource production horizon is relatively short*, or when the resource production horizon is long but *resource revenue would represent a relatively small share of total revenue*, long-run fiscal sustainability and intertemporal equity consideration ought to be paramount. In this case, the preferred fiscal rule would be de-linked from the natural resource revenue stream. In particular, the *nonresource primary balance* can provide a useful fiscal anchor, provided it is set in line with long-term sustainability benchmarks and calibrated in the short term depending on cyclical conditions. Norway and Timor-Leste use fiscal rules based on the PIH and have accumulated substantial savings in their respective SWFs.

A GENERAL EQUILIBRIUM MODEL WITH
A SOVEREIGN WEALTH FUND

The discussion so far has made it clear that an SWF can be an important supporting element in the design of a coherent fiscal framework. To see how the macroeconomic and fiscal implications of spending resource revenues can be assessed, this section presents an analytical tool—a dynamic general equilibrium model with an SWF—suitable for RRDCs. The SWF in the model is a financing fund that is fully integrated with the government budget. Fiscal surpluses are saved in the SWF, and SWF resources are drawn down to help finance fiscal deficits.

The model presented here modifies the DIGNAR (debt, investment, growth, and natural resource) model in Melina et al. (2015), allowing a government to allocate resource revenues as social transfers in addition to public investment. DIGNAR combines the model-based debt sustainability framework in Buffie et al. (2012) with the natural resource model in Berg et al. (2013). Like those two models, DIGNAR incorporates an investment-growth nexus and several conspicuous economic characteristics of developing countries, including a large share of hand-to-mouth households, investment inefficiency, and limited absorptive capacity. Also, DIGNAR has a rather detailed fiscal specification, including an SWF and a variety of debt instruments to jointly finance spending plans in RRDCs.

MODEL DESCRIPTION

DIGNAR is a real (i.e., no nominal rigidities), annual model of a small open economy with a natural resource sector. The description here focuses on the model's key features; for a full description of the DIGNAR model, see Melina et al. (2015).[8]

HOUSEHOLDS

The model has two types of households: (i) forward-looking, optimizing households with access to financial and capital markets, and (ii) liquidity-constrained, hand-to-mouth households that consume all their disposable income every period. A large share of hand-to-mouth implies that resource revenues transferred directly to them can immediately boost their consumption.

FIRMS

There are three production sectors: (i) nontraded goods; (ii) nonresource traded goods; and (iii) natural resources. As most natural resource production is capital intensive and a large part of its investment in developing countries is financed by foreigners, the setup of resource production is simplified in the model: its production does not employ labor, capital, or intermediate goods; all resource output is exported; and its profits are sent abroad. Total resource output is subject to a royalty tax, a modeling simplification as tax schemes on resource revenues are more complex in reality (International Monetary Fund 2012a). The paths of royalty rates in the model are backed out to target the projected resource revenues–to–gross-domestic-product (GDP) ratios obtained outside the model.

Firms in the two nonresource production sectors are perfectly competitive. They produce output using Cobb-Douglas technology with constant returns to scale of private capital and labor. Public capital is also an input in production, which increases the productivity of private inputs and can crowd in private investment.

To capture potential Dutch disease from spending resource revenues, total factor productivity (TFP) in the traded goods sector exhibits learning-by-doing externalities. Spending resource revenues domestically can result in real appreciation, hurting the competitiveness of the traded goods sector and lowering its output. Following van Wijnbergen (1984) and Berg et al. (2010), TFP in the traded goods sector depends on its output of the previous year. With some persistence in TFP, Dutch disease can linger before productive public capital is built up to reverse the negative impact on traded output.

GOVERNMENT

Each period, the government collects taxes (from consumers and in the form of royalties on resource sector production), receives foreign grants and aid, and issues debt to finance its expenditures on government consumption, public investment, transfers, and debt service. As in Buffie et al. (2012), the model distinguishes among domestic debt, external commercial debt, and external concessional debt. Depending on fiscal approaches, domestic and external commercial debt accumulates endogenously, whereas the path of external concessional debt is taken exogenously because the latter is decided by international donors. In the simulations we present, the alternative fiscal approaches focus on investing resource revenue and distributing it as transfers, and the consumption tax rate is the instrument that adjusts to maintain debt sustainability.

A SOVEREIGN WEALTH FUND INTEGRATED IN A FISCAL FRAMEWORK

The highlight of the fiscal specification in DIGNAR is the inclusion of an SWF that can save resource wealth and help smooth government spending. Given exogenous paths of resource revenues, public investment, and transfers and the steady-state values for other fiscal variables, any surpluses are accumulated in an SWF. When negative resource revenue shocks hit (resulting from either unexpectedly low production or prices), the fund is drawn down to support predetermined spending levels. In the case that the fund does not have sufficient savings to cover revenue shortfalls (or reach a lower bound that the government chooses to maintain), the government resorts to borrowing. In the simulations for Liberia and Kazakhstan, the governments borrow from external commercial markets when needed.

INVESTMENT EFFICIENCY AND ABSORPTIVE CAPACITY CONSTRAINTS

One main concern for scaling up public investment in developing countries is low public investment efficiency and limited absorptive capacity (e.g., Pritchett 2000; Collier et al. 2010; van der Ploeg 2012). In DIGNAR, one dollar of investment is converted to much less than one dollar of installed public capital, reflecting investment inefficiency. Moreover, scaling up investment spending too quickly can further lower efficiency, reflecting costs associated with absorptive capacity constraints.

COUNTRY APPLICATIONS: LIBERIA

Liberia is a fragile, low-income country, endowed with iron ore, gold, diamonds, and potentially petroleum. Although the fiscal mining revenue has remained low (around 2–4 percent of GDP) since production of iron ore resumed in 2011, the potential for the mining sector is significant, provided current investment plans are implemented (Deléchat et al. 2017). The combination of Liberia's resource wealth and urgent needs to build capital and improve the living conditions of a large poor population highlights the fiscal challenges faced by many fragile countries to allocate valuable resource wealth. At present, Liberia manages its resource wealth through the budget but in an ad-hoc manner. Anticipating larger resource flows from new mining projects and, possibly, petroleum, the authorities have started to consider alternative fiscal frameworks to best harness natural resource wealth. However, the long gestation periods of mining projects and uncertainty as to when production will be ramped up add to the difficulties in projecting future natural resource revenue.

Figure 9.1 presents the simulation results of three fiscal approaches for Liberia under the baseline: a relatively conservative scenario of resource revenues that assumes continuing production from mining

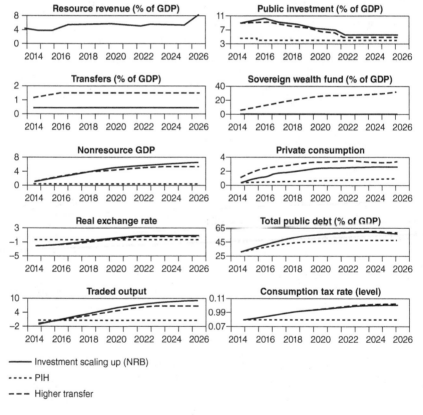

Figure 9.1   Various fiscal approaches to allocating resource revenues: Liberia. GDP, gross domestic product; NRB, nonresource balance; PIH, permanent income hypothesis.

projects already under exploitation and a relatively small flow of fiscal mining revenue remaining around 2 to 3 percent of GDP over the projection period. The first approach (solid lines) analyzed is a public investment path derived from a fiscal rule based on the sustainable NRB target. Under this rule, public investment is scaled up early on to 10 to 11 percent of GDP and later declines to a level merely sufficient to replenish depreciated capital. In contrast, the second approach (narrow dashes) follows the conventionally advised PIH rule, which restricts and smooths current spending (both consumption and capital spending) at a low level equal to the annuity value of total resource wealth (e.g., Davis et al. 2001). The third approach (wide dashes) analyzes the trade-offs between investment and transfer spending by lowering public investment to permanently increase transfers from 0.5 to 1.5 percent of GDP. Unless specified in parentheses, the units in the figures are in percent deviation from a path assuming that the economy grows at a constant rate.

A comparison of the NRB and PIH approaches illustrates the trade-offs between saving in an SWF versus spending to build productive capital. Under the PIH framework, public investment is kept low, at about 3 to 4 percent of GDP, and the SWF gradually increases its value, approaching 40 percent of GDP by 2025. A low level of investment entails little additional growth in nonresource GDP and private consumption, however, and the rise in public debt is due only to projected increases in concessional debt. On the contrary, investing under the NRB, nonresource GDP and private consumption rise much above the trend-growth path. However, an SWF cannot be established, and public debt rises, reaching 60 percent of GDP. A higher debt triggers increases in the consumption tax rate, which suppresses private consumption to some extent, offsetting some growth benefits from more public capital. Given the high level of public debt, the NRB investing approach exposes the economy to the risks of unsustainable debt, especially when the tax rate increase cannot be implemented or revenue inflows fall short of the projection assumed here. For a country like Liberia, resorting to nonconcessional borrowing might also be restricted, so that the public investment scaling-up would have to be more gradual. This highlights the importance of alternative strategies to expand fiscal space, including by increasing the efficiency of public investment ("investing in investment," as in Collier [2009]), and increasing nonresource revenue through a broadening of the tax base and improvements in tax administration.

Although NRB investing can increase private consumption, it does so only gradually, along with the public capital buildup. As the poverty headcount for Liberia is the highest among RRDCs—95 percent of the population live with $2 a day (International Monetary Fund 2012b)— the simulations also compare investing resource revenue with providing social transfers. These are modeled in DIGNAR as cash transfers to all households but in practice could be delivered as targeted social safety nets to protect the most vulnerable. Relative to NRB investing, simulation results show that increasing transfers merely by 1 percent of GDP (therefore reducing investment spending by the same amount), private consumption is higher by about 1 percent of the steady-state consumption level throughout the simulation horizon. Yet, the difference in non-resource GDP between NRB investing and higher transfers is trivial, especially in the early years.[9]

Since private consumption can be used to approximate the welfare of an economy, balancing between capital building and increased social transfers to households is an important consideration when allocating resource revenues in a fragile country. The analysis focuses on investment in public capital and transfers. Other options, such as education and health spending, may be analyzed by modifying the model to add human capital.

COUNTRY APPLICATION: KAZAKHSTAN

Since independence in 1991, discoveries of oil reserves and development of transport infrastructure to new markets have substantially increased oil production in Kazakhstan and made the country one of the top twenty oil producers in the world. During the 2003–08 oil price boom, the government pursued a conservative fiscal approach of paying down debt and saving a large part of oil windfalls in an SWF (the National Fund of the Republic of Kazakhstan). Unlike several RRDCs that experienced economic turmoil during the 2008–09 crisis (e.g., Angola, Mongolia), Kazakhstan used the savings in the fund to finance a large stimulus package, which mitigated the economic downturn (Minasyan and Yang 2013).

Using oil wealth to facilitate economic development and diversification has been a long-term objective of the Kazakhstani government. The simulation results presented demonstrate how DIGNAR can be used as a planning tool to reach a certain growth objective while accommodating the saving objective of an SWF.[10]

Figure 9.2 presents the simulation results of two fiscal approaches for Kazakhstan under a high (left column) and low (right column) oil price scenario with two investment scaling-up plans. The high oil price scenario

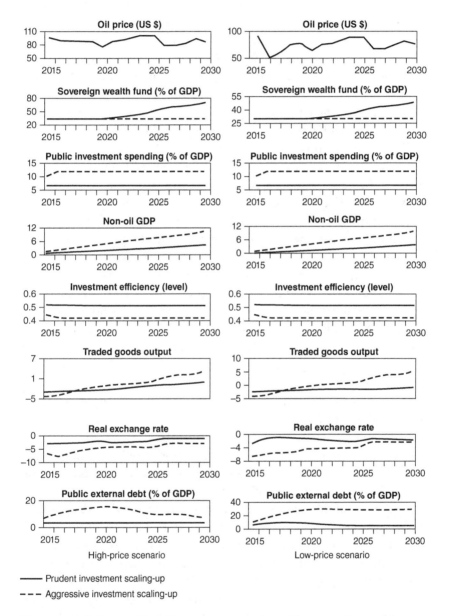

Figure 9.2   Saving and investing resource revenues with a sovereign wealth fund: Kazakhstan. GDP, gross domestic product.

is in line with the projection of oil prices (e.g., the projection recorded in the April database of the World Economic Outlook [International Monetary Fund 2013]) often seen before the declining trend since October 2014. The low-price scenario incorporates large negative oil price shocks, as observed in 2008 and around the end of 2014.

The simulations assume that the Kazakhstani government does not exhaust all its savings in the SWF to finance investment scaling-up; thus, the government would start borrowing in international financial markets, even though the fund holds substantial savings and the borrowing rate is higher than the interest rate earned by the fund.[11] The minimum level of saving in the fund is assumed to be 30 percent of GDP.

With prudent investing (solid lines), public investment is fixed at 6.4 percent of GDP and the SWF assets could reach about 70 percent of GDP by 2030 under a high-price scenario and 50 percent of GDP under a low-price scenario. On the other hand, with aggressive investing (dotted-dashed lines), public investment increases substantially and is maintained at 12 percent of GDP, reaching the goal of raising the growth rate of nonresource GDP by one percentage point above the trend-growth path. Even under the high-price scenario, the government accumulates no additional savings in the fund, but the amount of additional external borrowing remains low, peaking at about 16 percent of GDP. Meanwhile, non-oil GDP, private investment, and consumption all substantially outperform these series' projected paths under the prudent investing strategy. The high level of investment, however, lowers public investment efficiency by about 20 percent (from 0.5, implying that $1 of spending yields $0.5 of installed capital, to 0.4) as limited absorptive capacity exacerbates existing investment inefficiencies. Moreover, aggressive investing leads to a larger real exchange rate appreciation and thus lowers traded output more, reflecting more severe Dutch disease before a higher public capital stock is built up to increase the productivity of the traded goods sector.

On the fiscal side, aggressive investing carries more risks than prudent investing. Under the low-price scenario, external commercial debt rises from below 10 percent of GDP to 30 percent of GDP. If larger and more persistent negative shocks than what are assumed here hit the economy, the government may have to tap into savings in the SWF to avoid excessive borrowing in order to support the investment plan. Under these circumstances, the economy could be left with few fiscal buffers to cope with future negative economic or revenue shocks.

GENERAL LESSONS

Several lessons can be derived from the country cases about managing volatile resource revenues in developing countries.

- For RRDCs, SWFs ought to be part of fiscal frameworks geared toward the sound management of natural resources to foster sustainable development. Recent research has highlighted that over the long run, capital-scarce, low-income countries with little access to international capital markets ought to consider a strategy of investing in domestic assets with a high social return, rather than investing in foreign financial assets. For these countries, benchmarks established on the basis of the PIH are not optimal.[12] When looking at fiscal frameworks that would allow using a combination of natural resource revenue and borrowing to finance much-needed infrastructure investment, model simulations show that fiscal rules based on the PIH translate into high savings accumulation into an SWF but a very conservative investment path. For most RRDCs, a gradual frontloading of public investment mindful of absorptive capacity constraints and debt sustainability would be preferred, compared to an overly conservative PIH.
- When defining operational fiscal anchors for RRDCs over the short or medium term, policymakers ought to consider a number of factors: (i) the length of the resource production horizon (whether long or relatively short); (ii) the likely size of the natural resource revenue (i.e., whether it represents a large or small share of total government revenue); and (iii) whether the uncertainty in projecting natural resource revenue comes mostly from commodity prices or also from production volumes, as is the case for extractive mining. Operational frameworks also ought to take into account individual countries' implementation and institutional capacity.
- There is a trade-off between scaling up public investment and maintaining debt sustainability when borrowing against future resource revenues to invest. Increasing public investment builds up productive public capital, which facilitates nonresource GDP growth. Investment scaling-up plans, however, should be mindful of the high uncertainty of future resource revenues. When unexpected, large negative oil price shocks hit, aggressive investing substantially increases borrowing needs, subjecting the economy to debt sustainability risks. In addition, a more aggressive investment plan lowers investment

efficiency and leads to more severe Dutch disease symptoms in the first few years. If, instead, investment plans are too conservative, as with the PIH investing in the Liberia application, the economy can accumulate significant savings in an SWF but cannot benefit from the growth opportunity brought by the resource wealth. These simulation results suggest that a moderate investment scaling-up path, commensurate with resource revenue flows, can strike a balance between growth objectives and achieving fiscal sustainability (as also highlighted in chapter 8).

- There is also a trade-off between scaling up public investment and sharing resource wealth with households as transfers. As most developing countries have a large poor population, providing transfers has an immediate effect on improving the standard of living of the population. While public investment can also boost private consumption, it does so indirectly through raising productivity and the wage rate, which in turn increases households' income and consumption. By contrast, transfers boost income immediately. As poor households tend to consume all their disposable income, their consumption also rises immediately, as shown in the Liberia simulation.[13]

- The importance of not neglecting and building a strong domestic revenue base cannot be emphasized enough. This is particularly true for countries like Liberia, where resource revenue is relatively small or the resource production horizon is relatively short, but also true for all RRDCs, given the volatility of natural resource revenue. Fiscal space for scaling up public investment also needs to be generated by expanding the nonrevenue tax base and controlling nonessential expenditure, as well as improving investment efficiency.

- Lastly, an SWF can serve as an effective fiscal buffer as well as a saving device. The minimum saving level, however, should not be set too high, as the borrowing rate for developing countries is often higher than the earning rate of an SWF. When resource revenues do not turn out to be as high as expected, public debt can pile up and fiscal adjustments, such as raising the consumption tax rates, become necessary. Fiscal adjustments, either through cutting government spending, such as transfers, or increasing tax rates have negative effects on consumption and nonresource GDP, offsetting the growth benefits from more productive public capital. In addition, fiscal adjustment may be politically difficult to accomplish in RRDCs, and this should also be considered when designing an investment strategy. By fully integrating an SWF with a government budget constraint, DIGNAR provides a coherent framework for planning medium-term fiscal strategies for managing resource revenues.

NOTES

1. This chapter is part of a research project on macroeconomic policy in low-income countries supported by U.K.'s Department for International Development (DFID). The views expressed in this chapter are those of the authors and do not necessarily represent those of the International Monetary Fund (IMF), IMF policy, the DFID, or DFID policy.

2. Recent reports by the Africa Progress Panel (2013) and the African Development Bank (2014) address how to harness the continent's natural resource wealth for all.

3. Timor-Leste, as one of the most natural resource–dependent countries in the world, established its Petroleum Fund in 2005. The Petroleum Fund Law sets the objectives of the Petroleum Fund to conservatively manage petroleum revenues. Its rules target the outflows from the fund up to the estimated sustainable income (to be 3 percent of petroleum wealth for a particular year). Transfers to the government budget starting from fiscal year 2012 have been substantially higher than the estimated sustainable income owing to capital investments mandated in Timor-Leste's Strategic Development Plan with a main objective of transforming the country from a low-income into an upper-middle-income country by 2030 (McKechnie 2013).

4. In capital-scarce developing countries, it may be useful to create investment funds to temporarily park funds until domestic investment projects are ready to be undertaken and to collect any returns from these investments (van den Bremer and van der Ploeg 2013).

5. The volatility or uncertainty attached to natural resource revenue comes from both price and volume fluctuations. Commodity prices in general and oil prices in particular are volatile and difficult to predict, while for some types of natural resources (e.g., minerals), other factors, such as long project gestation periods, difficult local environments, and an arbitrary ramping-up of production by mining companies, contribute to high uncertainty regarding future production volumes (Deléchat et al. 2017).

6. Structural primary balance is the difference between the cyclically adjusted government revenue and spending excluding interest payment. Thus, calculating structural balance requires an estimation of what revenues and spending would be if the economy were at its potential.

7. Botswana's Sustainable Budget Index requires all current spending to be covered by nonresource revenue, with diamond revenue allocated to public investment, health, and education or saved in the Pula Fund.

8. For the modification of the DIGNAR to allow for using resource revenues as social transfers, see Deléchat et al. 2017.

9. Compared to NRB investing, the approach with higher transfers generates more private consumption but crowds in less private investment. In the longer horizon, more public capital accumulated under NRB investing produces slightly more nonresource GDP than the approach with higher transfers.

10. The simulation presented for Kazakhstan follows the exercise in Minasyan and Yang (2013).

11. The calibration assumes that the SWF earns an annual real return of 2.7 percent, based on the average return of Norway's Government Pension Fund Global from 1997 to 2011 (Gros and Mayer 2012), and the real annual borrowing rate of external commercial debt is assumed to be 5 percent.

12. These are benchmarks that allow only spending the annuity value of the future resource revenue stream while saving the rest of the windfall in financial assets in an SWF to guarantee intergenerational consumption and fiscal sustainability.

13. In poor countries, transfers may not work to raise certain types of consumption without parallel public investment. For example, to increase consumption of medical services, public investment to build health care facilities would be needed.

REFERENCES

African Development Bank. 2014. "From Fragility to Resilience: Managing Natural Resources in Fragile States in Africa." Tunis: African Development Bank.

Africa Progress Panel. 2013. "Equity in Extractives: Stewarding Africa's Natural Resources for All," Africa Progress Report 2013. Geneva: Africa Progress Panel.

Arestoff, F., and C. Hurlin. 2006. "Estimates of Government Net Capital Stocks for 26 Developing Countries, 1970–2002," World Bank Policy Research Working Paper 3858. Washington, DC: World Bank.

Barnett, S., and R. Ossowski. 2003. "Operational Aspects of Fiscal Policy in Oil-Producing Countries." In *Fiscal Policy Formulation and Implementation in Oil-Producing Countries*, edited by J. M. Davis, R. Ossowski, and A. Fedelino, 48–81. Washington, DC: International Monetary Fund.

Baunsgaard, T., M. Villafuerte, M. Poplawski-Ribeiro, and C. Richmond. 2012. "Fiscal Frameworks for Resource Rich Developing Countries," IMF Staff Discussion Note 12/04. Washington, DC: International Monetary Fund.

Berg, A., J. Gottschalk, R. Portillo, and L.-F. Zanna. 2010. "The Macroeconomics of Medium-Term Aid Scaling-up Scenarios," IMF Working Paper 10/160. Washington, DC: International Monetary Fund.

Berg, A., R. Portillo, S. S. Yang, and L.-F. Zanna. 2013. "Public Investment in Resource-Abundant Developing Countries," *IMF Economic Review* 61, no.1: 92–129.

Bhattacharyya, S., and P. Collier. 2011. "Public Capital in Resource-Rich Economies: Is There a Curse?" CSAE Working Paper 2011–14. Oxford: Centre for the Study of African Economies.

Buffie, E., A. Berg, C. Pattillo, R. Portillo, and L.-F. Zanna. 2012. "Public Investment, Growth, and Debt Sustainability: Putting Together the Pieces," IMF Working Paper 12/144. Washington, DC: International Monetary Fund.

Collier, P. 2009. "Still the Bottom Billion," *Finance and Development*, June, 4–7.

Collier, P., F. van der Ploeg, M. Spence, and A. J. Venables. 2010. "Managing Resource Revenues in Developing Economies," *IMF Staff Papers* 57, no. 1: 84–118.

Davis, J., R. Ossowski, J. Daniel, and S. Barnett. 2001. "Stabilization and Savings Funds for Nonrenewable Resources: Experiences and Fiscal Policy Implications," Occasional Paper 205. Washington, DC: International Monetary Fund.

Deléchat, Corinne, Shu-Chun S. Yang, Will Clark, Pranav Gupta, Malangu Kabedi-Mbuyi, Mesmin Koulet-Vickot, Carla Macario, Toomas Orav, Manuel Rosales, Rene Tapsoba, Dmitry Zhdankin. 2017. "Harnessing Resource Wealth for Inclusive Growth in Fragile Western African States," *Journal of African Economies 2017* (advanced online edition).

Gelb, A. 1988. *Oil Windfalls: Blessing or Curse.* Oxford: Oxford University Press.

Gros, D., and T. Mayer. 2012, "A Sovereign Wealth Fund to Lift Germany's Curse of Excess Savings," CEPS Policy Brief No. 280. Brussels: Centre for European Policy Studies.

International Monetary Fund. 2012a. "Macroeconomic Policy Frameworks for Resource-Rich Developing Countries." Washington, DC: International Monetary Fund.

——. 2012b. "Fiscal Regimes for Extractive Industries: Design and Implementation." Washington, DC: International Monetary Fund.

——. 2013. World Economic Outlook [online database]. Washington, DC: International Monetary Fund. www.imf.org/external/pubs/ft/weo/2013/02/weodata/index.aspx.

McKechnie, A. 2013. "Managing Natural Resource Revenues: The Timor-Leste Petroleum Fund," Research Report. London: Overseas Development Institute.

Melina, G., S. S. Yang, and L. F. Zanna. 2015. "Debt Sustainability, Public Investment, and Natural Resources in Developing Countries: The DIGNAR Model," *Economic Modelling*, 52, Part B: 630–649.

Minasyan, G., and S. S. Yang. 2013. "Leveraging Oil Wealth for Development in Kazakhstan: Opportunities and Challenges," Selected Issues, IMF Country Report No. 13/291. Washington, DC: International Monetary Fund.

Pritchett, L. 2000. "The Tyranny of Concepts: CUDIE (Cumulated, Depreciated, Investment Effort) Is Not Capital," *Journal of Economic Growth* 5, no. 4: 361–384.

Sachs, J. D., and A. M. Warner. 1999. "The Big Push, Natural Resource Booms and Growth," *Journal of Development Economics* 59, no. 1: 43–76.

——. 2001. "The Curse of Natural Resources," *European Economic Review* 45, no. 4–6: 827–838.

Van den Bremer, T. S., and F. van der Ploeg. 2013. "Managing and Harnessing Volatile Oil Windfalls," *IMF Economic Review* 61, no. 1: 130–167.

Van der Ploeg, F. 2011. "Natural Resources: Curse or Blessing?" *Journal of Economic Literature* 49, no. 2: 366–420.

——. 2012. "Bottlenecks in Ramping Up Public Investment," *International Tax and Public Finance* 19, no. 4: 509–538.

Van der Ploeg, F., and A. J. Venables. 2011. "Harnessing Windfall Revenues: Optimal Policies for Resource-Rich Developing Economies," *The Economic Journal* 121, no. 551: 1–30.

Van Wijnbergen, S. 1984. "The 'Dutch Disease': A Disease After All?" *The Economic Journal* 94, no. 373: 41–55.

Warner, A. 2014. "Public Investment as an Engine of Growth," IMF Working Paper 14/148. Washington, DC: International Monetary Fund.

CHAPTER 10

The Role of the Nigeria Sovereign Investment Authority in a New Era of Fiscal Responsibility

Uche Orji and Stella Ojekwe-Onyejeli

Nigeria Sovereign Investment Authority

The establishment of the Nigeria Sovereign Investment Authority (NSIA, or "Authority") has the potential to be a game changer in the way Nigeria manages it public revenues. Despite a lengthy period of growth in non-oil sectors of the economy, oil revenues remain the most significant source of government income, bringing with it the mixed blessings many other resource-dependent countries have experienced. Nigeria has experienced its fair share of political and economic instability, owing in large part to the volatility of oil and its impact on fiscal policy (a topic dealt with in chapters 1, 5, and 9). The NSIA forms an integral part of a new era of fiscal responsibility in Nigeria.

After receiving its mandate from the Nigerian government, the NSIA took a number of steps during its first year of operations in 2013 to establish a truly world-class sovereign investment institution with clear investment rules and principles, transparent benchmarks, active disclosure of investment policies and performance, and a dedicated and highly professional staff. While the size of assets under NSIA management is relatively small compared to the size of the Nigerian economy and budget, the fund's asset base is expected to grow over time as oil revenues grow, in particular after the current commodity price downturn and the institution establishes a track record for the independent, professional management of state assets.

In this chapter, we describe the process that led to the establishment of the NSIA and the three funds under its management, as well as the policies, strategies, and governance arrangement that have been put in place to ensure that the Authority becomes a world-class sovereign investment institution. In the following section, we provide an overview of the history of oil revenue management in Nigeria and the institutional and legislative reforms that took place to create the NSIA. We next outline the operational rules stipulated by legislation for the transfer of funds to and from the NSIA. We then consider the respective investment policies and strategies of the three funds under the NSIA's management: the Future Generations Fund (a typical savings fund), the Stabilisation Fund (a classic commodity–revenue stabilization fund), and the Nigeria Infrastructure Fund (one of the growing number of sovereign development funds). Finally, we consider the governance, management, and oversight arrangements around the NSIA, before concluding with some reflections on the lessons to be learned for other countries from the establishment and ongoing development of the Authority.

BACKGROUND AND INCEPTION

Commercially viable oil reserves were first discovered in Nigeria in 1956, and oil production commenced in 1958, two years prior to Nigeria gaining independence from Great Britain. By the time of the 1970s oil price shocks, Nigeria was already a significant global oil producer, and oil had become a mainstay of the Nigerian economy. However, far from providing a catalyst for sustained economic development and growth, these massive (but often short-lived) revenue windfalls triggered bouts of economic instability, political turmoil, and conflict over the decades. While there has been a significant rise in new African oil producers and large investments in oil exploration and development on the continent, Nigeria remains the largest oil producer in the region, ahead of Angola and Algeria (KPMG 2015). With considerable proven oil reserves, oil will remain a major part of the Nigerian economy for years to come. Revenues derived from oil and gas still account for the overwhelming majority of Nigerian fiscal revenues and foreign exchange earnings—in recent years, on average, around 80 percent of budget revenues have been derived from hydrocarbons. This dependence on oil remains a source of considerable economic volatility, political controversy, and contestation in Nigeria. The establishment of the NSIA to manage three separate sovereign funds has the potential to relieve some of these tensions and contribute to managing Nigeria's oil wealth and other government revenues in a more stable, sustainable, and productive manner.

The governance and institutions around Nigerian oil revenues underwent a significant change in 2004 with the establishment of the Excess

Crude Account, a segregated fiscal account intended to ring-fence and stabilize volatile oil revenues and provide an equitable basis for sharing oil revenues among Nigeria's numerous state governments. The value of the Excess Crude Account reached $5.1 billion in its first year, before rising to as much as $20 billion by late 2008 owing to sharply rising oil prices. However, a mere year and a half later, in June 2010, the account was depleted to less than $4 billion as a result of the collapse in global oil prices following the global financial crisis, transfers to Nigerian states to cover their deficits, and a number of unaccounted withdrawals. In recent years, even as oil revenues have recovered, the Excess Crude Account has continued to dwindle. The Excess Crude Account's lack of prudent, transparent operational rules laid the groundwork for the establishment of the NSIA. In May 2011, the Nigerian Senate passed the *Nigeria Sovereign Investment Authority Act*, with the House following suit one week later, thereby ratifying the law. Progress toward establishing the NSIA was delayed by legal challenges by a group of state governors, but once these cases were dismissed, the Authority's board of directors and chairperson were announced in August 2012, followed by the appointment of the managing director in October.

The law made provision for the NSIA to manage three distinct funds: the Nigeria Infrastructure Fund, the Stabilisation Fund, and the Future Generations Fund. As their names suggest, the Nigeria Infrastructure Fund has a domestic focus on investments in long-term infrastructure, the Stabilisation Fund invests in highly liquid, safe assets in order to provide a buffer against macroeconomic and fiscal volatility arising from oil dependence, and the Future Generations Fund invests in a diversified portfolio of international assets to preserve some of today's revenue windfalls for future generations. The legally mandated objectives of the three funds, included in the *Nigeria Sovereign Investment Authority Act*,[1] are as follows:

- Provide stabilization support to the federation revenue in times of economic stress (Stabilisation Fund).
- Invest in a diversified portfolio of appropriate growth investments in order to provide future generations of Nigerians a solid savings base for such a time as the hydrocarbon reserves in Nigeria are exhausted (Future Generations Fund).
- Invest in infrastructure projects in Nigeria that meet our targeted financial returns and contribute to the development of essential infrastructure (Nigeria Infrastructure Fund).

In December 2012, the NSIA released a document outlining the basic characteristic of its operational strategy, followed by a release of further details regarding the rules and formulas for allocating capital among the three funds under its management in March 2013. The fund's first investments and deployment of capital commenced in June 2013.

THE ALLOCATION OF FUNDS TO AND FROM THE NIGERIA SOVEREIGN INVESTMENT AUTHORITY

The initial $1 billion provided as seed capital to the NSIA was contributed via the Excess Crude Account by the various layers of the Nigerian government—that is, the federal, state, and local governments—in accordance with a distribution formula included in the separate *Allocation of Revenue Act*.[2] In February 2014, a transfer of an additional $550 million in third-party assets was made to the Authority, bringing its total assets under management to $1.55 billion. The additional third-party assets are to be managed on behalf of Nigerian Bulk Electricity Trading PLC and the Debt Management Office in the sum of $350 million and $200 million, respectively. The federal government has repeatedly expressed the desire for the fund's asset base to grow significantly in the coming years, even despite the decline in oil prices in the second half of 2014.

Ongoing funding of the NSIA may be provided from surplus revenues from the Federation Account, the primary budget account that receives all oil-related revenues and from which all subsequent distributions are made.[3] Figure 10.1 shows the legislated flow of funds from initial oil revenues to the NSIA and its three funds. The implication of these provisions is that state and local governments receive their respective shares of oil revenue only in line with the assumed benchmark oil price in a given year's federal budget. Revenues exceeding the budgeted amount, minus the budget smoothing amount, are transferred to the NSIA.

The *Nigeria Sovereign Investment Authority Act* also contains a provision pertaining to the maximum size of the assets under the institution's management. The law empowers the board of directors to appoint "recognized professionals and academics" to conduct "actuarial assessments of the demands for the proceeds of the Future Generations Fund" and determine "infrastructure and capacity requirements" that will need proceeds from the Nigeria Infrastructure Fund. These assessments, which the law states are to be conducted every two years, will be used to determine

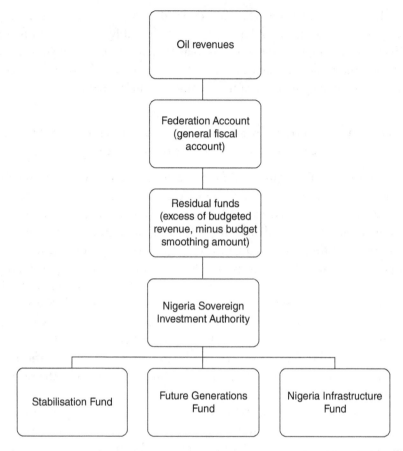

Figure 10.1   The allocation of oil revenues to the Nigeria Sovereign Investment Authority.

a "ceiling percentage of gross domestic product" for the assets under the management of both funds.[4]

The authority for allocating capital among the three funds under NSIA management resides with the NSIA's own board of directors. The only legal provision is that each of the three funds may receive no less than 20 percent of revenues under any allocation. The initial $1 billion in assets allocated to the NSIA was allocated as follows: $400 million each to the Nigeria Infrastructure Fund and the Future Generations Fund and $200 million to the Stabilisation Fund.

The law also establishes the basis for the potential transfer of funds and income from the NSIA back to the government. The Stabilisation Fund is intended to be a cash balance and is the smallest of the three funds under

NSIA management. The Stabilisation Fund may be drawn upon if the provisioned budgetary smoothing amount maintained in the Federation Account is insufficient to stabilize the budget and economy owing to oil prices falling below the budgeted price. Neither the Future Generations Fund nor the Nigeria Infrastructure Fund is intended to provide investment income to the government on a regular (e.g., annual or quarterly) basis: the law requires realized profits, interest, and dividends to be reinvested in existing or new assets of both funds. The law does, however, allow for the NSIA board of directors to "declare a distribution out of uninvested and uncommitted" funds. Such distributions can be made only if the Authority (i) has recorded a profit in each fund for at least five years; (ii) recorded profits in the year of the distribution; and (iii) has sufficient funds to meet its own operational needs. Distributions require a unanimous vote by the NSIA board of directors and are capped at 60 percent of profits.[5]

INVESTMENT RULES AND POLICIES

The *Nigeria Sovereign Investment Authority Act* delegates significant responsibility for investment rules, policies, and practices to the Authority's board of directors. The law does not, for example, specify a target return or a list of eligible assets for the Future Generations Fund or the Nigeria Infrastructure Fund, but states only that the NSIA may hold "such currencies as the Board may from time to time determine consistent with the objectives of the Authority."[6] The law requires the board of directors to develop an annual five-year rolling investment plan for the two funds. The NSIA has taken a number of initiatives to develop investment policies, notably the formulation of investment policy statements for all three funds under its management. In addition, a number of additional disclosures have been made through regular press conferences and statements. In December 2012, for example, the NSIA released a statement outlining the broad investment strategies and operations of the three funds (these documents remain publicly accessible through the NSIA website). Cambridge Associates, one of the world's leading global investment consultants, has been employed to advise the NSIA across all three funds.

FUTURE GENERATIONS FUND

The Future Generations Fund has a target annual return, measured in U.S. dollars, of U.S. inflation plus 4 percent. This is to be achieved against a broad risk guideline of "a desire to minimize (probability less than 10 percent) the possibility of an annual loss in excess of 20 percent." The Future Generations Fund invests in foreign assets and will pursue an outsourced model until internal investment capacity is enhanced. The fund's target portfolio is highly diversified and includes assets and asset classes organized in three categories according to their role in the overall portfolio, namely growth assets, inflation, and deflation hedges (table 10.1). The investment policy statement of the Future Generations Fund provides extensive information regarding all critical elements of the investment process, including time horizons (the fund's investment horizon is stated as being 20 years), manager concentration, investment benchmarks, liquidity requirements, investment beliefs, and security lending policies. The fund appointed its first external managers in December 2013.

Table 10.1   Asset allocation and benchmarks of Nigeria's Future Generations Fund

Asset allocation	Policy target	Benchmark
Growth assets	**80%**	**MSCI All Country World Index**
Developed equities	10%	MSCI World Index
Emerging and frontier equities	15%	MSCI Emerging Markets Index
Private equity, venture capital, and value-added real estate	25%	Cambridge Associates U.S. Private Equity Index
Absolute return	25%	HFRI Event-Driven (Total) Index
Other diversifiers	5%	TBD
Hedging assets: inflation	**15%**	**Weighted composite**
Commodities	5%	S&P GSCI (Equal Weight)
Hard assets	10%	50% FTSE EPRA/NAREIT Developed Real Estate Index, 50% CA Private Natural Resources Benchmark
Hedging assets: deflation	**5%**	**Citigroup World Government Bond Index (US$ Hedged)**
Cash	5%	U.S. T-bill

Abbreviations: CA, Cambridge Associates; EPRA/NAREIT, European Public Real Estate Association/National Association of Real Estate Investment Trusts; FTSE, Financial Times Stock Exchange 100 Index; HFRI, Hedge Fund Research, Inc.; MSCI, Morgan Stanley Capital International; S&P GSCI, Standard & Poor's Global Financial Centres Index; TBD, to be determined.

STABILISATION FUND

The Stabilisation Fund is intended to be an internally managed cash fund (however, mandates are currently being outsourced as the NSIA builds internal investment expertise). Rather than investing exclusively in investment-grade sovereign debt instruments, the Stabilisation Fund is also permitted to invest in high-quality investment-grade corporate bonds with one- to three-year maturities. The latter, which account for 75 percent of the fund's asset allocation, are liquid enough to serve the stabilization objectives of the fund (in combination with the remaining 25 percent that is invested in U.S. Treasury bills and short-term Treasuries) while still leaving some room for returns and portfolio growth. Table 10.2. shows the Stabilisation Fund's target asset allocation and respective benchmarks.

NIGERIA INFRASTRUCTURE FUND

The Nigeria Infrastructure Fund is a development-focused fund that will target investment opportunities that balance financial and strategic benefits. The *Nigeria Sovereign Investment Authority Act* makes explicit the fact that "the Authority may apply a lower target internal rate of return to social infrastructure investments made by the Nigerian Infrastructure Fund." Consequently, the NSIA has announced a subfund that "will hold up to 10 percent of the assets in the Nigeria Infrastructure Fund aimed at segments of the economy for which economic returns are not the primary drivers."[7] The Nigeria Infrastructure Fund's investment policy statement notes that its assets "shall be invested for the long term, which is understood to mean an investment horizon of more than 20 years through multiple economic and market cycles, and in recognition of the long-term nature of infrastructure investments." The annual target return of the fund, excluding special provisions for development projects, is U.S. inflation plus 5 percent.

Table 10.2 Asset allocation and benchmarks of Nigeria's Stabilisation Fund

Asset allocation	Policy target	Benchmark
Growth assets	75%	Barclays 1–3 Year Corporate Bond
Investment-grade corporate bonds, 1–3 years		Barclays 1–3 Year Corporate Bond
Hedge assets	25%	Barclays 1–3 Year Treasury Bond
US t-bills		91-Day Treasury Bill Index
US treasuries, 1–3 years		Barclays 1–3 Year Treasury Bond

Given the nature of infrastructure investing, co-investment is a particular area of emphasis for the fund, which has already announced significant joint investments with the likes of General Electric and multilateral institutions, such as the International Finance Corporation and the Africa Finance Corporation. The fund has also invested in leading infrastructure and development projects and initiatives in Nigeria, including the Fund for Agricultural Finance in Nigeria, the Nigeria Mortgage Refinance Company, and the Second Niger Bridge Project. As part of the investment policy statement, the NSIA has allocated 1.5 percent of the Nigeria Infrastructure Fund's capital toward project development funding in recognition of the need to co-develop projects given the early stage of the infrastructure investment sector in the country.

The NSIA will produce rolling five-year investment plans for the Nigeria Infrastructure Fund. During the development of the Nigeria Infrastructure Fund's first five-year plan in 2013, the NSIA identified an initial list of thirteen target areas within the infrastructure sector, which has been narrowed down to five sectors: agriculture, real estate, motorways, power, and health care. The NSIA has incorporated dedicated subsidiaries to help it execute investments in these priority areas, and the list of focus areas and dedicated subsidiaries may grow as the fund develops and expands. Possible focus sectors beyond the current five include water resources, free trade zones, manufacturing, rail transportation, aviation, and mining. Figure 10.2 shows the five current focus sectors of the fund in the center of the circle and potential additional areas of interest to the fund around the focus sectors. The selection criteria for identifying the focus areas for the fund are as follows:

- Sectors that align with national priorities;
- Projects with attractive commercial and social returns;
- Sectors in which the NSIA can attract private capital or unlock private sector potential; and
- Sectors in which the regulatory environment is conducive.

GOVERNANCE, MANAGEMENT, AND OVERSIGHT OF THE NIGERIA SOVEREIGN INVESTMENT AUTHORITY

The NSIA is a lean institution, given the size of the assets under its management (both current and prospective). As of late 2013, the Authority

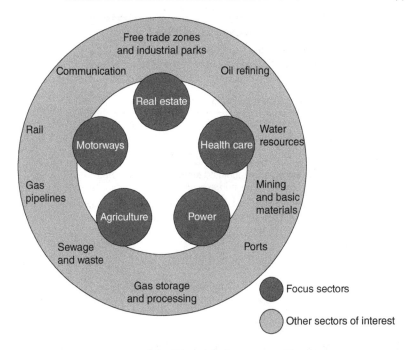

Figure 10.2   Focus sectors of the Nigeria Infrastructure Fund.

had only fifteen employees—although this number is expected to rise as the fund's assets grow, current plans are to grow the institution to no more than twenty-five full-time staff. The governance structure includes a governing council, a board of directors, and five board committees, as shown in figure 10.3. The governing council operates as a high-level advisory and oversight body and is chaired by the president. The council also includes the ministers of finance and national planning; state governors; the federal attorney general; the governor of the Central Bank of Nigeria; the chief economic adviser to the president; the chairperson of the Revenue Mobilisation, Allocation, and Fiscal Commission; and four private sector representatives.

The board of directors includes the Authority's nonexecutive chairperson, managing director, two executive directors, and five nonexecutive directors. It is important to note the degree of independence and investment professionalism that arises from the fact that the board of directors does not include any holders of political office and consists of individuals with strong private sector backgrounds in finance and investment. The board of directors has established five standing committees, dedicated to

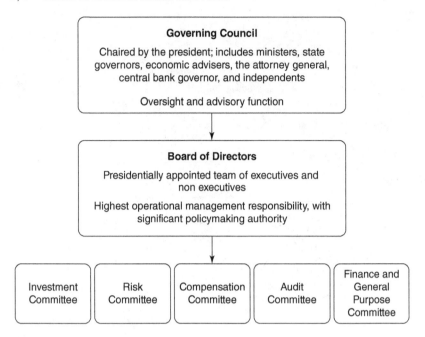

Figure 10.3   **The governance structure of the Nigeria Sovereign Investment Authority.**

specific aspects of the investment and management process. These committees report to the board and its chairperson (who does not sit on any of the committees):

- **Investment Committee:** assists the board in overseeing the investment processes, strategies, and policies of the NSIA (including external manager selection and monitoring).
- **Risk Committee:** assists the board in overseeing the identification and management of risks arising from the investments pursued by the NSIA and ensures that appropriate risk management controls are implemented, monitored, and regularly assessed.
- **Compensation Committee:** assists the board in ensuring that the compensation structure for the NSIA's employees is consistent with the institution's long-term objectives.
- **Audit Committee:** assists the board in overseeing the NSIA's accounting and financial reporting policies and practices, compliance programs, internal controls, and general compliance with applicable laws and regulations.

- **Finance and General Purpose Committee:** oversees the financial, operational, and administrative functions of the NSIA.

The board of directors is the most senior management structure within the Authority and holds a considerable degree of authority. Among the key powers that reside with the board of directors are the following:

- The allocation of received capital between the three funds (subject to legally defined minimum contributions);
- The determination of all critical eligible assets, target returns, asset allocation, benchmarks, and risk limits;
- The approval of the distribution of uninvested funds; and
- The appointment of expert panels to determine the maximum size of funds under the NSIA's management.

The legislation establishing the NSIA also makes several provisions ensuring the Authority is publicly and politically accountable. The main legal requirement for accountability is the *Nigeria Sovereign Investment Authority Act*'s provision that the NSIA submit a detailed annual report to the president, the cabinet, and members of the governing council. The annual report, together with quarterly financial reports and key policy documents prepared by the NSIA, must be made accessible to the public, which is done through media campaigns, press briefings, and the NSIA's website; for example, a summarized version of the annual report is to be printed at the Authority's expense in the two most widely circulated newspapers in Nigeria. The Act requires that all remuneration and cost allowances of the board of directors be presented in the annual report.

Legislators also considered the NSIA's standing as a world-class global sovereign wealth fund (SWF) as important. Consequently, the Act also requires the NSIA to "develop policies and procedures for communicating its investment objectives in a manner generally consistent with the guiding objectives underpinning the Santiago Principles."[8] The NSIA has become a member of the International Forum of Sovereign Wealth Funds, which was formed through the process that led to the establishment of the Santiago Principles and uses the meetings of this group to benchmark its policies, strategies, and operations against global peers. The NSIA has also received a favorable rating in terms of transparency by independent observers, including in the Linaburg-Maduell Transparency Index developed by the Sovereign Wealth Fund Institute.[9] Additional accountability and disclosure measures include regular internal audits, as well as annual external audits that meet international reporting standards and the requirement that the board of directors develop annual five-year rolling investment plans for the Nigeria Infrastructure Fund and the Future Generations Fund, over which it holds significant investment discretion.

CONCLUSION

The creation of the NSIA has the potential to contribute significantly to the dawning of a new era of fiscal responsibility in Nigeria. We have outlined the origins and inception of the NSIA and the three funds under its management, as well as the steps taken by the Authority to establish an institution that meets international best practices in terms of institutional design and governance. As of the end of 2014, the NSIA had total assets under management of $1.55 billion, which is still small given the magnitude of Nigeria's oil revenues. The Nigerian authorities and the NSIA itself have adopted a cautious and thorough approach to the development of this important institution and its policy, strategy, and operational frameworks. As Nigeria continues to generate oil revenues, the asset base of the NSIA is expected to grow, along with its internal investment capacity and expertise. A particularly important test of the NSIA's contribution will be whether it receives a significant portion of the oil revenues that arise in the aftermath of positive oil price shocks—and the extent to which it contributes to the stability of the Nigerian economy in the current period of lower oil prices and reduced revenues.

A number of other African countries that are establishing SWFs, or are considering doing so, have much to learn from the process Nigeria has gone through—and continues to go through—in establishing and building its funds and official investment institutions. The NSIA, both through its enabling legislation and the steps its board and management have taken since the Authority was established, has embraced the principles of high levels of disclosure, transparency about internal investment and management processes, and clarity around the distinctiveness of the objectives and strategies of its three funds. Nigeria's embrace of a three-pronged sovereign fund strategy—combining a stabilization fund, domestic infrastructure development fund, and an internationally invested savings fund—is likely to appeal to policymakers and legislators in other African countries (indeed, Ghana and Angola have introduced similar strategies). Of particular note in this regard is the NSIA's clear delineation of the different objectives, strategies, and performance targets of each of its three funds, which is essential in order to avoid confusion and conflict.

NOTES

1. See the *Nigeria Sovereign Investment Authority Act*, available at http://nsia.com.ng/wp-content/uploads/2013/02/NSIA_ACT.pdf.

2. See the *Allocation of Revenue Act*, available at http://lawnigeria.com/Lawsofthe-Federation/ALLOCATION-OF-REVENUE-(FEDERATION-ACCOUNT,-ETC.)-ACT.html.

3. The formulas used to derive these transfers are fairly complex. Surpluses on the Federation Account are defined in the relevant legislation as "residual funds above the budget smoothing amount." Residual funds are in turn defined as "revenue received into the Federation Account other than the projected federation hydrocarbon revenue for the relevant period," whereas the budgetary smoothing amount is defined as "an amount equal to 10 percent of monthly residual funding up to a cumulative maximum amount at any one time of 2.5 percent of the projected federation hydrocarbon revenue for the year." See Articles 30 and 58 of the *Nigeria Sovereign Investment Authority Act* for further details.

4. See Article 31, *Nigeria Sovereign Investment Authority Act*.

5. See Articles 34 and 35, *Nigeria Sovereign Investment Authority Act*.

6. See Article 33, *Nigeria Sovereign Investment Authority Act*.

7. This statement was released December 20, 2012.

8. See Article 49, *Nigeria Sovereign Investment Authority Act*.

9. See "Linaburg-Maduell Transparency Index," Sovereign Wealth Fund Institute, www.swfinstitute.org/statistics-research/linaburg-maduell-transparency-index/.

REFERENCES

KPMG. 2015. "Oil and Gas in Africa," Sector Report, www.kpmg.com/Africa/en/IssuesAndInsights/Articles-Publications/General-Industries-Publications/Documents/Oil%20and%20Gas%20sector%20report%202015.pdf.

PART III

Toward the New Frontiers of
Sovereign Investment

CHAPTER 11

Responsible Investment at AIMCo

Alison Schneider

Alberta Investment Management Corporation

Responsible investment incorporates environmental, social, and governance (ESG) factors into investment processes in order to generate long-term, sustainable financial value (United Nations Principles for Responsible Investment 2006) The responsible investment value proposition focuses on the triple bottom line: economic, environmental, and social value for investors, the market, and society as a whole. Responsible investment aligns with the groundbreaking 1987 Brundtland Commission's definition of *sustainable development* as "development which meets the needs of the current generations without compromising the ability of future generations to meet their own needs" (Brundtland et al. 1987). Demand for responsible investment has been driven by multiple factors: the erosion of public confidence in financial institutions following the global financial crisis, public concern for the environment amid climate change, and the glare of social media on questionable corporate practices. The United Nations Principles for Responsible Investment (UNPRI), established in 2006, have had a transformative effect on the responsible investment landscape, galvanizing investors to commit to six investment principles (box 11.1). In this chapter, I discuss how Alberta Investment Management Corporation (AIMCo), one of Canada's largest and most diversified institutional investors approaches responsible investment and its journey of ESG integration to date.

Box 11.1: The United Nations Principles of Responsible Investment

The United Nations Principles of Responsible Investment (UNPRI) serve as a global investor forum to exchange best responsible investment practices and hold signatories to account by requiring them to report annually. Since its inception in 2006, the UNPRI have grown to include 1,500 asset owners and investment management signatories, with $62 trillion in assets under management, accounting for approximately 24 percent of global investible assets (United Nations Principles of Responsible Investment, 2016). The six principles are as follows:

Principle 1: Incorporate ESG into investment analysis and decision making.
Principle 2: Be active owners and incorporate ESG into ownership policies and practices.
Principle 3: Seek appropriate disclosure on ESG issues from invested entities.
Principle 4: Promote acceptance and implementation within the investment industry.
Principle 5: Work together to enhance effectiveness in implementing the Principles.
Principle 6: Report on activities and progress.

AN OVERVIEW OF AIMCO AND ITS RESPONSIBLE INVESTMENT PHILOSOPHY

The Alberta Investment Management Corporation was established as a Crown corporation in 2007 by the government of the province of Alberta to manage a distinct group of provincial pension plans, government funds, and special purpose funds. As of December 31, 2015, AIMCo had approximately CDN$90 billion (US$62 billion) in assets under management invested on behalf of twenty-six clients, including Albertan public pension plans, Canada's largest endowment system, the day-to-day operating balances of the province of Alberta, and the Alberta Heritage Savings Trust Fund, a special purpose fund established in 1976 to invest a portion of Alberta's nonrenewable oil and gas resources to fund critical infrastructure, scholarships, and medical research (as described in chapter 13). AIMCo is a global investor, and its asset allocation includes public equity, fixed-income securities, private equity, mortgages, real estate and infrastructure assets. The organization's long-term investment horizon and a strategy of "patient capital" underpin a conservative risk profile, which aligns with the central tenets of responsible investment.

Institutional investors are charged with stewarding client and pension beneficiaries' funds to capture risk-adjusted returns in the face of increasing complexity, including ESG regulations, climate change, and globalization. Corporate assets and liabilities are no longer viewed as purely financial, making it difficult for traditional financial metrics to price risk and return appropriately. Accordingly, investors have to go beyond financial information gathering and analysis to properly assess asset value. AIMCo practices active ownership, realizing it can potentially influence company behavior by how it votes on its publicly traded shares, its communications strategy, and through advocacy efforts, conducted alone or with its peers. AIMCo took a significant step in formalizing its responsible investment journey when it became a signatory to the UNPRI in 2010. The implementation of responsible investment and the impact of ESG factors on risk and return vary across asset classes, but AIMCo's guiding philosophy remains the same: the consideration of ESG factors enables better investment decision making and supports long-term stakeholder value.

AIMCo's fiduciary duty is to act reasonably and in the best interests of its clients to deliver long-term return on investment as set out by the *Alberta Investment Management Corporation Act* (Province of Alberta 2007). The concept of fiduciary duty is governed by what society considers reasonable, which in and of itself is an evolutionary process. Leading academics and governance organizations, such as the International Corporate Governance Network, continue to advocate for fiduciary investors to duly consider the impact of their investment decisions on future generations and on systemic risk (Lydenberg 2013). The goal of responsible investment is inextricably tied to fulfillment of a fund's fiduciary duty, whereas the strategy to integrate ESG factors into financial analysis aligns with a long-term investment horizon in keeping with the future sustainability of the fund.

Responsible investment can be understood as a process of identifying ESG assets and liabilities and assessing the potential impact of ESG factors on investment risk and performance. Figure 11.1 presents several key

Assets		Liabilities
• Ecological efficiencies • Climate resiliency • Waste/energy recovery • Environmental management systems	**Environmental**	• High carbon footprint • Contamination • Poor waste management • Environmental mismanagement
• Stakeholder consultation • Employee satisfaction • Worker safety • Responsible sourcing	**Social**	• Public opposition • Accidents and incidents • Labor unrest • Human rights violations
• Board quality • Risk management • Pay for performance • Proactive communication • Robust internal audit	**Governance**	• Poor board quality • Reputational risk • Egregious compensation • Lack of disclosure • Financial restatements

Figure 11.1   Environmental, social, and governance assets and liabilities.

Source: AIMCo 2014 Responsible Investment Report.

ESG metrics that AIMCo commonly considers for companies across its holdings from an asset–liability perspective.

The business case for paying attention to ESG factors is increasingly considered compelling, particularly for long-term investors. The laundry list of risks traditionally deemed "extra-financial" are increasingly being viewed as mainstream, with potential financial impacts. These include environmental factors, or "E-factors," such as a company's climate change readiness and its environmental resource management; social factors, or "S-factors," such as the quality of a company's stakeholder relations, its track record on human rights and occupational health and safety; and governance factors, or "G-factors," such as lack of director independence, outlandish executive compensation packages not linked to performance, inappropriate non-audit fees, and poor ESG disclosure. Overarching risks that reach across ESG categories include legal and regulatory risk, geopolitical risk, and reputational risk (figure 11.2) Deeper analysis reveals ever more risk layers and risk outcomes, such as potential stranded-asset risk, the risk of negative externalities, and globalization. For example, in anticipation of higher carbon pricing scenarios, the number of companies using an internal price on carbon to

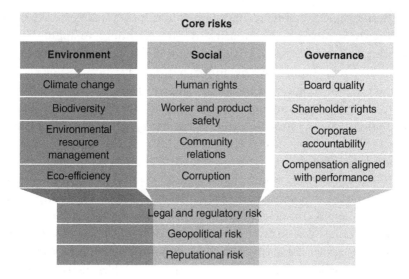

Figure 11.2   AIMCo's core environmental, social, and governance risk framework.

Source: AIMCo 2014 Responsible Investment Report.

determine future project viability tripled between 2014 and 2015 (Carbon Disclosure Project 2015).

A number of academic studies have helped illustrate and document the business case for responsible investment and the integration of ESG factors in the investment process. In the event of a choice between investment options with similar return-on-investment characteristics, the option with the better ESG assessment generally provides the positive differentiator and a lower risk profile over the long term, in alignment with clients' preference for lower risk (Bouslah, Kryzanowski, and M'Zali 2011; Oikonomou, Brooks, and Pavelin 2012). Similarly, an ESG-tilted portfolio has been demonstrated to offer insurance-like protection, which may result in a higher credit rating and a lower cost of debt. (Oikonomou, Brooks, and Pavelin 2014; Godfrey, Merrill, and Hansen 2009). A 2013 Deutsche Bank meta-study demonstrated that the cost of capital is lower for companies with higher ESG scores; however, higher overall ESG scores for companies were not necessarily correlated with investment outperformance or underperformance (Jussa et al. 2013). Indeed, certain ESG metrics tend to have a greater impact on financial performance than others. For instance, several studies demonstrate that companies with higher percentages of women on their boards outperform those with fewer to no women on their boards in developed country markets (Carter & Wagner 2011).

Responsible investment practitioners routinely track key ESG metrics across industries, with industry-specific weightings, to appropriately capture risk and returns in ESG scorecards and in portfolio monitoring. Guenster et al. (2011) have demonstrated that significant value can be gained by investing in the most eco-efficient firms. The authors found that eco-efficient companies experienced an upward price correction in share price over time, indicating that the market eventually assigns greater value to operational eco-efficiencies as disclosed by companies. Consideration of key ESG metrics can reveal alpha (abnormal return) that is overlooked by traditional investing strategies. Anand (2013) has demonstrated that a statistically significant positive relationship exists between certain corporate governance metrics and company valuation. More specifically, a positive relationship exists for the criteria of board composition, ownership structure, the presence of institutional shareholders, compensation structure, disclosure, and shareholder rights. Academic research across a broad spectrum of governance practices, therefore, suggests the importance of governance to firm and shareholder value.

The market's reaction, or "market sentiment," to disclosed ESG risk further impacts asset value. The Internet and its universal reach has forever changed how investors and the wider public receive information—negative news, whether it be an oil spill (environmental), a factory collapse (social), or evidence of corporate malfeasance (governance), is circulated earlier and more rapidly, reaching a wider audience and impacting share prices, increasing reputational and financial risk and market volatility. The resultant market sentiment impacts stock markets, financial benchmarks, and asset value. No company is immune to these risks.

AIMCO'S FIVE PILLARS OF RESPONSIBLE INVESTMENT

AIMCo's Responsible Investment pillars provide the structure and foundation for the implementation of its philosophy, with each pillar supporting one or more of the UNPRI principles. These principles are (1) responsible investment structure; (2) investment process; (3) engagement processes; (4) reporting and communications; and (5) advocacy and collaboration.

PILLAR 1: AIMCO'S RESPONSIBLE INVESTMENT STRUCTURE

The Responsible Investment team reports directly to the chief investment officer and functions as an umbrella department reaching across the organization. Ultimate oversight of responsible investment rests with AIMCo's board, which approves the responsible investment policy. The AIMCo Responsible Investment Committee, which is chaired by the CEO and features cross-departmental representation, is responsible for broad oversight of AIMCo's responsible investment strategy, activities, and procedures. The AIMCo Responsible Investment Team is responsible for the day-to-day implementation of the responsible investment program. The responsible investment structure comprises the following guiding documents: the Responsible Investment Policy, the Proxy Voting Guidelines, the Engagement Guidelines, and the Exclusions Guidelines.

PILLAR 2: INVESTMENT PROCESS

The integration of ESG factors into AIMCo's investment processes is central to the implementation of its responsible investment philosophy. ESG integration occurs to varying degrees across all AIMCo managed asset classes at various investment phases—from investment screening, due diligence, monitoring and exits. A significant portion of AIMCo's responsible investment departmental activity is concentrated on proxy voting for AIMCo's holdings in publicly traded companies. The Responsible Investment team also conducts portfolio analytics to track changes in ESG ratings across certain portfolios. All asset classes report on how they integrate ESG factors into investment processes in the annual Principles for Responsible Investment (PRI) survey, and two (real estate and infrastructure) have adopted their own bespoke sustainability guidelines, which they implement.

PILLAR 3: ENGAGEMENT PROCESSES

By engaging with companies, AIMCo builds trust relationships, fosters corporate accountability, and promotes shareholder value. The engagement process is both tactical and strategic, proactive and reactive; AIMCo strongly prefers a strategy of "voice over exit" to engage with a company to effect positive change, rather than divesting and reducing the investible universe. Where possible, AIMCo collaborates with like-minded investors, enhancing its ability to influence company behavior. The Engagement Guidelines define AIMCo's engagement approach, desired outcomes, priority issues, and criteria and processes for engagement, as well as escalation strategies and reporting protocols. These vary by geographic market, asset class, industry, ownership level, the perceived egregious nature of an issue, trend, and regulation and are case dependent.

PILLAR 4: REPORTING AND COMMUNICATIONS

By publicly reporting on its responsible investment activities, AIMCo demonstrates the same level of transparency and accountability expected from its investee companies. AIMCo's annual report, the Responsible Investment Report, PRI Transparency Report, proxy voting records, voting rationales, advocacy letters, white papers, and all related governing documents are publicly available and posted on AIMCo's website. Clients also receive quarterly Responsible Investment reports and regular in person presentations.

PILLAR 5: ADVOCACY AND COLLABORATION

As an active member of the Canadian and international responsible investment community, AIMCo is regularly invited to contribute to public policy debate. This includes industry consultations initiated by federal and provincial bodies; requests for comments on proposed changes to securities regulations, law, or guiding documents for member or other international organizations. By participating in the development of improved policies and regulations, institutional investors contribute to a healthy, stable financial system to the benefit of all stakeholders over the long term.

IMPLEMENTING RESPONSIBLE INVESTMENT

There is a growing expectation that, considering institutional investors collectively steward an ever larger share of assets relative to the size the global economy, they have commensurate responsibilities to address systemic risk and to advocate on behalf of the public good to effect corporate behavior change (Urwin 2011). The development of responsible investment as an organizational function is an exercise in change management for many funds, as traditional finance and "business as usual" must adapt to include consideration and integration of ESG factors across the investment decision–making process. Implementation of ESG factors into investment processes varies across asset classes, by whether the asset is directly or externally managed, and by whether it is actively or passively invested. The expectation that one ever arrives at full ESG integration is flawed: ESG integration is focused on investment processes and so is iterative. AIMCo's implementation strategy is guided by the following theoretical approaches to responsible investment (see Mercer 2009 for a more general discussion):

- **Universal owner:** The expectation for investors to act in the public interest aligns with AIMCo's advocacy activities; for instance, AIMCo routinely comments on proposed changes to regulation, such as the Ontario Securities Commission's Bill 58-101 requiring companies to disclose their processes to recruit women to boards and executive positions. The fact that institutional investors own the lion's share of the world economy—PRI signatories alone steward $60 trillion or 75 percent of global gross domestic product (GDP)—holds them to a higher standard of care. Fiduciary duty for institutional investors includes the duty to consider systemic triple-bottom-line risk (financial, environmental, and social factors). Moreover, if institutional investors invest in entities that increase systemic risk, this impacts financial benchmarks, creates unintended consequences, and results in a lose–lose situation for all.
- **Norms-based approach:** AIMCo seeks to invest in companies that uphold internationally accepted norms of good behavior, such as those contained in the Organisation for Economic Co-operation and Development (OECD) Guidelines, the United Nations Conference on Trade and Development (UNCTAD) Principles and Policies, the International Labour Organization (ILO) Standards and the UN Guiding Principles. The norms-based approach compares firms' ordinary business practices with normative practices for the industry and the geographic market to satisfy AIMCo's base level requirements and/or identify areas for improvement.
- **Best practices:** By identifying best ESG industry practices and engaging with industry leaders, AIMCo is better able to understand which factors create success. These practices can then be promoted in AIMCo's communications with other investee companies, setting higher expectations overall.
- **Negative screening:** AIMCo employs "negative screens," which means that certain companies or industries are excluded from its investment universe as applied to direct investments.
- **Positively themed:** AIMCo invests in alternative energy, agriculture, sustainable real estate, timberlands, and core infrastructure investments.

These investments may be considered positively themed from a sustainability perspective. The underlying assets are variously focused on solutions to societal issues such as achieving eco-efficiencies; developing core, climate-resilient infrastructure; and offsetting carbon emissions.

These widely used theoretical approaches serve as a backdrop to the various differentiating strategies AIMCo employs in its responsible investment activities, some of which I discuss next, along with some salient responsible investment trends.

EXCLUSIONS

Exclusions are a structural feature of responsible investment that informs the investment process. AIMCo is the only Canadian institutional investor with a tobacco exclusion. The *Alberta Cancer Prevention Legacy Act* (Province of Alberta, 2006) stipulates that the securities of specified government funds under AIMCo's management may not be invested in the tobacco industry. The Alberta Heritage Fund's Statement of Investment Policy and Goals also explicitly states that fund monies may not be directly invested in the tobacco industry. This exclusion was applied across all direct investments to achieve efficiencies. AIMCo is subject to statutory investment restrictions, such as the *United Nations Act* and the *Special Economic Measures Act*, enacted by the Canadian federal government imposing geographic sanctions. These restrictions include companies that are engaged in activities prohibited by international treaties or agreements to which Canada is a party, such as the *Ottawa Treaty* excluding weapons of mass destruction and the *Convention on Cluster Munitions*. The exclusions list is refreshed quarterly, at which point a formerly excluded company may re-enter AIMCo's investment universe, should the conditions for exclusion no longer apply.

PROXY VOTING

The right to vote on one's shares is a fundamental shareholder right. Proxy voting is a significant responsible investment activity important to the investment process. AIMCo voted on almost CDN\$35 billion worth of publicly traded shares in 2015, representing over 20,000 ballot proposals across 2,433 publicly traded companies. Given the size and geographic diversity of these public holdings, proxy voting is conducted electronically. Each ballot item is reviewed internally, and, although AIMCo takes voting recommendations from proxy service research providers into account, it ultimately makes its own voting decisions. While the vast majority of proxy votes are "plain vanilla," or ordinary, motions, some necessitate deeper inquiry or trigger a company engagement.

The proxy voting guidelines describe AIMCo's guiding principles with respect to director elections, shareholder rights, executive compensation, audit, capital structure, takeover protection, and reporting and disclosure. However, these guidelines cannot possibly capture the intricacies of each voting decision across vastly different markets. As such, AIMCo reserves the right to vote on a case-by-case basis, and generally expects companies to uphold their country-specific corporate governance codes and any internationally applicable standards, such as the United Nations Guiding Principles (UNGP). For instance, board independence norms vary by market: all else being equal, AIMCo could hypothetically support all board members at a company in South Korea featuring only two out of ten independent board members while voting against the entire nominations committee at a Canadian company given the same level of director independence.

SHAREHOLDER PROPOSALS

Shareholder proposals are submitted by shareholders for voting at annual and special meetings, subject to market-specific minimum holdings and advance notice requirements. The frequency of and support for shareholder proposals reflect evolving regional and global shareholder concerns. AIMCo supports timely, reasonable shareholder proposals that uphold corporate governance principles, such as board quality, diversity, appropriate levels of ESG disclosure, and pay aligned with performance. Figure 11.3 illustrates the numbers of ESG- and compensation-related shareholder proposals AIMCo has voted on in recent years. Overall support of shareholder proposals was 51 percent in 2014–15. Not all ESG-related shareholder proposals are routinely supported; for example, if a shareholder proposal requests the company to disclose an environmental report and the company already does so, there is no cogent reason to support the proposal. Shareholder proposals that are duplicative, overly restrictive, poorly worded and subject to interpretation, or that give unrealistic time frames for compliance are not supported. Governance-themed shareholder proposals continue to dominate overall. The three most

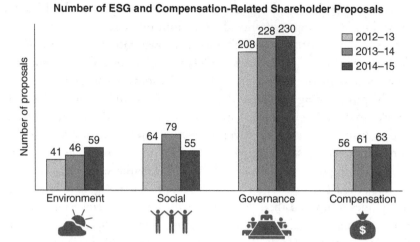

Figure 11.3   Shareholder proposals by theme, voted on by AIMCo.

common governance-themed shareholder proposals witnessed in calendar year 2015 were regarding disclosure of political lobbying activities; the right of shareholders to nominate directors, subject to minimum holdings requirements (referred to as "proxy access"); and calls for an independent chairperson of the board.

Although compensation-themed shareholder proposals typically fall within the category of governance, they are treated separately in figure 11.3, as they represent a significant portion (15 percent) of AIMCo's shareholder proposals. The rising number of compensation-related proposals reflects growing shareholder concern with equitable executive compensation. Compensation-themed shareholder proposals generally call for changes to compensation structure and alignment with company performance. Last proxy season, AIMCo witnessed a slight decrease in the number of overall ESG shareholder proposals, due to a 30 percent drop in socially themed shareholder proposals. This reflects improvements in boards' gender diversity and in company disclosures of political contributions, which are common themes for social shareholder proposals. Environmental shareholder proposals increased 28 percent over the previous year, reflecting growing public concern with companies' environmental stewardship. Shareholder proposals calling for climate-related reporting have become increasingly frequent in the wake of the twenty-first session of the Paris Conference of the Parties in November 2015.

ENGAGEMENT

Engagement is integral to responsible investment. Firms displaying problematic, undisclosed, or particularly robust ESG practices may be selected for engagement. The AIMCo Responsible Investment Committee identifies focus areas to drive the engagement process. At the time of writing these focus ares are: Climate change (environmental), supply chain risk (social), and shareholder rights (governance). As a precondition of engagement, one of the following criteria will generally apply: (1) a level of materiality, defined either as a level of AIMCo's financial exposure to the firm (percent ownership of issuer or absolute exposure) or of the perceived egregiousness of the issue; (2) the company exhibits issues within AIMCo's ESG focus areas; or (3) a reasonable probability of success. Proactive engagements attempt to anticipate an issue by identifying best practices or by minimizing AIMCo's exposure to ESG risk. Reactive engagement is also possible if a company's policies or ESG activities raise operational, financial, environmental, or social risks beyond an acceptable level.

ADVOCACY

AIMCo is a leading member of the global responsible investment community through its active membership in the International Corporate Governance Network, the UNPRI, the Canadian Coalition of Good Governance, the Responsible Investment Association, and the Pension Investment Association of Canada, among others. Participation and leadership in these groups fosters sharing of best practices and stimulates problem solving and the development of new initiatives. In alignment with its fiduciary duty, AIMCo determines which initiatives to support, such as the need for greater board diversity, and encourages the Government of Canada to actively contribute to global climate negotiations. Advocacy letters are posted on AIMCo's website.

ASSET CLASS–SPECIFIC STRATEGIES

Identifying ESG risks and opportunities across the investment process is vital to the success of ESG integration. The business case for incorporating ESG considerations is especially important for investment strategies that are longer term, more highly concentrated and capital intensive.

Within public equities at AIMCo one such strategy is named High Conviction Equities. "High-conviction equities" is the name of a targeted public equities strategy that is highly concentrated and characterized by long holding periods to allow us to realize the underlying assets' intrinsic value. The portfolio managers target firms that may be underperforming financially yet are deemed "restorable" and poised for long-term capital appreciation. The root cause of underperformance may be attributed to weaker corporate governance and/or ineffective corporate strategy. The investment philosophy can best be described as a contrarian, value-based style designed to minimize downside owing to a focus on "margin of safety" investing where market price is significantly below portfolio managers' estimation of intrinsic value. Abnormal returns tend to be higher for these concentrated portfolios (van Nieuwerburgh and Veldkamp 2010) over the course of a full market cycle; this is in contradiction with modern portfolio theory, which states that abnormal returns should be zero (Markowitz 1952).

In 2012, the real estate portfolio became the first asset class under AIMCo's management to adopt its own bespoke internal sustainability policy, reflecting the strong business case of this asset class. Environmental performance improvements not only drive down operating costs, but also reduce exposure to utility price volatility and result in increased tenant satisfaction and loyalty. As a result, the portfolio has high levels of green-building certifications, which drives premium rental rates, lengthens lease terms, and produces higher resale values than conventional buildings. Using a baseline of 2010 for environmental performance, AIMCo's Canadian real estate portfolio has saved tenants over CDN $9.5 million through increased efficiencies in power, gas, and water usage. A significant proportion of the real estate portfolio's Canadian investments achieve Leadership in Energy and Environmental Design (LEED) and/or Building Environmental Standards (BOMA BEST) certification.

Infrastructure offers scalable, resilient pathways to sustainable economic growth. Infrastructure investments are an integral part of a diversified investment management strategy, as they are a good hedge to inflation, provide an excellent match to pension liabilities, and are global and long term in nature. AIMCo's CDN$5.2 billion infrastructure portfolio is composed primarily of diversified long-term equity positions in assets with regulated returns or long-term contracted revenues across Australia, Canada, Chile, Europe, India, the United Kingdom, and the United States; across many infrastructure categories, such as transportation and energy; and across many infrastructure subcategories, such as toll roads and wind power. The need for robust ESG data is important for AIMCo's infrastructure assets, as they are highly illiquid, requiring large capital investment and rigorous due diligence to appropriately price and mitigate risks. In September 2015, AIMCo cofounded a new sustainability benchmarking initiative specific to infrastructure, Global Real Estate Sustainability Benchmark (GRESB) Infrastructure, in collaboration with a group of institutional investors to enable the systematic ESG evaluation of our global infrastructure assets.

We are starting to see evidence of a changing investment landscape for fixed income with green bonds offered more commonly across several jurisdictions. AIMCo invested in the first green bonds issued by a government in Canada to raise funds for environmental projects, such as solar power, wind power, public transportation, climate-resilient infrastructure, flood protection, and reforestation—namely, those issued by the province of Ontario in October 2014.

CONCLUSION

Responsible investment is evolving globally and is now considered mainstream in developed countries, as evidenced by the upward trajectory of UNPRI membership, growing public demand for responsible investment, and a compelling business case. By examining the ESG performance of its investee companies, and of the investment universe, AIMCo can potentially impact the risk-adjusted returns of its investment portfolios, or even improve overall financial performance. Responsible investment can be a value driver over the long term and offers investors a distinct competitive advantage. Practitioners may lead academics in determining which ESG criteria have greater risk–return impacts by industry sector and subsector, as they have the advantage of access to real-time data across holdings.

The five-pillar approach to responsible investment adopted by AIMCo fully aligns with UNPRI's aspirational principles by incorporating ESG factors into investment analysis to reduce risk, improve corporate governance, and contribute to long-term investment returns. The implementation of responsible investment and the relative impact of ESG factors vary by asset class, but AIMCo's guiding philosophy remains the same: The consideration of ESG factors and related information enables better investment decisions and supports long-term, stable stakeholder value. AIMCo is focused on making a positive impact on investee firms' corporate governance and will continue to focus on engagement to improve investment performance and to enhance and protect its investments.

Institutional investors have a key advocacy role to play globally in promoting shareholder rights and to improve their respective regulatory and proxy voting systems. Despite building awareness of responsible investment, integration of ESG factors into investment decisions is uneven across institutional investors, across markets, and across asset classes. This is a reflection of various and changing cultural protocols, regulatory regimes, stakeholder demand, the availability and quality of ESG measurement tools, industry ESG disclosure conventions, and investors' organizational strategies. It is important to keep in mind that even for the most advanced investors, responsible investment is an iterative process— it remains a journey rather than a destination.

REFERENCES

Anand, A. 2013. "The Value of Governance," *The Program on Ethics and Law in Business*. Toronto, ON: University of Toronto.

Bouslah, K., L. Kryzanowski, and B. M'Zali. 2011. "Relationship Between Firm Risk and Individual Dimensions of Social Performance," *Proceedings of the Annual Conference of the Administrative Science Association of Canada* 32, no. 1: 105–122.

Brundtland, G., and World Commission on Environment and Development. 1987. *Our Common Future: Report of the World Commission On Environment and Development*. Oxford: Oxford University Press.

Carbon Disclosure Project. 2015. "Putting a Price on Risk: Carbon Pricing in the Corporate World," www.cdp.net/CDPResults/carbon-pricing-in-the-corporate-world.pdf.

Carter, N. and Wagner, H. 2011 "The Bottom Line: Corporate Performance and Women's Representation on Boards (2004-2008)", Catalyst, 2011. http://www.catalyst.org/system/files/the_bottom_line_corporate_performance_and_women%27s_representation_on_boards_%282004-2008%29.pdf

Godfrey, P., C. Merrill, and J. Hansen. 2009. "The Relationship Between Corporate Social Responsibility and Shareholder Value: An Empirical Test of the Risk Management Hypothesis," *Strategic Management Journal* 30, no. 4: 425–445.

Guenster, N., R. Bauer, J. Derwall, and K. Koedijk. 2011. "The Economic Value of Corporate Eco-Efficiency," *European Financial Management* 17, no. 4: 679–704.

Jussa, J., R. Cahan, M. A. Alvarez, S. Wang, Y. Luo, and Z. Chen. 2013. "The Socially Responsible Quant," *Deutsche Bank Markets Research*, April 24.

Lyndenberg, S. 2013. *Reason, Rationality and Fiduciary Duty*. Cambridge: Hauser Center for Nonprofit Organizations.

Markowitz, H. 1952. "Portfolio Selection." *The Journal of Finance* 7, no. 1: 77–91.

Mercer. 2009. "Shedding Light on Responsible investment: Approaches, Returns and Impacts." London: Mercer.

Oikonomou, I., C. Brooks, and S. Pavelin. 2012. "The Impact of Corporate Social Performance on Financial Risk and Utility: A Longitudinal Analysis," *Financial Management* 41, no. 2: 483–515.

——. 2014. "The Effects of Corporate Social Performance on the Cost of Corporate Debt and Credit Ratings," *Financial Review* 49, no. 1: 49–75.

Province of Alberta. 2006. "Statutes of Alberta, 2006, Chapter A-26.5," *Alberta Cancer Prevention Legacy Act.* www.qp.alberta.ca/documents/Acts/A14P2.pdf.

——. 2007. "Statutes of Alberta, 2007, Chapter A-26.5," *Alberta Investment Management Corporation Act.* www.qp.alberta.ca/documents/Acts/A26p5.pdf.

——. 2015. "Revised Statutes of Alberta, 2000, Chapter A-23." *Heritage Savings Trust Fund Act.* www.qp.alberta.ca/documents/Acts/A23.pdf.

United Nations Principles of Responsible Investment. 2006. "United Nations Principles for Responsible Investment (UNPRI)," www.unpri.org.

United Nations Principles of Responsible Investment. 2016. "About the PRI," https://www.unpri.org/about.

Urwin, R. 2011. "Pension Funds as Universal Owners: Opportunity Beckons and Leadership Calls," *International Journal of Pension Management* 4, no. 11): 26–33.

Van Nieuwerburgh, S., and L. Veldkamp. 2010. "Information Acquisition and Portfolio Under-Diversification," *The Review of Economic Studies* 77, no. 2: 779–805.

CHAPTER 12

Sovereign Wealth Funds and Long-Term Investments in Infrastructure

WHY THE GLARING ABSENCE?[1]

Sanjay Peters
Columbia University

In recent years, a troubling imbalance has bedeviled economists. A seeming global savings glut has ballooned, generated largely by sovereign wealth funds (SWFs) from emerging-market regions in Asia and the Middle East that export manufactured goods or commodities. At the same time, there has been a massive rise in the need for infrastructure investment, particularly in developing countries. Yet, the savings are not flowing to the investments where they are needed.

Sovereign wealth funds managed $7.1 trillion in 2014, an amount that has more than doubled since 2007 (Sovereign Wealth Fund Institute 2015). Meanwhile, it is estimated that sustaining global gross domestic product (GDP) growth on the current track until 2030 would require $57 trillion in infrastructure investments, an increase of 60 percent from $37 trillion in the last two decades (Dobbs et al. 2013). If just 10 percent of SWF assets were to be earmarked for infrastructure development, these needs would be easier to meet and the impact on global GDP growth and poverty reduction could be bigger than other sources of large-scale private investments.

This mismatch is particularly puzzling because the savings, highly concentrated among SWFs, insurance companies, and pension funds, and the required investments share similarly long-term investment objectives. Having matching time horizons between the investors and the projects reduces the need for financial intermediation,[2] which removes another layer of complexity and cost in project financing. So what is stopping those trillions of dollars from finding these strong investment opportunities, such as in infrastructure?

There are numerous obstacles that prevent the efficient flow of capital from countries with high savings to countries with strong investment opportunities in infrastructure. Inadequate institutions, information asymmetries, adverse incentives, and poor governance are just a few examples. In many developing countries—especially commodity-exporting and agriculture-based economies in Africa—political risks, poor governance, corruption, and conflict present even greater hurdles to infrastructure investment.

Although the objectives of SWFs are typically not short-term oriented, the main strategic focus of certain types of SWF requires ready access to liquid assets to address foreseen or unforeseen market disruptions. For example, SWFs in commodity-driven economies such as Chile (a major exporter of copper) function as stabilization funds in case of a commodity price crash. Sovereign wealth funds that function primarily as stabilization funds are reluctant to seek riskier investments, such as equity stakes in private companies or real estate, let alone invest in long-term infrastructure projects, especially in countries that appear risky for the reasons discussed earlier. Even if such investments yield higher returns *on average*, the lack of access to liquidity with such investments is an obstacle, as there may be difficulty obtaining immediate access to financial resources when urgently required. Other types of SWF, including monetary reserve investment funds and savings funds, share similar liquidity concerns, but to a much lesser degree.

• The concern about access to liquid assets is very legitimate; however, the mismatch in savings and need for investment could nonetheless still be addressed if SWFs were to earmark even a relatively small percentage of their total assets under management to infrastructure investments. Because of the anticipated growth in SWF assets, an investment size of as little as 5 percent would be a meaningful step in bridging the savings to the investments and to national economic growth, global GDP growth, and to transforming the lives of hundreds of millions of people, particularly in developing countries. Apart from the problem of liquidity that deters long-term investors such as SWFs to invest in infrastructure, some of the main obstacles to infrastructure investments listed earlier are gradually disappearing.

• However, referring to the dilemma as a "mismatch" may be overly simplistic given the context in which most of these SWFs operate their risk and return budget. The main issue is not about how much should be earmarked toward infrastructure investments, but intrinsically why, what objective this fulfills, and how this translates to portfolio diversification given the overall investment objectives of these funds. Hence, to answer this question without considering the context of each and every SWF's investment policy is somewhat narrow in scope. For example, it could be argued that the problem for SWFs is not just a question of liquidity. Each and every asset class serves a purpose. SWFs need to be presented with compelling arguments about what purpose infrastructure serves within their overall asset allocation. In other words, what bucket should infrastructure as an asset class come under: return enhancement, risk mitigating, inflation hedging or tail risk? Liquidity does play a role but not to the extent that many of us consider it to be the main inhibiting factor. Second, infrastructure as an asset class itself is quite opaque: even though SWFs keep their allocations secret, their devotion to transparency is limitless. Infrastructure requires very careful monitoring, there is a J curve in play, and returns are by definition long term—despite the fact that a lot of SWFs report in terms of their investment objectives being very long term. They are extremely sensitive to durational investments, especially illiquid ones like infrastructure. The return demands are often unrealistic as the price or liquidity premium demanded needs to match their appetite for risk. Third, there are often very few truly well-managed infrastructure investment opportunities out there at one time. Capacity is a critical issue for those very attractive managers, and by the time it is open for distribution, capacity constraints force managers to close the fund and start a completely new one. Hence, the underlying issue around why SWFs fail to allocate increasingly higher amounts to this asset class is that the supply is not limitless, and the very well-managed projects are often filled before one can get access to them. It is therefore incumbent on both policy authorities as well as private managers to mitigate these risks by coming together to provide the fertile ground for these investment opportunities to take place. Public authorities should provide the guarantee for private investors to come with confidence to seed projects. At least when this happens, the investors are left to consider only the critical parameters behind their appetite to invest (i.e., risk and return).

On the political front, many African countries are realizing that poor governance, corruption, and conflict are obstacles to foreign direct investments, particularly in infrastructure, and are taking measures to mitigate these issues. A Country Policy and Institutional Assessment Africa review in 2015 found steady progress in strengthening governance policies, especially in budgetary and financial management (World Bank 2015a). Anticorruption initiatives, such as the African Governance Monitoring and Advocacy Project and the African Parliamentarians Network Against Corruption, are also making measurable impacts in the fight against corruption in governance. With the exception of a small number of African countries, in particular Libya and South Sudan, Africa as a whole has seen a significant drop in political and military conflict, according a report by the Institute for Security Studies (Cilliers 2015).

In general terms, the obstacles posed by infrastructure investments are shrinking, and there is a growing awareness among fund managers that traditional patterns of safe investment strategies by SWFs are inadequate due to very low, if not negative, real yields as a result of global central banks' interest rate policies and quantitative easing programs. The mindless "search for yield," while exposing SWFs to considerable risk, has proven to be even more counterproductive due to a lack of consistent investment strategy. Moreover, investing in conservative instruments such as Treasury bills to avoid liquidity risk and commodity boom–bust cycles is not particularly effective in the long term: SWFs can *stabilize* their wealth only if financial assets are held in countercyclical investments (countercyclical, that is, to the underlying asset; e.g., the price of copper), which they are not. Otherwise, in a prolonged commodity price decline, the assets under management can experience significant drawdown. On the other hand, large-scale infrastructure investments offer advantages of stable long-term real returns, which have a low correlation with other asset classes (Inderst 2010).[3]

Because large infrastructure initiatives can be part of government stimulus programs during a downturn when the private sectors are scaling back, infrastructure investment may exhibit countercyclical patterns that carry sig nificant diversification effects. This type of countercyclical investment initiative has been unfolding in China since early 2015; to combat declining economic growth, the Chinese government has been accelerating 300 infrastructure projects valued at $1.1 trillion in order to spur economic growth, according to Bloomberg News (2016). Private sector funding would meaningfully benefit from government support during periods of economic slump.

Though it has long been recognized that the long-term returns to equity exceed those to debt by more than an amount that can be justified by risk aversion (the equity premium puzzle), only a small—if growing—number of SWFs have started to allocate a larger share of their assets to equity investments. Beyond these two broad asset classes, however, there has been relatively little exploration into other very large asset classes, such as real estate or infrastructure. These asset classes, however, are natural targets for SWFs, given their long-term orientation (as also discussed in chapters 4, 6, and 14).[4]

In this chapter, we build on an earlier paper (Arezki et al. 2014), presented in Bellagio, Italy, at a specialized conference organized by the Rockefeller Foundation. This paper, which we will refer to as the "Bellagio paper," offers a detailed survey of the state of SWFs and their long-term investment behavior and explains why their involvement in infrastructure investments in developing countries has been so glaringly low. It concludes that the SWFs' reluctance to venture more actively into global infrastructure is largely due to risk aversion. The Bellagio paper also makes a strong case for the need of a new independent global infrastructure investment platform to complement ongoing efforts by the European Investment Bank, the New Partnership for Africa's Development, the European Bank for Reconstruction and Development, and other development banks to promote infrastructure investments. We describe how such a platform could provide a framework for risk management and allocation.

We build on the Bellagio paper by further exploring how the Global Infrastructure Investment Platform (GIIP) can help overcome some of the remaining key challenges specific to developing countries—and to African countries in particular.

EMERGING AFRICA: AN ILLUSTRATION OF INFRASTRUCTURE INVESTMENT OPPORTUNITIES AND NEEDS

The assets that could underlie the economic transformation that is taking place in Africa remain largely underrepresented in the portfolios of SWFs. Africa has been the world's second-fastest growing region after China in recent years. The continent has enormous needs for infrastructure investments if it is to continue growing and developing. Sovereign wealth funds are uniquely positioned to make these investments, given their long-term investment horizons. These combined factors suggest that SWFs should be making more investments in infrastructure in the region than they have been.

Growth in Africa has been accompanied by political change. Since the early 1990s, direct multiparty elections have been held in more than forty Sub-Saharan African countries, and, for many of them, these were the first multiparty elections to have occurred after gaining independence in the 1960s. These trends suggest that democratic reforms are underway in many African countries (Peters 2011). There are also signs of a notable reduction in regulatory risk and an increase in investor protection (Deloitte 2013).

AFRICA'S INVESTMENT NEEDS

Infrastructure remains massively underdeveloped on the continent. Africa has urgent needs, particularly in transport, water, and electricity, sectors that usually involve a major component of public funding, unlike telecommunications, which early on attracted investment from the private sector. Without these investments, Africa will not be able to continue to realize its economic potential. According the World Bank, the infrastructure investment gap in Africa until 2020 will average $93 billion per year (Foster and Garamendia 2010); however, this figure may be even greater, given the forecast for high population growth in the region. While Europe's population is estimated to decline by 60 million by 2050, Africa is estimated grow by another 900 million during the same period.

INFRASTRUCTURE INVESTMENT IS ESPECIALLY NEEDED IN THE FOLLOWING KEY AREAS:

- **Energy**: Installed power generation capacity needs to increase from present levels of 125 gigawatts (comparable with that of the United Kingdom) to almost 700 gigawatts in 2040 (Programme for Infrastructure Development in Africa [PIDA] 2011). According to the International Energy Agency (2014), "an estimated 620 million people in Sub-Saharan Africa do not have access to electricity, and for those that do have it, supply is often insufficient, unreliable and among the most costly in the world."
- **Transport**: Demand volumes will increase around six to eight times and up to fourteen times for some landlocked countries by 2040. Port throughput will rise from 265 million tons in 2009 to more than 2 billion tons in 2040 (PIDA 2011).

- **Water:** Needs will push Africa's existing river basins—including the Nile, Niger, Orange, and Volta basins—to the ecological brink (PIDA 2011).
- **Information and communications technology:** Demand will swell by a factor of twenty before 2020 as Africa catches up with broadband. Demand for international bandwidth, around 300 gigabits per second in 2009, will reach six terabits per second by 2018 (PIDA 2011). As of 2014, Africa's international bandwidth had reached three terabits, which is ten times the 2009 bandwidth. In 2010, only 10 percent of Africans had online access; this figure doubled in four years to 20 percent. This rapid growth is expected to continue for the next two decades (World Telecommunications/ICT Indicators Database 2014).

There are several drivers of these growing infrastructure needs. One major contributing factor is population growth (Africa has the fasting growing population in the world). Another major factor is that many countries are experiencing economic transformation—moving from agriculture to the manufacturing sector. Growing urbanization across African countries is also creating huge demands. For example, there is strong demand for road modernization in Angola, Namibia, and Zambia, where untarred roads account for 70 to 90 percent of all roads, making the exorbitant transportation costs, in literal terms, a major road block to promoting urbanization (Naidoo 2007). For more recent data on paved and unpaved roads in Africa as a whole when compared to other low income countries, see Foster and Garamendia 2010, and Gutman, Chattopadhyay, and Sy 2015. The demand created by growing urbanization is not limited to the current decade.

WHY SOVEREIGN WEALTH FUNDS SHOULD INVEST IN INFRASTRUCTURE IN AFRICA

Sovereign wealth funds may well find infrastructure investments in Africa particularly attractive in coming decades. Compared with other long-term investors, SWFs may have some comparative advantages, allowing them to obtain differential returns, and this may be especially important if other investment opportunities are foreclosed (Turkisch 2011).

1. SWF investments can be leveraged with private sector investments. SWFs may "signal" relative safety, but their political influence (their

connection with governments and the global political processes) may *make* it safer for investment. When the political environment is believed to be safer, other private-sector investors will be attracted to enter.

2. Developing markets may seem more attractive as developed countries raise barriers to state-backed investors owing to the perceived threat to national sovereignty.

3. As SWFs are not subject to quarterly earnings reports, they can invest in illiquid and long-maturity assets that private institutions are unable to undertake. The shortage of suppliers of long-term investors should yield them a long-term investment premium.

4. Lastly, investing in Africa's infrastructure development is a way to diversify in assets that have little correlation with the global stock and bond markets (Idzorek and Armstrong 2009).

According to a recent World Bank report (2015b), as of 2014, more than 2,200 Chinese enterprises were operating in Sub-Saharan Africa, yet most of them are private firms. In addition, large-scale investments from the Middle East into Africa have grown notably over the past decade, but the main source has been private investors, as opposed to SWFs. There are multiple drivers of these investments: As wages rise in China, for instance, Chinese firms are looking for low-cost production sites elsewhere in the world. Firms in the Middle East may feel that geographical proximity gives them an informational advantage, not to mention cultural links around Islam. Some of the investment may be politically driven—pushed by governments to strengthen the political bonds between the two regions and to enhance influence. For the African recipient of these funds, SWFs also have distinct advantages. Sovereign wealth funds will not only con-tribute with large-sized investments, but also reduce the volatility of these capital flows and the short-termism associated with private investors. The great needs in African infrastructure investments combined with the comparative advantage of SWFs in providing such funding may yield a successful partnership that is conducive to high-return expectations.

SOURCES OF FUNDS FOR AFRICA

The past decade has also witnessed strong investments from many parts of the world, and in many arenas. For example, there have been strong investments from Middle Eastern countries, including Abu Dhabi,

Dubai, Kuwait, Qatar, and Saudi Arabia, to Africa in oil and gas, the telecommunications sector, and agricultural cultivation (Hardy 2014).

China, which has pursued an integrated and multilateral approach through the leadership of the China Development Bank, has provided about two-thirds of Africa's new spending on infrastructure since 2007. These funds come not only in the form of aid, but also through a number of other channels and financial instruments by China's various state institutions (e.g., SWFs) (Organisation for Economic Co-operation and Development [OECD] 2012).

For infrastructure investments, China has sometimes provided resource-backed loans, through financial institutions such as the China Development Bank, as nonconcessional loans to African governments. In return, the recipient country of resource-backed loans contracts Chinese companies to build the infrastructure projects and also extends the conditions and the rights to extract natural resources (e.g., mining, oil extraction). China's financing of Africa's infrastructure rose dramatically in the years prior to the global financial crisis (OECD 2012).

But, infrastructure is only a small part of overall investment. A Brookings Institution study by Chen, Dollar, and Tang (2015) points to the United Nations Conference on Trade and Development's World Investment Report for 2015, which shows that, contrary to popular perception, China's role in overall foreign investment in Africa is sometimes overstated. In 2014, for example, only 4.4 percent of total foreign direct investment (FDI) flowing into Africa originated from China. Foreign direct investment from the European Union, the U.S., and even South Africa exceeded the size of FDI from China to the continent over the same period.

EVER-PRESENT RISK

The favorable trends indicated earlier that make Africa a more attractive destination for FDI, however, do not mean that investment risks in Africa are no longer present. Complex labor markets, poor infrastructure, currency volatility, poor supply of skilled labor and management, social challenges, high transaction costs, inadequate political and legal frameworks, difficulty in monitoring and measuring social impacts and enforcement mechanisms, all serve as major deterrents to FDI (Roose, Bishoi, and Schena 2012). Poor policy coordination and planning, as well as inadequate operational performance in such areas as the power sector in Africa, are also pervasive and similarly deter investment. Most importantly, default rates are also extremely high (Collier and Gunning 1999). Together, these shortcomings limit "the enabling environment for long-term planning" and investment (OECD 2012).

There is clearly a major need to address infrastructure inadequacies in Africa, and this acute demand offers strong opportunities for SWFs and other long-term investors. African countries would also benefit enormously from the involvement of long-term investors to address shortages in infrastructure development. Yet, there are numerous obstacles to convert such possibilities into reality from a policy design, execution, maintenance, and monitoring perspective. An independent infrastructure investment platform, such as the one we propose here, would underwrite investor risks and address clear coordination failures.

Having outlined the needs, as well as the opportunities, around infrastructure investments in Africa, we now present a proposal for the operation of an independent international platform involving a multitude of actors through which long-term investors, including but not limited to SWFs, can raise their investments in this asset class in Africa (and indeed in countries in other regions requiring investments in this area).

THE GLOBAL INFRASTRUCTURE INVESTMENT PLATFORM

Despite the encouraging trends in growth, one key factor that is holding back investors, including SWFs, is the perception of high risk associated with investing in the least-developed countries. Generally speaking, there is a major lack of transparency, coordination, and information about investment opportunities in global infrastructure, coupled with legal, governance, and monitoring challenges. These types of barriers are the major reason why private investors are often disinclined to make such investments. All investors—SWFs, as well as pension funds, insurance companies, and development banks—face major challenges in assessing and mitigating the risks associated with long-term investments in infrastructure. GIIP offers new ways of addressing all of the various challenges mentioned here through a more open and independent investment platform.[5]

The GIIP is not a multilateral agency, an arm of development banks, a think tank, or a private financial institution. Essentially, its aim is to operate as an independent special-purpose entity,[6] to bring together all relevant parties involved in long-term infrastructure investments in a transparent manner. These parties include sovereigns, ratings agencies, environmental agencies, legal firms, SWFs, pension funds, insurance companies, international financial institutions, and regional development banks. The GIIP would identify all agencies involved in a given infrastructure project and follow the development of the project through each stage of the concession period (normally anywhere from ten to thirty years).

The most importance function of the GIIP is to mitigate investment risks and to perform all tasks required to convert a potential project in Africa into an investable asset.

PUBLIC SECTOR ALTERNATIVES

Various initiatives to promote infrastructure have been pursued by organizations such as the Asian Infrastructure Investment Bank (AIIB), the European Bank for Reconstruction and Development, the New Development Bank (NDB), the World Bank, and others. Table 12.1 illustrates the existing models, as described by Gutman et al. (2015).

The Global Infrastructure Facility, under the World Bank, became operational in April 2015, and the AIIB is leading the charge in developing an infrastructure investment platform in the Asia–Pacific region. The AIIB and NDB were primarily founded on an understanding that the old model characterizing the World Bank and other multilateral institutions might not be fully appropriate for the twenty-first century. The NDB, for instance, focused on creating special investment funds, which would invest in a particular range of investment projects, with a particular risk profile, attractive to particular classes of investors. It serves an important function by engaging with special investment funds, bringing together an array of potential investors, from SWFs to pension funds, and even high-net-worth individual investors. The NDB employs modern financial techniques to provide an array of investment products—using structured finance in a responsible way to allocate risk and securitization to pool risks.

The governance structure within the mentioned different funds is generally regarded as being adaptable and responsive to the concerns of the investors.

VALUE-ADDED OF AN INDEPENDENT GLOBAL INFRASTRUCTURE INVESTMENT PLATFORM

Another infrastructure investment platform, such as the GIIP, may therefore seem redundant and run the risk of largely overlapping with the existing

Table 12.1 Development bank investment platforms for potential infrastructure investments

	EIB	EBRD	WB	AIIB	NDB
Official purpose	Bring about European integration and social cohesion	Use investment as a tool to help build market economies	Reduce worldwide poverty	Provide finance to infrastructure projects in the Asia–Pacific region	Mobilize resources for infrastructure and sustainable development in the BRICS countries and other emerging economies
Shareholders	EU member states	64 countries and 2 EU institutions; the U.S. is the largest shareholder	188 member countries; the top 5 countries by voting power are the U.S., Japan, China, Germany, and France; thus, dominated by American, European, and Japanese interests	22 Asian countries; China holds the major stake	The BRICS countries: Brazil, Russia, India, China, and South Africa
Inception and initial mission	Nonprofit long-term lending institution established in 1958 under the Treaty of Rome	Founded in April 1991 during the dissolution of the Soviet Union to support countries of the former Eastern Bloc in the process of establishing their private sectors	One of the key Bretton Woods institutions founded in 1944 to increase cooperation on an international scale	Founded in 2014, as China was frustrated with the slow pace of reforms and governance of the American, European, and Japanese members	The idea for setting up the bank was first proposed in 2012 at the fourth BRICS summit. The agreement on provision of a legal basis was signed in July 2014 and entered into force in July 2015. The NDB was formerly known as the BRICS Development Bank.

Abbreviations: ADB, African Development Bank; AIIB, Asian Infrastructure Investment Bank; BRICS, Brazil, Russia, India, China, and South Africa; EBRD, European Bank for Reconstruction and Development; EIB, European Investment Bank; EU, European Union; NDB, New Development Bank; WB, World Bank.

Note: The "alphabet soup" of international development banks is getting larger and larger. This table compares five of them.

organizations in terms of functionality, but the sheer scale of infrastructure investment needs over the next three to four decades dwarfs the combined capacity of the existing organizations. For example, the World Bank estimates that the emerging-market and developing economies require more than $1 trillion each year, while the Global Infrastructure Facility has an initial capitalization of only $100 million as of 2015. The total capital capacity of the NDB stands at $100 billion—one-tenth of the estimated infrastructure financing need. In addition to adding capital capacity to the global pool of financing available for infrastructure investment, a nongovernmental investment platform has several other advantages. First, the nonpolitical nature of GIIP may give it an advantage—potential investors would not worry, for instance, that the destination of investments was influenced by politics.[7] Second, the GIIP can become a reliable source for unbiased research and recommendations by operating as a platform independent of any sovereigns or investors, thus avoiding conflicts of interest.[8] Last, the GIIP can gain a higher degree of consistency, (as opposed to infrastructure investment platforms that are directly attached to governmental institutions such as the World Bank or the China Infrastructure Investment Bank (launched by the Chinese Government)), because its financing sources are not subject to regime change or political instability.[9]

STRUCTURE OF THE GLOBAL INFRASTRUCTURE INVESTMENT PLATFORM

The GIIP is a platform charged with coordinating actors, aggregating projects, and raising funds from long-term investors. The basic configuration of the proposed infrastructure platform is shown in figure 12.1. The platform is essentially an institutional framework designed to create special-purpose entities that invest in infrastructure projects and issue claims against the income stream from these projects to investors. As with securitizations for other asset classes, we conceive the special-purpose entity as an independent organization that holds and services infrastructure assets against which asset-backed claims have been issued, but the special-purpose entity is managed by the GIIP.

While the basic intermediation principles behind the proposed platform are similar to other forms of pass-through securitization structures, there are fundamental specific characteristics that will take shape according to the nature of infrastructure assets, the specific risks associated with these assets, and the nature of the main parties involved in infrastructure investments.

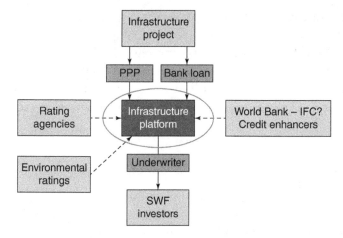

Figure 12.1 Infrastructure investment platform. IFC, International Finance Corporation; PPP, public–private partnership; SWF, sovereign wealth fund.

BARE-BONES OUTLINE OF A GLOBAL INFRASTRUCTURE INVESTMENT PLATFORM

A GIIP originates projects (or identifies good projects designed by others), brings them together with long-term investors, and designs a framework for risk allocation that lowers the overall cost of finance consistent with the risks the country is willing to bear. Financial and reputational risks are managed by operational oversight by the GIIP, even if it does not operate the project directly.

1. SWFs and pension funds would bring the pool of savings;
2. Governments would propose to match the savings with projects, based on their investment plans and development strategy; and
3. Risk mitigation and allocation would be done not just in the usual ways through structured finance and securitization, but through the use of guarantee funds (e.g., the Multilateral Investment Guarantee Agency), guarantees from multilateral development banks (MDBs), and possibly private foundations.

ORIGINATION

A first key distinguishing characteristic of infrastructure projects compared with, for example, commercial real estate is that the origination of an infrastructure project would typically involve a government agency in the host country, whether the project is set up entirely as a publicly owned utility or as a public–private partnership (PPP).

The World Bank, multilateral and regional development banks, as well as private foundations and the anticipated NDB (or BRICS [Brazil, Russia, India, China, and South Africa] bank) could play a very important role in project preparation and technical assistance to recipient or host country governments.

SUBSIDIZATION AND COLLATERALIZATION

Another distinguishing feature of investment projects is that many are not viable commercial ventures. Infrastructure investments such as roads, railways, airports, water and sanitation, and electricity generation are justified by the development externalities they generate.

For example, the costs of constructing a bridge may far exceed the present discounted value of toll revenues, yet the bridge is a worthwhile infrastructure investment because of all the related economic development benefits it will generate. The construction costs of the bridge have to be funded somehow, and investors will demand a market rate of return for the funds they invest in the project. Therefore, a specific question for infrastructure projects is how the cash flows the project generates—whether in the form of toll revenues or public subsidies—are determined—and how the transfer of these cash flows to the special-purpose entity is enforced.

One potential benefit of the infrastructure platform structure for host countries is that it may be able to facilitate the assignment of specific revenues to an infrastructure project, thus giving a higher-seniority protection to investors in the project relative to other investors in the host country's (unsecured) sovereign debt.

The assignment of revenues, for example, provides a form of collateral protection to investors in the project through an enforceable long-term PPP contract. This can allow host countries to fund their infrastructure investments at a lower cost.

One of the existing obstacles to infrastructure investments is the debt-overhang problem these countries face, which makes infrastructure investments funded through sovereign debt issues sometimes prohibitively expensive. In other words, the funding of infrastructure projects with a specific assignment of cash flows to the project provides the host countries similar benefits to *covered bond* financing arrangements for real estate investments by banks. The holders of the covered bonds have higher protections than other bank creditors and are therefore willing to purchase these bonds at a higher price. At the same time, bank issuers of covered bonds have stronger incentives to ensure that the real estate investments they originate are sufficiently safe, as they carry a disproportionate share of the downside risk.

WAREHOUSING AND SECURITIZATION

Once a conforming infrastructure project has been identified, it can be warehoused for securitization by the platform. At this stage, MDBs can play another essential role: credit enhancement and bridge financing. No matter how carefully infrastructure projects are vetted, substantial risks remain for investors. To begin with, there is the risk of construction delays and cost overruns. Continuous monitoring of construction progress and access to bridge financing are essential at this stage, and both can be provided by development banks. Once the project has been completed, the remaining risks are operational, political, and currency risk. Ideally, SWFs would prefer to have no exposure to either political or currency risk and to have minimal exposure to operational risk. Development banks and other multilateral agencies can play an important role in absorbing these risks by providing guarantees and holding on to a junior tranche in the securitization of infrastructure assets.

By concentrating on their role as guarantors, development banks can thus leverage their capital to significantly scale up infrastructure investments. They are also best placed to absorb this risk, as they have the greatest experience with and leverage on host governments in enforcing promised repayments of infrastructure loans. Finally, by co-investing in infrastructure projects with other long-term investors in this way, they can augment the pressure they exert on delinquent host governments to obtain promised repayments. Indeed, by putting themselves in the position of a gateway to global infrastructure funding, they wield significant power just by their ability to cut off further access to funds for future projects in the event that a host government defaults on promised repayments of infrastructure loans.

Along with the credit-enhancement role of development banks, another important group of participants in securitization are credit rating agencies (CRAs). At least in the early phases of the development of this investment vehicle, it is likely that SWF investors will require an

AAA rating to invest in infrastructure-asset-backed securities. The rating agencies, in collaboration with the development banks, can set guidelines and protocols for obtaining the AAA rating, which can be made available in advance to the senior tranches of these infrastructure-backed bonds.[10] This would significantly improve SWFs' access to this asset class. Similarly, one can envision a key role for environmental ratings agencies at this stage in determining which infrastructure projects have the least environmental impact and the greatest social development impact.

The GIIP can be made to play a more important role and have greater flexibility than this bare-bones description might suggest. The GIIP should be set up so that origination of investments can be initiated by investors, not just by host country governments and development banks. Moreover, the GIIP should have a planning role, mapping out whole infrastructure networks for Africa in which individual projects can become "bankable."

GOVERNANCE OF THE GLOBAL INFRASTRUCTURE INVESTMENT PLATFORM

The importance of governance is gradually becoming widely recognized. An independent and transparent governance structure could lend stability and be seen as attractive to long-term investors, as it would provide them with a heightened sense of legal security when undertaking investments with payback periods of ten to thirty years. The board would consist of members from the investment community (SWFs and pension funds), from the recipient countries, and from the World Bank and other official multilateral agencies. Clear guidelines governing conflicts of interest and environmental and social safeguards would need to be formulated.

The initial organizational structure of the GIIP could be modeled on the U.K.'s Pension Infrastructure Platform (PIP). The PIP started with pension funds as founding investors to seed the fund with capital, which targets long-term infrastructure development projects. This structure sought to form a pool of assets of meaningful size to be free from stricter investment regulations on pension funds. The GIIP could initially be formed in the same way by soliciting SWFs and MDBs as the founding investors. On one hand, the commitment of the SWFs and the MDBs would lend strong credibility to the platform; with the information network available to the MDBs and the strong financial backing of the SWFs, the platform would be able to ensure that a pipeline of projects is available over time and that the projects are thoroughly vetted and rated before being securitized. On the other hand, this arrangement also offers unique incentives to the SWFs, given that some emerging-market SWFs have hit road blocks in investment initiatives in developed markets owing to direct or indirect protectionism. By teaming up with the MDBs and making investment through the GIIP, SWFs could alleviate and circumvent distrust by host nations and achieve broader market access around world.

An operation template available to the GIIP is the Canadian syndication model. The Canada Pension Plan Investment Board (CPPIB) and the Ontario Teachers' Pension Plan (OTPP) were designed to allow both small and large institutional investors to gain access to infrastructure investments otherwise too labor or risk intensive. To do so, one of these large institutional investors, such as the OTPP, takes the lead and invests directly in an infrastructure asset. The lead then creates an opt-in by structuring a vehicle and setting a minimum investment level for each additional stakeholder. Each investor then does its own due diligence and decides whether to invest at the set price. Larger entities with in-house infrastructure investment teams can make multiple investments in infrastructure assets while diversifying their risk. This approach gives them the ability to invest in larger projects even if they do not have the appetite or capacity to carry out a large-scale single project on their own. The institutional investor divests substantial amounts of the risk. By spreading risk among stakeholders, this approach reduces the problem of direct investors shying away from a project because of the concentration of risk. There are, however, no extra fees for the lead investors; there are no management or performance fees because each subsequent investor pays only the lead investor's pro-rata costs (plus the investment). Smaller investors without in-house infrastructure experts could invest directly with only a pro-rata share of the costs of the lead investor—much less than the fees from traditional fund structures. The syndication model could be structured such that no investors have any fiduciary responsibility to any other investor—requiring, as noted, every investor to exercise their own due diligence. Further, while the smaller investors must be responsible for their own due diligence, in practice, the lead investor will have already done a great deal of that work, giving the smaller investors something to build from. (Alternatively, the lead investors could undertake fiduciary responsibilities, for which they would be appropriately compensated.)

RISK MITIGATION

There are many risks associated with infrastructure projects, which may loom especially large in the minds of investors given the long-term nature of these projects.

The risk of nationalization today is minimal, but this risk could be easily handled through the World Bank's Multilateral Guarantee Investment Agency. National guarantee agencies (e.g., the Overseas Private Investment Corporation) and development banks could also play the role of guarantor.

Multilateral development bank participation in a project not only mitigates nationalization risk, but also mitigates the risk of actions that significantly and inappropriately reduce the value of an asset. Some of the international and regional lending institutions could also collaborate with each other to act as guarantors should a natural disaster or war take place.

Securitization and tranching of risks, prudently done, may enable greater participation in the investments, not only by pooling and limiting risks (for those who want risks to be limited in certain ways), but also by facilitating exits from the fund should that become necessary. (Provisions for exit, especially in periods where mass withdrawals might be a threat, would have to be carefully drawn.)

Solving important global challenges often requires innovative solutions involving the coordination of sometimes radically different actors. An acknowledgement of the virtue of plurality and diversity among members of the governing board guides the conceptualization of the GIIP, as do recent examples of promising collaborations to deal with similar large-scale development investments. In 2014, JPMorgan Chase and the Bill and Melinda Gates Foundation formed an investment fund that backs the late-stage development of technologies to fight killer diseases in low-income countries. This private financing seeks to address the fact that global health funding barely grew in 2015. Given the risks of investing in the clinical development of new technologies, the Bill and Melinda Gates Foundation and the Swedish International Development Cooperation Agency have committed to partially offsetting potential losses in the fund, which seeks financial return for investors by targeting technologies with public health applications in both developed and emerging markets. Lion's Head Global Partners LLP, a London-based asset manager specializing in sustainable development, is responsible for originating, managing, and exiting the fund's portfolio investments.

DEFAULT AND ENFORCEMENT

Another key question regarding infrastructure investments is how contracts associated with long-term projects can be enforced.

The specific assignment of cash flows to an infrastructure project does not necessarily mean that the cash flow transfer to investors will always be enforced. Investors' lack of power for contract enforcement in infrastructure projects is another key distinguishing characteristic of these investments, which must be taken into account by the GIIP. For most asset-backed securities (whether backed by commercial or real estate assets, auto loans or credit card debt), the investors' rights in case of default are straightforward, even if the costs of default can be substantial. If there is a default on an asset that backs an asset-backed security, the special-purpose entity in charge of servicing the asset has the right to liquidate the asset and take ownership of either the asset or the proceeds from the sale of the asset. Such rights, however, are typically not available for infrastructure projects. Thus, a key question is what can be done in the event of default on payments for an infrastructure project—or to reduce the risk of such a default.

A closely related issue is what options are available to investors of asset-backed securities when the special-purpose entity that has issued the securities defaults on the promised payments. Here again, investors' rights are straightforward. Following the default of the special-purpose entity, investors can resolve the entity in bankruptcy and recover the liquidation value of the assets. In principle, the same rights can be offered to investors in infrastructure-asset-backed securities, although careful consideration would have to be shown to identifying the appropriate court systems in a given country or region, should legal jurisdiction be required to resolve the failing projects.

The participation of regional and multilateral development banks (such as the World Bank, the European Bank for Reconstruction and Development, and private foundations) in the proposed independent infrastructure platform is essential to facilitate and guarantee the enforcement of promised payments under the infrastructure investment contracts. Multilateral development banks, in particular, can play a critical role in enhancing the infrastructure platform. They are uniquely placed to perform due diligence at the origination of new infrastructure projects. Multilateral development banks have a high concentration of infrastructure engineering expertise and are thus well placed to assess the technical viability of the investments under consideration and to offer assistance to host nations at the project preparation phase. They have also accumulated the know-how to assess the community, social, and environmental impact of such projects, as well as the financial capabilities of host country governments to subsidize such projects.

CONFRONTING CHALLENGES AND THE PERCEPTION OF EXCESSIVE RISK

There are of course certain risks SWFs take on by investing in infrastructure projects and some compelling reasons they may be unwilling to take them on. The GIIP is structured to assuage these concerns. If, despite the great investment of time and resources in creating the GIIP, it fails to gain the legitimacy sought by SWFs and countries seeking large investments in infrastructure, any other future efforts in this area of investment will also suffer. In this section, we consider a number of anticipated challenges and briefly discuss the broad outlines of how these may be addressed.

Many SWFs tend to mainly pursue projects that are ascribed the highest ratings by credit ratings agencies. The reality is that risks exist in just about every context, and where there is lower risk, the payoff also tends to be lower. The required skill is in being able to manage risk effectively and to reduce failure. The GIIP could be seen as a public good that can help limit potential failure by harnessing the skills required to invest successfully in infrastructure. The investment risk posed by a lack of technical expertise in SWFs in managing large-scale infrastructure projects could be addressed by the GIIP, as a consequence of having a large pool of participants with a broad range of experience and technical know-how regarding the management of such projects. Moreover, the GIIP would also serve as an important source of information about new infrastructure projects that are open for public competition. Such a platform would reduce the risk for investors because the host country or countries seeking funding and technical and management expertise for large-scale infrastructure initiatives would also be required to provide clear, complete, and detailed information about the projects for which they are seeking bids. Many leading SWFs might have plenty of funds to invest but be unaware or poorly informed about a number of potentially highly profitable infrastructure projects on the international market.

Some large-scale, long-term infrastructure projects are spread across a number of countries within a developing region, some of them with higher risk ratings owing to unstable political and legal institutions.

Sovereign wealth funds would be able to diversify their risks through securitization of their investments across a broad range of projects by partnering, for example, with SWFs from other regions, institutional investors, regional development banks, and international investment banks and by gaining the endorsement and support of the World Bank in its role as guarantor in the event of a risk of nationalization of long-term projects through regime change or other disasters related to climate or other causes. The legality and compliance by all parties involved in given projects would also be well defined, and therefore enforceable, in case of a breach in agreements. Many of these examples are cited in the Bellagio paper (Arezki et al. 2014). For a comprehensive and thorough analysis of how these structural features associated with the GIIP may be of relevance to Africa, see the Brookings Institution research by Gutman et al. (2015).

While access to infrastructure investments is unambiguously beneficial to the host country, the investment returns to the investor, just like returns on any other conventional investments, can be highly variable and volatile. Inderst (2010) argues that, although infrastructure investments follow the traditional capital asset pricing theory, where higher expected risk is associated with higher expected return, infrastructure investments exhibit much higher variability in expected returns for a given level of risk compared with conventional fixed income and equity investments. This is indeed a challenge in terms of managing investor expectations, but the GIIP is in a unique position to design risk mitigation strategies because of the breadth of the investment projects it expects to screen, and also because of the diversification it facilitates. To enhance this role, the GIIP can identify types of projects that demonstrate negatively correlated returns and bundle them together, much in the same way that a conventional equity/fixed income portfolio is built to eliminate idiosyncratic risks. A further extension of this approach is to combine projects with predictable early cash flows with those that do not expect cash flows until much later. This would make it easier for ratings agency models to come up with consistent ratings for a project bundle. With these tools, the GIIP could mitigate the idiosyncratic risks inherent in individual projects and offer a diversified bundle that earns returns commensurate with the systemic risk in infrastructure investment.

Another risk is that developing countries and SWFs may perceive the GIIP as a Western construct designed to extract high returns on investments and to exploit their economies and capital and could thus be reluctant to join. One way to overcome this negative perception is to consult these core participants, most of who are from developing countries, as early as possible and to have them collaborate in the formulation of mission and vision statements and the fundamental governance structure of the GIIP.

The need for sustainable and responsible investment poses another challenge to the GIIP in terms of reputational risk. Growth at the cost of the environment, particularly as the world has begun to reel from the effects of climate change, is unsustainable and no longer accepted. Therefore, when screening infrastructure projects, the GIIP must take into account both the social and environmental impacts of the projects. The environmental consideration also provides opportunities, since there is already an increasing demand for sustainable infrastructure assets. Bhattacharya, Oppenheim, and Stern (2015) estimate that the sustainable infrastructure assets required over the next fifteen years will be around $90 trillion.

CONCLUSION

We have proposed an independent Global Infrastructure Investment Platform to channel capital, especially from SWFs, into much-needed investments in infrastructure, and put forward a general list of tentative steps toward the creation of the GIIP. We propose a focus on SWFs as key investors because they have the deepest pockets and a long-term outlook. The GIIP would play an important role in shrinking the gap between the current global savings glut and the growing need for infrastructure investments. In principle, it would be mutually advantageous for both the investors—offering them higher returns over longer periods of time than existing assets—and the host country, where high-return investment projects are currently going unfunded. There are, of course, a large number of institutional and policy challenges associated with the creation of the GIIP. We have suggested, however, that most of these seemingly impossible barriers are surmountable. We have presented a detailed outline of the GIIP to discuss the various operational challenges, enormous commitment, expertise, and goodwill that will be required from many partners to ensure the success of such an initiative. The acknowledgement that something is hugely difficult should not deter one from taking on the challenge. In the case of the GIIP, the benefits appear to far exceed the costs in whatever shape or form they may manifest themselves.

The first step would be to identify a group of SWFs, pension funds, insurance funds, development banks, and foundations that would be interested in exploring this project further. Ideally, the founding sponsors would represent all regions of the world. A second step would be to team up with a group of development banks that would take on the role of guarantors.

The start-up phase of the GIIP would likely combine both bottom-up and top-down processes, in which a private initiative would be supported by a coalition of willing governments and development banks. To kickstart the process as a first step, seed funding from foundations and other supporting actors would allow a team of infrastructure experts, investment bankers, and international investment lawyers to establish the legal structure of the GIIP and gather templates for investment agreements, as well as identify a first set of projects that could be funded. The initial phase of operation of the GIIP would begin with a pilot project that focuses on a particular country, region, or small subset of countries. This pilot project could then be scaled up to include other countries where there is strong demand for long-term investments in infrastructure. Based on the outcome of the pilot project, other countries would, we hope, be encouraged to use the GIIP to attract long-term investments from SWFs. Eventually, the GIIP would not only promote development in a very significant way, but also provide SWFs with information about attractive investment opportunities. Regional organizations should play a prominent role in the platform.

Who would be the first mover to take the initiative to encourage investments through an international investment platform? Should it be SWFs, governments, pension funds, international financial institutions, financial intermediaries, or developing countries seeking funding for vital projects? The GIIP could clearly serve as the catalyst for coordination among these parties. Further, some safeguard mechanisms, such as insurance, monitoring, and auditing, could be employed to enhance coordination.

The organizations backing the platform, both as facilitators and guarantors, should be comprised of a healthy mix of cultures and nationalities to lessen the risks of both perceived and real exclusion. The guarantees expected to be offered by multilateral organizations (e.g., the World Bank's Multilateral Investment Guarantee Agency) would consist of insurance against defaults of infrastructure projects owing to political unrest

(Irwin 2007). Investors such as SWFs are likely to want maximum monitoring of long-term projects in the infrastructure development they take on. Meanwhile, countries or individual companies managing the projects are likely to want minimum monitoring. Therefore, the best outcome for all parties concerned would be to have the monitoring, as well as the auditing process, carried out by an independent party or organization.

Both the guarantors and investors would agree on the contours of the appropriate governance structure of the GIIP and target return for investors. Further, they would determine whether investments are made through a closed- or open-ended fund, the modality of the guarantee, and a calendar for the start of the operation and its potential evolution as the platform grows.

NOTES

1. The core of the discussion regarding the GIIP is drawn from an earlier paper presented by R. Arezki, P. Bolton, F. Samama, and S. Peters, in Bellagio, Italy, in May 2014, with the generous support of the Rockefeller Foundation. The author has also benefited greatly from useful input from Joseph Sitglitz to restructure the key arguments put forward in this chapter. The author would especially like to thank Rumi Masih for discussions on SWFs and Weigang Yuan and Eamon Kircher-Allen for valuable research assistance.

2. Pension funds typically match their liabilities to investment assets to minimize reinvestment risk. However, very long life-span assets have limited supply. Through financial intermediation, short-term assets can be linked to synthetically create long-dated assets. Pension funds incur additional costs for financial institutions to assume the reinvestment risk in this maturity transformation process.

3. Of course, the overall return to such investments will typically depend on the overall economic performance of the country.

4. Part of the reason for this failure is institutional: Most of the funds have relatively small teams of managers, who have expertise primarily in managing portfolios of liquid, publicly traded securities. They lack expertise in less liquid markets, such as real estate and infrastructure—and may be more reluctant or even unable to assess when these markets have become less risky. This chapter focuses on an alternative explanation.

5. The Bellagio paper provides a thorough and detailed review of lessons learned from past experiences. It should be noted that similar ideas as those exposed in this paper underlie the founding of the new infrastructure banks.

6. The specific proposal put forward in the Bellagio paper has the GIIP hosted at Columbia University.

7. This advantage is perhaps overstated: Large participants on both sides of the market potentially could exercise influence over a private GIIP.

8. This advantage is weakened, especially if the GIIP becomes a profit-making organization. It is well known that the research of investment banks is often biased.

9. This point, too, can be overstated: Multilateral institutions operate in a way that is influenced by a change in political regime—except for that of the U.S. (in the case of the World Bank).

10. We are not "Pollyanna-ish" about the accuracy of the ratings of the CRAs. We simply note that under current institutional arrangements, they are a central part of the securitization process.

REFERENCES

Arezki, R., P. Bolton, S. Peters, and F. Samama. 2014. "Sovereign Wealth Funds and Long-Term Investments: A Proposal for a Global Infrastructure Investment Platform (GIIP)." Paper presented at the Bellagio Center Conference, "Funding the Infrastructure Gap", Bellagio, Italy, May 2014.

Bhattacharya, A., J. Oppenheim, and N. Stern. 2015. "Driving Sustainable Development Through Better Infrastructure: Key Elements of a Transformation Program." Washington, DC: The Brookings Institution.

Bloomberg News. 2016. "China Said to Accelerate $1 Trillion in Projects to Spur GDP," *Bloomberg News*, January 6. www.bloomberg.com/news/articles/2015-01-05/china-said-to-accelerate-1-trillion-in-projects-to-spur-growth.

Chen, W., D. Dollar, and H. Tang. 2015. "China's Direct Investment in Africa: Reality versus Myth." Washington, DC: The Brookings Institution.

Cilliers, J. 2015. "Conflict Trends in Africa: A Turn for the Better in 2015?" Accessed April 2015. Pretoria, South Africa: Institute for Security Studies. www.issafrica.org/iss-today/conflict-trends-in-africa-a-turn-for-the-better-in-2015.

Collier, P., and J. W. Gunning. 1999. "Explaining African Economic Performance," *Journal of Economic Literature* 37, no. 1: 64–111.

Deloitte. 2013. "Where Next on the Road Ahead? Deloitte Infrastructure Investors Survey 2013." London: Deloitte.

Dobbs, R., H. Pohl, D.-Y. Lin, J. Mischke, N. Garemo, J. Hexter, S. Matzinger, R. Palter, and R. Nanavatty. 2013. "Infrastructure Productivity: How to Save $1 Trillion a Year." Brussels: McKinsey Global Institute. www.mckinsey.com/insights/engineering_construction/infrastructure_productivity.

Foster, V., and C. B. Garamendia, eds. 2010. "Africa's Infrastructure: A Time for Transformation." Washington, DC: World Bank.

Gutman, J., S. Chattopadhyay, and A. Sy. 2015. "Financing African Infrastructure: Can the World Deliver?" Washington, DC: The Brookings Institution.

Hardy, S. 2014. "Africa's Middle East Moment," *The Majalla*, May 16. http://eng.majalla.com/2014/05/article55249951.

Idzorek, T., and C. Armstrong. 2009. "Infrastructure and Strategic Asset Allocation: Is Infrastructure an Asset Class?" Washington, DC: Ibbotson Associates/Morningstar.

Inderst, G. 2010. "Infrastructure as an Asset Class," *European Investment Bank Papers* 15 (1): 70–105.

International Energy Agency. 2014. "World Energy Outlook 2014." Paris: International Energy Agency.

Irwin, T. C. 2007. "Government Guarantees Allocating and Valuing Risk in Privately Financed Infrastructure Projects." Washington, DC: International Bank for Reconstruction and Development/World Bank.

Naidoo, E. 2007. "Why Invest in Africa?" TED Talks video. July 31. www.ted.com /talks/euvin_naidoo_on_investing_in_africa?language=en.

Organisation for Economic Co-operation and Development. 2012. "Mapping Support for Africa's Infrastructure Investment." Paris: Organisation for Economic Co-operation and Development.

Peters, S. 2011. "Emerging Africa: The New Frontier for Global Trade," *Economics, Management and Financial Markets* 6, no. 1: 44–56.

Programme for Infrastructure Development in Africa. 2011. "Interconnecting, Integrating and Transforming a Continent." Côte d'Ivoire, Africa: Programme for Infrastructure Development in Africa.

Roose, N., K. Bishoi, and P. J. Schena. 2012. "Sovereign Investment Vehicles and the Case for Social Returns: Toward a Research Agenda." Medford, MA: Tufts University.

Sovereign Wealth Fund Institute. 2015. "Linaburg-Maduell Transparency Index," www.swfinstitute.org/statistics-research/linaburg-maduell-transparency-index/.

Turkisch, E. 2011. "Sovereign Wealth Funds as Investors in Africa: Opportunities and Barriers," OECD Development Centre Working Paper No. 303. Paris: OECD Publishing.

World Bank. 2015a. "Assessing Africa's Policies and Institutions." Washington, DC: World Bank.

——. 2015b. "China and Africa: Expanding Economic Ties in an Evolving Global Context." Washington, DC: World Bank.

World Telecommunications/ICT Indicators Database [online database]. 2014. Geneva: International Telecommunications Union; 18th edition. www.itu.int/en/ITU-D /Statistics/Pages/default.aspx.

CHAPTER 13

North America's Sovereign Wealth Funds

ORIGINS, MODELS, AND LESSONS

Malan Rietveld
Columbia Center on Sustainable Investment

Compared with their global peers, the sovereign wealth funds (SWFs) of the United States and Canada have received nowhere near the amount of public scrutiny and in-depth academic analysis. Over the past decade, policymakers and academics have devoted growing attention to the commodity-based sovereign funds of Abu Dhabi, Kuwait, Norway, Qatar, and Saudi Arabia, as well those of China, Hong Kong, Korea, and Singapore, which derive their assets from the accumulation of excess foreign exchange reserves. However, their North American counterparts—being smaller in size, more conventionally governed and invested, and owned by subnational rather than sovereign governments—have remained uncontroversial and largely out of the spotlight.

In this chapter, I address this shortcoming by providing a comparative perspective on the growing number of North American subnational SWFs. North American sovereign funds provide useful case studies for a number of reasons. First, they have a long, and largely successful, track record. This allows for the identification of policies that have either stood the test of time or evolved as required by the funds' own growth and changing economic context. Indeed, the Texas permanent funds may be considered the world's oldest SWFs, having been established in the mid-nineteenth century. The commodities boom of the 1970s led to a "second wave" of funds in Alabama, Alaska, Louisiana, Montana, and Wyoming, and the Canadian province of Alberta, which are now established resource-based SWFs, managing and overseeing portfolios worth billions of dollars.

Second, the number of North American funds is growing. The shale oil and gas revolution in recent years has resulted in the creation of the North Dakota Legacy Fund in 2010 and increased interest in the establishment of similar funds in Ohio, Pennsylvania, and West Virginia (see Cauchon 2012; Boettner et al. 2012; Petsko 2014). Meanwhile in Canada, the prospect of oil sands and natural gas developments has led to fledgling funds in British Columbia, the Northwest Territories, Quebec, and Saskatchewan (McKinnon 2013; Poelzer 2015). The lessons and experiences of their more established North American counterparts are likely to greatly influence the establishment and evolution of these fledgling funds, given the similar political and institutional contexts in which they are emerging.

A third reason for studying North American funds is the fact that their governance and operational structures are interesting—and, in a number of instances, unique. Operationally, North American resource funds tend to have lean internal structures, requiring small groups of in-house staff, in exchange for a high degree of reliance on external fund managers and professional investment consultants. However, despite their comparatively lean structures, North American funds—particularly the more established ones—have adopted highly diversified and complex portfolios with significant allocations to alternative asset classes in search of higher expected returns (a characteristic they share with American university endowments and foundations). From a governance perspective, many North American funds could be regarded as less independent from government than some of the global SWFs. However, the widely articulated concerns regarding a lack of independence are tempered by exceptional degrees of transparency, public credibility, and adherence to clear rules.

I begin with a brief discussion of the origins and purpose of the most important North American sovereign funds and then proceed with a two-fold analytical focus. First, I consider the governance structures of these funds—both the internal and external institutional arrangements that determine the allocation, use, and investment of the funds' assets and income. Second, I discuss the operational models these funds have embraced with respect to the achievement of their investment mandates. Following this, I identify striking trends in the governance and organization of these funds' investment operations. Finally, I outline a number of lessons to be learned from and policy implications for the North American SWF model.

ORIGINS, OBJECTIVES, AND PURPOSES

The definition of *sovereign wealth fund* is no simple task: Considerable differences exist about where to draw the categorical boundaries around a variety of different types of funds that fit somewhere on a notional scale of public ownership, resource-revenue foundations, long-term investment horizons, and arm's length management—all of which are features commonly associated with SWFs (see Alsweilem et al. 2015 for a detailed discussion). In this chapter, I consider only funds that are capitalized through the public proceeds of natural resources, have some form of independence from the political and budgetary process, and relatively long-term investment mandates (negatively defined, not simply cash-like fiscal buffers in the annual budget). Using these definitional criteria, this chapter focuses on ten established funds, as shown in table 13.1.

Table 13.1 Leading North American sovereign wealth funds

Fund	Year of inception	Size of assets (US$bn)	Funding source
Texas Permanent School Fund	1876 (1854)[a]	33.8	Revenue of assigned public land (predominantly from oil and gas)
Texas Permanent University Fund	1876	17.5	Revenue of assigned public land (predominantly from oil and gas)
New Mexico Land Grant Permanent Fund	1912	14.5	Revenue of assigned public land (predominantly from oil and gas)
New Mexico Severance Tax Permanent Fund	1973	4.6	Severance taxes from oil, gas, and other natural resources
Permanent Wyoming Mineral Trust Fund	1975	7.1	Severance taxes on minerals, oil, and gas
Alaska Permanent Fund	1976	52	25% of mineral lease rentals, royalties, royalty sales, and net profit shares
Alberta Heritage Savings Trust Fund	1976	13.5	Largely discretionary transfers of nonrenewable revenues
Montana Coal Severance Tax Fund	1976	0.6	Severance taxes on coal
Alabama Trust Fund	1985	2.5	Royalty taxes on oil and gas
Louisiana Education Quality Trust Fund	1986	1.3	Revenue of assigned public land (predominantly from oil and gas)
North Dakota Legacy Fund	2010	3.3	Oil and gas revenues (and retained earnings, until 2017)

[a]In 1876, the Texas Permanent School Fund replaced the Special School Fund, which was established in 1854.

Sources: Official public documents, latest information as of December 2015.

The permanent fund model dominates the North American SWF landscape. Under this model, SWFs operate as both income and future generations savings funds. First, they generate annual revenue based on the inflation-adjusted returns generated on the financial portfolio, while, second, ensuring that this income-generating capacity is maintained for future generations by protecting the fund's principal capital from its two largest threats: withdrawals and erosion through inflation. Given that the funds discussed in this chapter are all funded by public revenues arising from the extraction of natural resources, they therefore perform the same overarching function: transforming a depleting asset in the form of commodity deposits into a permanent form of wealth (capital held in a financial portfolio) and income (real returns generated on those financial assets).

Within this basic permanent fund model, there are important differences with respect to how the income generated by the funds are allocated. Broadly, such income is allocated to the general budget, earmarked for specific spending priorities in the budget (e.g., education, health care, and infrastructure maintenance) or the needs of their owners (notably, public school and university systems). The remainder of this section discusses the historic origins of these funds, starting with the establishment of the original American permanent funds in Texas in the mid-nineteenth century, as well as the allocation of their income.

THE PIONEERS: THE TEXAS AND NEW MEXICO PERMANENT FUNDS

Texas's two SWFs—the Texas Permanent School Fund and the Texas Permanent University Fund—are among the oldest public investment institutions in the United States, dating back to the formation of the state in its current form. Both funds were established under the state constitution in 1876—only a decade after civilian government was restored in the state, following the state's secession from Mexico, the collapse of the autonomous Republic of Texas in 1946, its subsequent annexation by the United States, and the turmoil of the post–Civil War reconstruction (in fact, the Texas Permanent School Fund's predecessor, the Special School Fund, dates back even further, having been established by the legislature in 1854).

The pioneering course charted by Texan legislators needs to be placed in its appropriate historic and economic context. In the early years of the formation of the new state, the government was at pains to attract people to the sparsely populated territory, making investments in human capital and education a priority. Texan schools and universities, and the promise of an education, was regarded as way to encourage migration to the territory and to develop the potential of existing residents. As part of the compromise that lead to Texas's accession to the United States in the mid-nineteenth century, the newly formed state (rather than the federal government) retained ownership of vast swathes of public land, the proceeds from which were subsequently earmarked to fund in-state education. The Texas State Constitution established two distinct SWFs—the Texas Permanent University Fund and the Texas Permanent School Fund (although the latter was simply a formalization of the existing Special School Fund)—through the appropriation of land grants (Texas State Constitution 1876).

While these lands initially yielded relatively small amounts of revenues from agricultural leases, the Texas oil boom at the beginning of the twentieth century changed the dynamic in a way that legislators could not have envisaged. The identification of significant hydrocarbon deposits on granted land initiated the allocation of billions of dollars over the course of the next century from land sales, oil and gas taxes, royalties, and rights to the Texas public school and university systems through their respective SWFs. Both Texan funds are typical permanent funds: SWFs that function as income and future generations savings funds, promoting statewide public education. They provide annual income to their owners (public schools and universities), based on returns generated on the financial portfolios, while ensuring that this can be maintained for future generations by protecting the fund's capital (or principal) from withdrawals and erosion through inflation.

The Texan example has been widely embraced by other state law makers and policymakers. The first state to follow the Texan model was New Mexico. As with the Texan permanent funds, the New Mexico Land Grant Permanent Fund has its origins in the inception of statehood and in the earmarking of the proceeds from the sale or lease of public lands for education. While the New Mexico Land Grant Permanent Fund was formally constituted only with the formation of statehood in 1912, its original seed capital in fact predates this, as funds held in trust that were granted by the federal government to the State of New Mexico under the Ferguson Act of 1898 and the New Mexico State Enabling Act of 1910 (New Mexico State Land Office 2015). While the fund is still widely referred to as the "New Mexico Land Grant Permanent Fund," it has also been enshrined as the "New Mexico Permanent School Fund" in the state constitution since 1958 (New Mexico State Constitution 1958). In addition to its investment management for this fund, the New Mexico State Investment Council also oversees the smaller Severance Tax Permanent Fund, a separate fund created by the New Mexico legislature in 1973 to save and invest severance tax revenues not being used that year to bond capital projects. These severance taxes originate from oil, gas, and other natural resources.

Being modeled on the permanent funds of neighboring Texas, the New Mexican permanent fund has similar objectives: to transform and preserve natural resource wealth in the form of financial assets, while also providing revenue for current and future generations. Educational institutions are the most significant beneficiaries of the fund's income (public schools own in excess of 80 percent of the fund's assets), while state hospitals, public buildings, state penitentiaries, and water resources have also received earmarked financial support from the fund's investment income (New Mexico State Investment Council 2015).

BORN FROM COMPROMISE: THE PERMANENT WYOMING MINERAL TRUST FUND

The second wave of North American SWFs emerged in the midst of the oil price boom of the mid-1970s, which saw the establishment of new funds in Alabama, Alaska, Montana, Wyoming, and the Canadian province of Alberta. The first among these was the Wyoming Permanent Mineral Trust Fund, established in 1975 following the passage of a constitutional amendment by the state legislature (Wyoming State Constitution 1975).

A striking—and insightful—feature of the legislative process around the creation of the Wyoming Permanent Mineral Trust Fund was that it required a moment of decisive leadership in the face of considerable political opposition. As oil and gas prices rose sharply and unexpectedly in the mid-1970s, the legislature attempted to introduce a large increase in the severance tax on mineral production in the state. An impasse between lawmakers and state governor Stanley Hathaway emerged in which Hathaway threatened to veto the bill raising the severance tax unless a permanent fund was established to manage resource revenue windfalls for the long term (Gorin 1991). The governor's apprehension was that legislators were looking to cash in on a temporary commodity production and price boom—a concern he sought to allay by directing a portion of that windfall to the long-term-oriented permanent fund.

Like the Texan and New Mexican funds, the Wyoming permanent fund is an income and future generations savings fund, based on an endowment model that provides annual revenue in the form of investment income, while ensuring that this can be maintained for future generations by protecting the fund's capital. The income from the Wyoming Permanent Mineral Trust Fund is, however, not earmarked for specific budgeted priorities, but rather flows into the state's General Fund (earmarking would require a constitutional amendment). The state does, however, also manage a number of smaller SWFs that are also capitalized through mineral royalties and earmarked for spending on education, notably the Common School Permanent Land Fund and the Excellence in Higher Education Endowment Fund (Wyoming State Treasurer's Office 2015).

FUNDING A DIVIDEND: THE ALASKA PERMANENT FUND

The largest North American SWF, the Alaska Permanent Fund, was established by an amendment to the state constitution in November 1976 (Alaska State Constitution 1976). The establishment of the fund was preceded by a public vote in which Alaskans voted strongly in favor of transferring a portion of resource revenues to the fund. The popularity of the proposal is widely attributed to negative public perceptions of the management of Alaska's first major oil revenue windfall from the sale of Prudhoe Bay for $900 million in 1969 (Groh and Erickson 1983). The legislation requires that a minimum of 25 percent of all mineral lease rentals, royalties, and federal mineral revenue sharing payments be transferred to the Alaska Permanent Fund.

While the Alaska Permanent Fund is, in the broadest sense, a classic income-cum-savings fund, like those of Texas, New Mexico, and Wyoming, its most famous and defining characteristic is the use of a portion of the fund's annual investment income to fund the "Alaskan Permanent Fund Dividend"—a direct transfer to every citizen of Alaska (subject to minimum age and residency requirements). This dividend is calculated based on 50 percent of the fund's earnings, based on a five-year moving average (Alaska State Constitution 1976). The remainder of the fund's earnings—but not its capital, which is constitutionally protected—may be appropriated through legislative action to the budget via the Earnings Reserve.

A CAUTIONARY TALE: THE ALBERTA HERITAGE SAVINGS TRUST FUND

The Alberta Heritage Savings Trust Fund was established in 1976 through a legislative act in response to rising oil revenues arising in the province. In the first two decades since its establishment, the Albertan fund had a distinctly different purpose from those of other resource-based SWFs in North America: it overtly and directly targeted investments within the province in order to "strengthen and diversify the economy, and improve Albertans' quality of life" (Province of Alberta 1976).

From the very start, the Alberta Heritage Savings Trust Fund suffered from two fatal flaws that greatly undermined its success until subsequent reforms were enacted: First, the investment selection criteria and institutional arrangements that governed in-province investments were poorly designed; second, the process through which oil revenues were transferred to the fund were nonbinding, quickly watered down, and ultimately dismantled when oil prices and revenues collapsed in the 1980s. These two design flaws have informed the policies and practices of various other North American funds, with lessons from Alberta often supporting the case for limiting the scope of political influence over local investments and ensuring that funds receive a greater share of revenues during boom periods.

With respect to the fiscal rules governing the flow of revenues in and out of the fund, compared with other North American resource-based SWFs, the Albertan fund has received only a small percentage of revenues, while the real value of its capital has historically been inadequately protected against a loss of purchasing power due to inflation. Warrack (2008) and Murphy and Clemens (2013) note that Alberta has historically lacked any formal requirement for depositing nonrenewable resource revenues into the fund—a sharp contrast with most American state permanent funds, where such transfers are required in the state constitutions rather than being a matter of executive discretion or annual legislative approval. According to Murphy and Clemens's calculations, "From 1977 to 2011, the Alberta Fund's cumulative net income (summing nominal yearly amounts over the period) was $31.3 billion. During the same period, the amount transferred out of the fund by the legislature was $29.6 billion—meaning virtually nothing was set aside for 'inflation-proofing' to keep the principal intact in real terms." Murphy and Clemens conclude, "Even with generous classifications, the government has deposited a mere 5.4 percent of resource revenues into the Fund during its history" (at least until the end of their sample period in 2011). The nonbinding nature of Alberta's funding rules is also evident from the decision to reduce resource revenue transfers to the fund from 30 percent to 15 percent in 1982, and then from 15 percent to zero in 1987.

While the original investment objectives of the fund were explicitly developmental, rather than purely commercial, this orientation (along with the inadequate fiscal rules) had the consequence of further draining the fund's capital. Various commentators have argued, more forcefully, that the domestic investments made by the fund suffered from deep-seated political biases, resulting in its investments amounting to inefficient subsidies. Murphy and Clemens (2013) argue that the fund's Canada Investment Division "engaged in questionable practices right from the start, granting loans to provincial governments at preferential rates," whereas Warrack (2008) notes that the Alberta Investment Division served as a "private placement banker for various provincial government-owned corporations, including Alberta Government Telephones. These loans totaled very large amounts, over half of Alberta Heritage Fund's total size . . . [and] insulated the fund and recipient Crown corporations from market forces and disciplines." Other critical accounts of the extent of political influence on the Alberta Heritage Savings Fund's investments, particularly its in-province investments, include Tupper and Gibbins (1992), Stevens (1993), Morton (2015), and Morton and McDonald (2015).

While the early history of the Albertan SWF is, therefore, widely regarded as an unhappy one, subsequent reforms have brought improvements. In 1996, the Alberta Heritage Savings Trust Fund Act was amended after a government survey revealed that the public wanted the fund to be used as a savings fund. This led to an amendment of the Alberta Heritage Savings Trust Fund Act, according to which the fund would no longer be used to make in-province investments, but rather to "provide prudent stewardship of the savings from Alberta's nonrenewable resources by providing the greatest financial returns on those savings for current and future generations of Albertans." Over time, management of the fund's assets has been moved to a highly professional, independent manager, the Alberta Investment Management Corporation.

More recently, the Fiscal Management Act of 2013 created the Contingency Account as a stabilization fund. The purpose of the Contingency Account is to provide budget financing in years where expenses exceed revenues. Once the Contingency Account reaches at least $5 billion, a set percentage of oil, gas, and mining revenues are distributed to the Alberta Heritage Savings Trust Fund and several other public investment funds targeted at scientific research and education. While these reforms are improvements on the frameworks that preceded them, a residual criticism of Albertan fiscal policies is the extent to which they remain largely discretionary rather than binding, with much of that discretionary power residing with the Alberta Treasury Board.

SMALLER-SCALE POOLED FUNDS: MONTANA, ALABAMA, AND LOUISIANA

A number of smaller funds were established in the late 1970s and 1980s in Montana, Alabama, and Louisiana. In Montana, the Coal Severance Tax Trust Fund (initially called the Coal Severance Tax Permanent Fund) was established in 1976, with the joint purpose of serving as a savings fund for future generations and as a local development fund. The fund receives 50 percent of coal severance tax collections, a rule that can be altered only by constitutional amendment. As of 2015, the Coal Severance Tax Trust Fund comprises five subtrusts, and capital contributions are distributed among the subtrusts at the discretion of the legislature. The principal of the fund is constitutionally protected and may be appropriated only with a two-thirds majority vote of each house of the legislature. Given the recent increase in state revenues from shale oil and gas development, it is notable that the fund does not receive oil and gas revenues, which are directly distributed among local governments, the state general fund, and various dedicated state accounts. While some portion of oil and gas revenues do flow into a variety of pooled investment funds under management of the Montana Board of Investments, the rules and procedures through which this happens are largely discretionary.

Alabama and Louisiana both have a number of state funds that are capitalized, at least to some degree, by the proceeds of natural resources. The Alabama Trust Fund was established in 1985 in response to offshore natural gas discoveries in 1978. The fund manages revenues from oil and gas royalty payments. The fund is under the jurisdiction of the

Treasury of the State of Alabama, which also manages a range of other state funds under a pooled investment program. Similarly, in Louisiana, the Louisiana Education Quality Trust Fund was created in 1986 to support primary, secondary, and higher education programs across the state. It, too, is managed as part of a pooled investment program by the state treasurer's office.

A RECENT ADDITION: THE NORTH DAKOTA LEGACY FUND

The first addition to the North American SWF landscape owing to the shale oil and gas revolution is the North Dakota Legacy Fund. The fund, modeled closely on the more established American permanent funds, was established in 2010 following a public vote for a constitutional amendment to provide that 30 percent of oil and gas gross production taxes and oil extraction taxes be transferred to the fund. The Legacy Fund's establishing documents explicitly note that the fund was created "due to the recognition that state revenue from the oil and gas industry will be derived over a finite time frame" and that revenues should be deferred "for the benefit of future generations" (North Dakota Legacy Fund 2011).

The fund has grown significantly since its inception, given the shale revenue windfall—its assets under management grew to just over $3.3 billion by November 2015. Earnings will be retained and added to its capital until 2017, when the fund's interest and income will start to be rolled into the state's general budget, as per the typical permanent fund model. Money from the principal will be able to be spent only if two-thirds of both houses of the state legislature approve (additionally, no more than 15 percent of the principal will be able to be spent in any two-year period).

INVESTMENT MANAGEMENT MODELS

While there is significant commonality in the fiscal rules and purposes of the North American SWFs, particularly the U.S. state funds, there is greater divergence between them with respect to the operational models for performing the investment management function. This section, and the summary provided in table 13.2, provide an overview of the most significant observations regarding the state of play among North America's SWFs in this important area of public investment management.

Table 13.2   Investment structures of the North American sovereign wealth funds

Fund	Investment authority	Investment objective
Texas Permanent School Fund	Texas Education Agency	The return objective is long term and focused on "fairly balancing the benefits between the current generation and future generations while preserving the real per capita value" of the fund.
Texas Permanent University Fund	The University of Texas Board of Regents (asset owner) contracts the University of Texas Investment Management Company (asset manager) to invest funds.	An average annual real return of 4.75 to 5.0 percent over a rolling ten-year period
New Mexico Land Grant Permanent Fund	New Mexico State Investment Council	Nominal return target of 7.5%, pursued through a diversified portfolio
New Mexico Severance Tax Permanent Fund	New Mexico State Investment Council	Nominal return target of 7.5%, pursued through a diversified portfolio
Permanent Wyoming Mineral Trust Fund	The Wyoming State Loan and Investment Board for investment policy, with responsibility for day-to-day operational management residing with the Wyoming State Treasurer	To produce maximized long-term investment income and capital gains while providing appropriate liquidity; the primary investment goals are capital appreciation, total return, and protection against inflation.
Alaska Permanent Fund	The Alaska Permanent Fund Corporation, a state-owned corporation dedicated to managing the fund's assets	Preserve the principal while maximizing total return with a view toward producing an average annual real rate of return of 5% over the long term
Alberta Heritage Savings Trust Fund	The Alberta Investment Management Corporation, a Crown corporation dedicated to managing the fund's assets (alongside other public and private provincial funds)	Target asset allocation is expected to earn an annual real return of 4.5 percent on average over a five-year period, after expenses.
Montana Coal Severance Tax Fund	Montana Board of Investments	Achieve a moderate yield advantage to the Barclays Capital Aggregate bond index

Table 13.2 *(continued)*

Fund	Investment authority	Investment objective
Alabama Heritage Trust Fund	Office of the State Treasurer (Alabama Trust Fund Board)	Long-term investment horizon, with short-term fluctuations considered "secondary to long-term investment results"
Louisiana Education Quality Trust Fund	Louisiana Treasury (Investment Department)	Equal weight on three objectives: income stability, capital growth, and capital preservation
North Dakota Legacy Fund	North Dakota State Investment Board	Current focus on capital preservation, with the expectation of gradual allocation to riskier asset classes

HEAVY USE OF EXTERNAL MANAGERS AND INVESTMENT CONSULTANTS

Investment management is a highly intermediated field, featuring a myriad of principal–agent relationships. It is not unusual to observe institutional investors, of which SWFs are a subset alongside pension funds, endowments, foundations, and insurance companies, make extensive use of external asset managers and professional investment consultants (Neal and Warren 2015). External asset managers are awarded fund management mandates for selected asset classes and strategies, whereas professional investment consultants typically provide highly standardized services in strategic asset allocation (i.e., portfolio construction based on modeled risk, return, and correlations between asset classes), external manager selection and monitoring, the purchase and maintenance of investment and risk management software, and a range of strategic and operational issues.

Many SWFs face challenges in attracting and retaining talent—most notably owing to the geographic remoteness of their head offices (typically located in small state capitals) and the limits of public sector compensation relative to that of the private sector. In such contexts, the heavy use of external managers and consultants is a practical necessity (see chapter 6 and Clark and Monk 2013). However, even when assessed within this peer group, it is striking that American SWFs have combined an exceptionally lean internal structure with an extensive use of both external managers and investment consultants. The implications of this operational model pertain to both cost and governance issues.

In terms of costs, while politics (and in some instances, geography) may impede the ability to attract and retain in-house talent—and compensate it accordingly—it is unclear whether the outsourced investment model is cost effective to the public sector and taxpayers. Fees paid to external managers can be extremely high, particularly when the investment mandates awarded to outside managers purport to offer "active" performance—that is, excess returns or "outperformance" over low-cost "passive" market benchmarks (see Malkiel 2013 for a recent overview of the extensive literature in this area). Prudent cost management of external management therefore requires a careful consideration of, first, the feasibility of building in-house expertise and competence versus the cost of fees paid to external managers, and, second, whether expensive active mandates with external asset managers are truly delivering their purported advantages and cannot be replaced with lower-cost passive alternatives.

The latter assumes greater urgency—as well as important governance implications—in light of another strong finding from the academic literature on finance: that the overwhelming share of the variation in investor returns is attributed to strategic asset allocation (as also discussed in chapters 4 and 14). A seminal contribution by Brinson, Hood, and Beebower (1986) found that more than 90 percent of the variation in investment performance is explained by strategic asset allocation. A clarification by Ibbotson and Kaplan (2000), using data from a large sample of U.S. mutual and pension funds, unpacked the evidence across three statistical dimensions: first, the variation in investment performance *within* a single fund over time (a time-series question), and second, the variation in investment performance *between* funds (a cross-sectional question). Ibbotson and Kaplan found that strategic asset allocation explained at least 40 percent of the variation between funds and a staggering 90 percent of the variation in performance within a fund over time.

The bottom line for any individual fund is that strategic asset allocation is incredibly important—it accounts for an overwhelming share of the success a fund will enjoy in generating investment returns, rather than whether it picks the "best" managers with the ability to outperform the market. Once they grasp this reality, the most important policy and governance question for SWFs becomes, Who determines the strategic asset allocation? An SWF's strategic asset allocation is its most important investment policy decision—and the authority over strategic asset allocation is, consequently, its most important governance question.

Two major observations can be made about North American SWFs, particularly the American permanent funds, with respect to their strategic asset allocation processes. First, North American SWFs (with the exception of the North Dakota fund, which is still in its inception) have highly diversified portfolios compared with other SWFs globally. North American SWFs, for example, have significant allocations beyond the conventional asset classes of public stocks and sovereign bonds into alternative asset classes, such as infrastructure, private equity, real estate, high-yield credit, and even hedge funds. They are not alone in this respect when compared with SWFs around the world (as also discussed in chapters 4 and 14), but these allocations place them among the more diversified and risk-oriented sovereign investors worldwide and expose them to higher fees (given the extent of external management) and potentially sharp losses (in exchange for expected higher average returns in the long run).

Second, as with their actual investment operations, North American SWFs tend to transfer a rather considerable amount of authority over strategic asset allocation to external entities in the form of professional investment consultants. Again, this is not a unique position—the use of consultants to advise on strategic asset allocation is widespread among institutional investors. However, North American SWFs, particularly those without dedicated independent management agencies, tend to make heavy use of consultants. Given the central importance of strategic asset allocation to long-run investment performance, this should be an area for medium- to long-term governance reform: the goals should be to raise the level of expertise and competence of the state investment structure so that they ultimately can take greater ownership of strategic asset allocation decisions.

While the use of external asset managers and investment consultants is widespread among North American SWFs, dedicated independent managers can reduce this reliance on external parties, as they have—at least in theory—the ability to assign dedicated resources to the development of internal investment management capacity. The North American landscape, however, features only a small number of cases where SWFs are managed by such authorities. In the next section, I consider the main differences between the dedicated, independent manager model and the more widespread practice of retaining the investment authority within the state treasury.

DEDICATED, INDEPENDENT INVESTMENT AUTHORITIES

Most of the world's established SWFs are managed by dedicated, independent investment authorities: The Abu Dhabi Investment Authority,

Norges Bank Investment Management, the Kuwait Investment Authority, the Qatar Investment Authority, and the Government of Singapore Investment Corporation are prominent examples. The logic behind the establishment of such arm's length authorities rests on both profound and purely pragmatic grounds. Most fundamentally, independent authorities are part of an institutional apparatus that helps ensure that investment decisions are not influenced by political interventions. Political factors help determine broad investment objectives, mandates, and risk tolerance—but investment authorities insulate the day-to-day investment process from damaging political influence and transfer it to an authority with technocratic expertise in capital markets and investment management. More pragmatic motivations include the ability to (i) award higher compensation to employees once the investment authority has been (at least partially) severed from the public sector; (ii) develop in-house investment expertise; and (iii) ultimately build a local investment authority with a proven track record and competence in order to attract external funds and assets (managed at a fee) and therefore achieve economies of scale.

The use of dedicated independent investment authorities is rather limited in the management of SWFs in the United States and Canada. The three most established examples are the Alaska Permanent Fund Corporation (APFC), the University of Texas Investment Management Corporation (UTIMCO), and the Alberta Investment Management Corporation (AIMCo) (see chapter 11). All three entities have well-developed governance structures, with a clear delineation between the board and the executive and their respective areas of authority and responsibility.

Certainly, the building of a dedicated, independent investment authority can be a costly exercise (note, too, that despite having a dedicated investment authority in place, the majority of the Alaska Permanent Fund's assets are managed by external managers). In all three cases, the comparatively large size of assets under management is clearly a key motivating factor: The Alaska Permanent Fund, at roughly $52 billion in assets under management (as of December 2015), is the largest SWF in North America, whereas in the cases of AIMCo and UTIMCO, the investment authority oversees the management of several other public sector funds, boosting the total size of assets under management for these organizations to around $55 billion (CDN$75 billion) for AIMCo (as of December 2015) and $35 billion for UTIMCO (as of November 2015).

STATE INVESTMENT BOARDS OR STATE INVESTMENT COUNCILS

A far more prevalent model is to retain investment management authority within a branch of the state treasury, typically through structures such as a state investment board or state investment council. This is the model for all American permanent funds (with the exception of the Alaska Permanent Fund and the Texas Permanent University Fund). The model has the advantage of considerable simplicity: The state treasury typically has an existing investment infrastructure in place to manage the state's cash flows, alongside existing debt and surplus assets (often including public sector pension and benefit schemes). Adding the management administration and investment oversight of a new permanent fund to such entities' list of responsibilities may therefore be a pragmatic—if potentially temporary—step.

State investment boards and councils are typically staffed by a small team of competent and credible technocrats with a track record of prudent management of state assets. Given the diversified asset allocation of most permanent funds, state investment boards and councils typically do not make the actual investments themselves, outside of the occasional passive cash and fixed income portfolios, but rather make use of the aforementioned external managers and consultants. Often, the relatively small size of the permanent funds, the ability to achieve economies of scale in operations (as a result of pooling with other state funds), and a path-dependent adherence to the status quo mean that permanent funds remain under this management structure for many years (as they have done in Alabama, Louisiana, Montana, New Mexico, and Wyoming).

At first glance, this arrangement is somewhat at odds with the received—and otherwise very sensible—wisdom on the governance of SWFs; namely, that their investment operations should be removed, as far possible, from executive office holders. However, in the case of most U.S. states, there are a number of mitigating factors influencing the choice of retaining management oversight of permanent funds within the state treasury (and thus under the nominal control of state treasurers):

- First and foremost, the placement of these funds with state treasuries has not come at the expense of transparency; rather, given American standards and expectations of accountable government, state investment boards and councils report frequently and extensively on their activities, investment performance, and internal decision making. Transparency helps offset potential concerns over undue political interference.

- Second, state investment boards and councils are typically staffed with officials who enjoy a high degree of public credibility, and their appointment generally requires broad-based legislative approval (although of course there are no guarantees that this tradition will be adhered to at all times).
- Third, while the extensive use of external asset managers and professional investment consultants has the downside of costs (fees to external fund managers) and governance (undermining true ownership of asset allocation decisions), it does protect against bad decisions and abuse, as these external companies are reputation-sensitive and bound by federal regulatory requirements to act in the best interest of their clients.
- Finally, rule-based investment is the overwhelming norm among North American funds, limiting the scope of executive discretion and undue interference.

In short, the placement of the investment responsibility of permanent funds within the state treasury is a credible, if imperfect, second-best solution. It has certain governance and cost drawbacks, but at the same time has the benefit of simplicity and insuring against undesired outcomes. However, some of the larger and more established U.S. state permanent funds are approaching a size and level of maturity where consideration should be given to the establishment of dedicated investment authorities to deepen their governance arrangement, so they can truly "own" long-term asset allocation choices and economize on costs.

LESSONS AND POLICY IMPLICATIONS

North American SWFs are well managed and well governed. With the exception of Alberta in the 1970s and 1980s, they have effectively accumulated assets in periods of booming resource revenues and reduced wasteful spending of revenue windfalls—something that few other countries and jurisdictions can claim. Today, a number of American states have healthy financial endowments that provide invaluable income, often for very important spending needs, that is funded by—but ultimately diversified from and uncorrelated with—resource revenues. North American SWFs are also competently and transparently run with respect to their investment policies and practices, while being insulated from overt and damaging political pressure on investment operations. There are some important differences, as outlined in this chapter, but in general the governance and operational models of North American SWFs work well and are worthy of emulation by incipient funds, including those under consideration by other North American states and provinces.

Despite this broadly positive assessment, a number of possible improvements and reforms can be identified, which should be seen in the light of the growing maturity and shifting economic realities of the North American SWFs.

RECOMMENDATION 1: EMBRACE MORE DYNAMIC, COUNTERCYCLICAL FISCAL RULES

The fiscal rules governing North American state permanent funds have the advantage of being institutionally robust and simple: Typically, a fixed percentage of saving from resource revenues is constitutionally mandated, whereas spending is based on real earnings. These rules serve the purpose of saving a share of windfalls in boom periods and providing stable income to the budget—which, as the early experience of Alberta and many other resource-rich countries shows, is no mean feat. Existing fiscal rules are, therefore, perhaps somewhat crude and mechanistic, but at least promote a base level of saving, fiscal prudence, and capital accumulation.

However, many permanent funds have reached a level of maturity where serious consideration should now be given to more cyclically adjusted, dynamic rules; that is, rules that promote higher savings in boom times and potentially higher (yet sustainable) draws on buffer or stabilization funds (which may or may not be part of the actual permanent fund). Another way of framing this idea—which is pertinent to a number of countries with SWFs worldwide—is to argue that the fiscal rules surrounding these funds should be better integrated with the medium-term budget process. Particularly with the growing prospect of a sustained period of lower commodity prices and revenues, many U.S. states are likely to feel fiscal pressures over the coming decade. A key objective of fiscal reforms should be to find a way for permanent funds and associated buffer funds to support spending and public investment in a way that is sustainable and avoids the depletion of previously accumulated savings.

RECOMMENDATION 2: PLACE GREATER
EMPHASIS ON STABILIZATION FUNDS

The North American SWF landscape is dominated by permanent funds, which operate as both income and future generations savings funds. Compared to other resource-dependent jurisdictions, much less emphasis is placed on an important second variant of SWFs; namely, buffer or stabilization funds, whose purpose is not to save assets and provide investment income over a long horizons, but rather to absorb positive shocks to revenue and support the budget in the event of unanticipated shortfalls. Such stabilization funds are critical to the successful implementation of countercyclical fiscal policy.

Most resource-rich states have the basic infrastructure and fiscal apparatus to achieve this reform. American state treasuries typically hold fiscal balances in the form of "budget reserves," "earnings reserves," and associated budget accounts (whereas, in Alberta, the Fiscal Management Act of 2013 created the Contingency Account as a stabilization fund). However, meaningful reforms of the role of these funds would focus on three areas: first, raising the profile of stabilization funds in the fiscal process; second, making the policies that govern the flow of revenues in and out of these stabilization funds more transparent and rule based; and, third, growing the size of assets held in these reserve accounts relative to the level of annual spending in the budget, so that they can provide a more meaningful degree of fiscal stability in volatile commodity-based economies.

Reforms in the role and operation of stabilization funds will be conducted as part the establishment of a more dynamic framework, as discussed earlier. A sound countercyclical, dynamic fiscal rule will bind spending, revenue forecasts, and the use of both stabilization and permanent fund assets and income in one unifying medium-term fiscal framework (see chapter 2 and Alsweilem et al. 2015).

RECOMMENDATION 3: GREATER OWNERSHIP OF CRITICAL
INVESTMENT DECISIONS

As stated earlier, for many state permanent funds, the heavy use of external managers is a pragmatic solution to relative skill shortages and public sector salary limitations. However, many funds also largely outsource a more important and fundamental area of investment; namely, strategic asset allocation. Academic research and past experience incontrovertibly demonstrate that it is strategic asset allocation—rather than short-term "tactical" decisions, market "timing," or security and manager selection—that drives long-term portfolio returns.

Permanent funds' reliance on established investment consultants to guide strategic asset allocation becomes less problematic if accompanied by greater ownership of these critical decisions by the entities charged with managing these funds—whether it be an independent management authority or investment council or board housed within state treasuries. In particular, this ownership needs to evolve around a deep analysis of how strategic asset allocation matches liabilities, fund-specific investment beliefs, and risk tolerance, as well as greater accountability and informed public and political consultation and engagement. In short, the current tendency to hand off responsibility to investment consultants risks "off-the-shelf" solutions that pay insufficient attention to the characteristics of specific funds, as well as "buck-passing" when things go wrong (even temporarily).

RECOMMENDATION 4: PRESSURE ON FEES FOR OUTSOURCED INVESTMENT SERVICES

North American SWFs would be well advised to join institutional investors worldwide in asking tougher questions about the value external managers are really adding and the level of fees they charge for their services (French 2008; Malkiel 2013). For many institutional investors—including leading SWFs—the realization that asset management fees are unduly high has resulted in two major trends: first, a much wider use of more cost-effective passive allocations (e.g., "tracker funds" and basic "enhanced index" strategies) where applicable, and second, over a more long-term horizon, efforts to build larger internal management teams and investment infrastructure (most obviously through a dedicated independent investment authority).

The former requires, at a minimum, the previously mentioned reforms in terms of greater ownership of asset allocation, as fund managers will lose the ability to pass blame for bad outcomes onto external asset managers. "Insourcing" asset management capacity most likely also requires lifting compensation constraints in order to attract and retain talent, and potentially very significant investments in trading and risk management infrastructure and information technology (IT). Many North American SWFs are now approaching a scale of assets under management where such investments are increasingly easy to justify. One way to galvanize public and political support for internal investments, and the costs associated with enabling them, is to make greater disclosures regarding the magnitude of fees paid to external managers, which for most permanent funds amounts to several hundred thousands of dollars annually. Another idea that U.S. state treasuries should actively explore is the possibility of pooling assets and investments together—or to co-invest between state permanent funds—as a way to achieve economies of scale and develop cost-effective in-house investment expertise.

CONCLUSION

In this chapter, I have addressed the relative paucity of comparative analysis of North American SWFs. While neither the United States nor Canada possesses a large national SWF to rival those of various European, Middle Eastern, and Asian nations, they are home to a significant number of subnational resource-based funds at the state or provincial level. Some of these funds are among the oldest and most established SWFs in the world, and the number and size of funds in North America has grown since the 1970s oil boom and, more recently, during the shale oil and gas and Canadian tar sands developments.

The chapter revealed the dominance of one particular model, pioneered more than a century and half ago in Texas: the permanent fund model. Under this model, funds operate as both an income and future generations savings fund: first, they generate annual revenue based on the inflation-adjusted returns generated on the financial portfolio, while, second, ensuring that this income-generating capacity is maintained for future generations by protecting the fund's capital from withdrawals and erosion through inflation. Alberta's failed experiment with establishing a local development and infrastructure fund in the 1970s and 1980s stands out as an exception to this model—and its apparent failure has informed other jurisdictions' decisions to place considerably less weight on such objectives (as well as motivating subsequent reforms to Alberta's own fund).

The North American SWF model has been a success. These funds have effectively accumulated assets in periods of booming resource revenues and reduced wasteful spending of revenue windfalls—something that few other countries and jurisdictions can claim. Today, a number of American states have healthy financial endowments that provide invaluable income—often for very important spending needs—and that are funded by, but ultimately diversified from and uncorrelated with, resource revenues. North American SWFs are also transparently run with respect to their investment practices, strategies, and performance. Finally, in large part, North American SWFs are well insulated from overt and damaging political pressure, particularly in the area of investment operations. There are some important differences, as discussed in this chapter, but, in general, the governance and operational models of North American SWFs work well and are worthy of emulation by incipient funds, including those under consideration by other states and provinces.

The preceding section did, however, identify important areas for reform—two of which pertain to the fiscal framework surrounding North American SWFs and another two of which pertain to their investment functions. With respect to the former, I argue it is high time for North American SWFs to develop a more dynamic, countercyclical fiscal rule, in which revenues are not simply mechanistically deposited into permanent funds, but rather allows for higher savings in boom periods and larger withdrawals—preferably via a buffer or stabilization fund—during leaner times. In general, more attention needs to be paid to the role and rule-based policies of stabilization funds, as the North American SWF landscape is essentially dominated by one type of fund: the permanent fund.

With respect to investment management operations and policies, I have suggested that the level of maturity now achieved by a number of North American SWFs requires their managers to take greater ownership of critical investment choices—notably, strategic asset allocation decisions, which are by far the most important determinants of long-term investment performance. Finally, while North American SWFs are likely to continue relying heavily on external asset managers, given the constraints they face with respect to geography and compensation of internal staff, they should join the international trend among institutional investors in asking tougher questions about the level of fees they are paying in relation to the value added by their managers. Practically, this may result in larger, low-fee passive investment strategies and, more gradually, efforts to reduce the barriers to building in-house investment expertise.

REFERENCES

Alaska State Constitution. 1976. http://w3.legis.state.ak.us/docs/pdf/citizens_guide.pdf.

Alsweilem, K., A. Cummine, M. Rietveld, and K. Tweedie. 2015. "Institutions and Policies for Managing Sovereign Wealth," Paper Series, April. Cambridge, MA: Belfer Center for Science and International Affairs, John F. Kennedy School of Government, Harvard University.

Boettner, T., J. Kriesky, R. McIlmoil, and E. Paulhus. 2012. "Creating an Economic Diversification Trust Fund: Turning Nonrenewable Natural Resources Into Sustainable Wealth for West Virginia." Charleston, WV: West Virginia Center on Budget & Policy.

Brinson, G., L. Hood, and G. Beebower. 1986. "Determinants of Portfolio Performance," *Financial Analysts Journal* 42, no. 4: 39–48.

Cauchon, D. 2012. "States Eye Trusts for New Oil, Gas Revenue," *USA Today*, November 19.

Clark, G., and A. Monk. 2013. "The Scope of Financial Institutions: In-sourcing, Outsourcing and Off-shoring," *Journal of Economic Geography* 13, no. 2: 279–298.

French, K. 2008. "Presidential Address: The Cost of Active Investing," *Journal of Finance* 63, no. 4: 1537–1573.

Gorin, S. 1991. "Wyoming's Wealth for Wyoming's People: Ernest Wilkerson and the Severance Tax, A Study in Wyoming Political History," *Annals of Wyoming* 63, no. 1.

Groh, C., and G. Erickson. 1983. "The Permanent Fund Dividend Program: Alaska's Noble Experiment," *Alaska Journal* (Summer).

Ibbotson, R., and P. Kaplan. 2000. "Does Asset Allocation Policy Explain 40, 90, or 100 Percent of Performance?" *Financial Analysts Journal* 56, no. 1: 26–33.

Malkiel, B. 2013. "Asset Management Fees and the Growth of Finance," *Journal of Economic Perspectives* 27, no. 2: 97–108.

McKinnon, P. 2013. "A Futures Fund for Saskatchewan," Report to Premier Brad Wall on the Saskatchewan Heritage Initiative. www.gov.sk.ca/adx/aspx/adxGetMedia .aspx?mediaId=2db41e74-30f1-4397-bf4f-fa051bc6182e&PN=Shared.

Morton, T. 2015. "Time to Politician-Proof the Heritage Fund," *The Globe and Mail*, January 8.

Morton, T., and M. McDonald. 2015. "The Siren Song of Economic Diversification: Alberta's Legacy of Loss," SPP Research Paper No. 8–13. Calgary, AB: School of Public Policy, University of Calgary.

Murphy, R., and J. Clemens. 2013. "Reforming Alberta's Heritage Fund: Lessons from Alaska and Norway." Vancouver, BC: Fraser Institute.

Neal, D., and G. Warren. 2015. "Long-Term Investing as an Agency Problem," Working Paper No. 063/2015. Sydney, Australia: Centre for International Finance and Regulation, University of Sydney.

New Mexico State Constitution. 1958. www.sos.state.nm.us/Public_Records_And _Publications/2013nmconst.pdf.

New Mexico State Investment Council. 2015. "SIC Beneficiaries," www.sic.state .nm.us/sic-beneficiaries.

New Mexico State Land Office. 2015. "Trust Beneficiaries," www.nmstatelands.org /trust-beneficiaries.aspx.

North Dakota Legacy Fund. 2011. "Investment Policy Statement," www.legis.nd.gov /assembly/62-2011/docs/pdf/lbso81111appendixh.pdf

Petsko, E. 2014. "Marcellus Legacy Fund a Lesser-known Funding Source," *Observer-Reporter*, January 11.

Poelzer, G. 2015. "What Crisis? Global Lessons from Norway for Managing Energy-Based Economies." Ottawa, ON: Macdonald-Laurier Institute.

Province of Alberta, 1976. *Alberta Heritage Savings Trust Fund Act.* www.qp.alberta.ca /documents/Acts/A23.pdf.

Stevens, D. 1993. *Corporate Autonomy and Institutional Control: The Crown Corporation as a Problem in Organization Design.* Montreal, QC: McGill-Queen's University Press.

Texas State Constitution. 1876. www.constitution.legis.state.tx.us/.

Tupper, A., and R. Gibbins. 1992. *Government and Politics in Alberta.* Edmonton, AB: University of Alberta Press.

Warrack, A. 2008. "Whither a Heritage Fund Public Dividend Policy?" In "Wealth Management Sovereign and Permanent Funds Around the World," Trustees' Papers Vol. No. 8. Juneau, AK: Alaska Permanent Fund Corporation.

Wilson, S., J. Penner, and A. Demyen. 2012. "A Call for a New Saskatchewan Heritage Fund?" Discussion Ppaper No. #109., Regina, SKCanada: Department of Economics, University of Regina.

Wyoming State Constitution. 1975. http://legisweb.state.wy.us/statutes/constitution .aspx.

Wyoming State Treasurer's Office. 2015. "State of Wyoming's Investment Portfolios: An Overview of Strategies." https://treasurer.state.wy.us/pdf/investmentstrate-gies1214.pdf.

CHAPTER 14

Sovereign Venture Funds

AN EMERGING FRONTIER IN SOVEREIGN WEALTH FUND MANAGEMENT

Javier Santiso

IE Business School

The nature and the policy implications of state capitalism are the core of the ongoing discussions on governments' role in economic development and growth. In recent years, sovereign wealth funds (SWFs) have gained prominence in the transformation from traditional thinking about government support of the economy to a new mindset, characterized by a greater appreciation of the catalytic role state investors can play in promoting economic development based on innovation and technology. As a number of contributors to this volume have discussed, a number of SWFs have started allocating increasing shares of their portfolios to domestic investments, while also demonstrating an increased appetite for alternative assets classes, notably private equity, and more direct and disintermediated forms of investment, including co-investments with other sovereign funds and long-term institutional investors. In this context, this chapter considers a somewhat underreported element of this trend; namely, the growing involvement of SWFs in innovation and technology sector investments. While the sums of capital involved remain small compared to SWFs' often massive portfolios, and while the phenomenon is arguably still largely limited to a small number of large and established funds, I suggest that we are now witnessing the emergence of new type of SWF, which I refer to as a sovereign venture fund.

EMERGING MARKETS AS EMERGING INNOVATION LEADERS

Before discussing the ways in which SWFs are increasingly becoming an instrument of state capitalism and government-led investment in innovation and technology, it is useful to consider the shift that has occurred more generally in recent decades: the rise of the emerging markets as technological powers and the general role governments have played in catalyzing this development. Until recently, innovation (particularly corporate innovation) was largely a Western story. Gradually, another model has started to emerge in which innovation is still conceived in the West but produced in emerging markets. Just in the last few years, however, a third model has started to emerge in which innovation is not just produced and sold from the emerging markets, but increasingly also conceived and exported from there.

In the economic geography of international trade, emerging markets are no longer exclusively low-cost, low-technology destinations. A number of well-known examples serve to underline the magnitude of the shift. In 1963, for example, South Korea exported goods, mainly agricultural and fishery products, at a value equivalent to roughly $600 million at current prices. In 2015, it exported more than $600 billion worth of goods, mainly electronics, machinery, chemical products, and shipping technology. One of the world's most research and development (R&D)-intensive companies, Samsung, is Korean. It consists of more than eighty companies and employs over 380,000 people around the world (Santiso 2015). The world's biggest supplier in the telecommunications industry is no longer an American, French or Swedish company, but a Chinese one: Huawei. In 2013, Huawei surpassed Apple, selling more smartphones and generating more profit than the California-based company (Cohan 2013). Although Silicon Valley is still the world's innovation and technology leader, China has taken the position of the world's second biggest venture capital hub. In Israel, there are more startups per capita than in any other country in the world, earning itself the title of "Startup Nation" (Senor and Singer 2009).

The Internet has traditionally been dominated by American multinationals. However, China's Tencent now has a market capitalization of $45 billion, putting it ahead of eBay and Yahoo. The Singaporean telecommunications operator, Singtel, is accelerating its acquisition of technology startups worldwide. This phenomenon is not confined to Asia. Russia's DST Group and South Africa's Naspers are prime non-Asian examples of emerging technology behemoths that derive revenues not only from their growing home and regional markets, but increasingly from other emerging markets worldwide.

SOVEREIGN WEALTH FUNDS AS AN
INSTRUMENT OF STATE CAPITALISM

State involvement in innovation is not new. Economic history provides many examples of the state kickstarting growth: Japan and South Korea in the 1950s, Germany in the 1870s, and the United States after the Revolutionary War. This is also true for the development of technology in past decades. Many of the innovations that are now familiar to us, such as the Internet, cloud computing, and augmented reality, were incubated by governments seeding capital or driven by government agencies. Silicon Valley was born largely with the aid of the American government, as explained by Lerner (2009), who also points out that the state—and particularly its military—was key to the rise of the Israeli "Startup Nation" through its famous Yozma program.

Similar to Lerner, Mazzucato (2013) highlights the state's historically huge role in boosting innovation in the Unites States, with particularly prominent roles in the "green revolution," biotechnology, pharmaceutical development, and "smart" mobile technology. For many SWFs, the initial foray into sectors that require and thrive on significant investments and transformative innovation and technology came through the telecommunications and media sectors. Consequently, many of the leading SWFs still have significant holdings in local telecommunications operators, contributing to the total investments in telecommunications and technology: for Malaysia's Khazanah, these sectors account for 26 percent of the portfolio; for Singapore's Temasek, they account for 23 percent; for the China Investment Corporation, they account for 16 percent; and for the United Arab Emirates' Mubadala, they account for 8 percent of the portfolio (based on data from the funds' annual reports). Historically, Temasek has been the great driver of Singtel, the Singapore operator, as Khazanah has been for Axiata, Malaysia's operator. Both Temasek and Kazkanah have driven their respective pushes to internationalize.

In response to this growing involvement in the venture, innovation, and technology sectors, SWFs have adapted their teams, processes, and investment committees to meet the challenges of a world where speed and informality, as well as private and illiquid deals, dominate. For instance, Singapore's Temasek created an entirely new team devoted exclusively to these types of investments, employing a speedier and more flexible decision-making process, adapted to the nature of venture and growth capital firms. (On changing governance structures and investment management adjustments, see chapter 4 and Al-Hassan et al. 2013).

According to Musacchio and Lazzarini (2015), a new form of state capitalism implies state-owned investors acquiring small noncontrolling stakes in strategic companies, sufficient for transferring knowledge. This model is being followed by SWFs and is referred to as the "ownership stake model." According to this model, SWF investments should include sufficient stakes to ensure a transfer of knowledge between the private recipient and the state-owned investor and to facilitate the state's soft control over strategic private companies through regulations and access to public financing.

Some scholars argue that the venture capital space offers an ideal long-term investment opportunity for SWFs, which by their nature are not stuck in short-term arbitrages or in need of liquidity (Bachher et al. 2014). Dyck and Morse (2011) suggest that investing in venture capital correlates with the objectives of the type of SWFs commonly labeled as "sovereign development funds," which look to maximize risk-adjusted returns through assembling diversified holdings and use investments to influence the domestic development path (as also described in chapter 6). They found that the ownership model is aligned with developmental agendas, particularly in finance, transportation, energy, and telecommunications.

SOVEREIGN WEALTH FUNDS 3.0:
THE EMERGENCE OF SOVEREIGN VENTURE FUNDS

The trend of state-backed funds entering the realm of technology and innovation investments challenges the view conventionally held in Silicon Valley that technology and innovation are instruments of the private sector. Instead, current developments reflect a more balanced approach, with private and public sectors both being instrumental in the rise of the Palo Alto, Tel Aviv, and Singapore technological and innovative ecosystems. The interest that SWFs have in the innovation and technology space is an expression of a dual strategy: economic development (or social returns) and pure financial returns. Seen in this historic light, the current trend does not necessarily signify a shift in the state's involvement in innovation as such, but in the investment instruments it uses. This is particularly manifested in SWF investment in venture capital. Many countries have already created or are creating what are being called "sovereign venture funds." Figure 14.1 gives an indication of the growth in SWF investments in the media, telecommunications, and new technologies sectors over the past six years. Singapore clearly dominates, but the geographical diversity of the funds is on the rise.

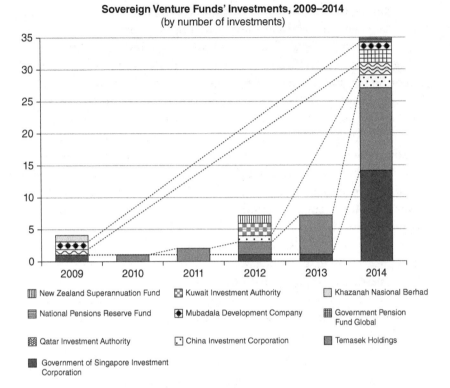

Sovereign Venture Funds' Investments, 2009–2014
(by number of investments)

Figure 14.1   Sovereign wealth fund investments in telecommunications, media, and new technologies, 2009 to 2014.

Source: Santiso 2015.

While sovereign venture funds assess deals based on standard financial criteria, they are also often pursued in order to meet strategic objectives: adding innovation value to their own portfolio of large traditional companies and also to their home countries. For example, when Singapore's Temasek invested in the financial technological company Markit ahead of its listing in London, it was first and foremost a financial bet, in pursuit of pure financial returns. But, simultaneously, the investment in a financial technology (FinTech) startup supports the developmental ambition of Singapore of becoming one of the world's leading financial centers.

These funds, which may be standalone entities or more likely part of a broader SWF portfolio, embrace different models in executing their venture investments. Some sovereign venture funds invest directly in startups, whereas others invest in private venture capital funds, which in turn invest in startups. Finally, investments by sovereign venture funds now include "unicorns"—startup software-based companies, such as Uber and Spotify, that have reached valuations in excess of $1 billion in record time. China has provided some of the most striking examples of this trend. In 2015, it announced the creation of a $6.5 billion government venture capital fund. At the same time, the ascent of the unicorns in China is fuelling the innovation and technology ecosystem, with the founders of these startups in turn investing in more technological companies, feeding a virtuous cycle. Regarding the trend to invest in startups, Singapore has taken the lead. Singapore's two SWFs, the Government of Singapore Investment Corporation and Temasek Holdings, have invested a total of $3.3 billion in startups between 2013 and 2015. Temasek is not just one of the biggest sovereign venture funds; it is also one of the most active investors and a leading market maker. In 2014, it invested relatively small amounts in China's second biggest e-commerce company, JD.com ($17.2 million) and another $12.8 million in Chinese cyber-security firm Cheetah Mobile. In April 2015, Temasek paid $48.1 million to acquire SVB India Finance, an Indian company that provides venture debt to startups. It also took part in a $250 million round together with venture capital funds such as General Atlantic, Index Ventures, and Felicis Ventures. In 2014, the Government of Singapore Investment Corporation took part in a $200 million round in Square, a payment FinTech startup. In the same year, it also invested in iParadigms, an American startup in the educational sector, as well as Lynx, a Brazilian company, and Flipkart of India.

Sovereign wealth funds from the Middle East are increasingly joining the trend of allocating to venture capital. In 2015, the Abu Dhabi Investment Council participated in an investment round of more than $400 million raised by Swedish musical streaming startup Spotify, catapulting its valuation to $8.4 billion. In 2014, this fund also invested in the American startup Coupons. Mubadala, another Emirati SWF, has holdings in the American startups Damballa (cyber security), AMD (semiconductor manufacturing), and Prodea Systems (digital services). Qatar Holding, a subsidiary of Qatar Investment Authority has invested in California-based startup Uber, the mobile-sharing economy app for urban transport. Qatar Holding also invested in Blackberry in November 2013 ($200 million) and in the French Internet company Vente-privée in December 2014 (for an undisclosed amount). Together with the venture capital fund New Enterprise Associates, it took part in a total round of $1.2 billion at the end of 2014, which values Uber at more than $41 billion. As previously mentioned, China is also highly active in the field of startup investment. The China Investment Corporation is a major seed funder for Alibaba, with an investment of more than €2 billion for a 5.6 percent equity stake in the startup. Table 14.1 summarizes the main investments of the sovereign venture funds in startups.

While much of the activity described is being led by SWFs from emerging markets, mirroring the broader geographic shift in innovation and technology investment discussed at the beginning of the chapter, there are also major SWFs from advanced economies active in this area. In 2014, New Zealand's SWF, the New Zealand Superannuation Fund, made a $60 million investment in the renewable energy startup LanzaTech, in which Khosla Ventures, the California-based fund, Siemens' venture capital investment arm, and the Malaysian Life Sciences Capital Fund have also invested. Also in 2014, the provincial government of Ontario and the federal government of Canada teamed up with a number of Canadian sovereign investors (notably the Canada Pension Plan Investment Board) and private banks and investors to create a $300 million venture capital fund, the Northleaf Venture Catalyst Fund.

What do we know about the emerging preferences of SWFs with respect to the myriad of investment models in innovation and technology? First, a study examining investments by large institutional investors between 1991 and 2011 found that when institutions invested in venture capital transactions alone, the returns tended to lag behind the fund benchmark (Fang, Ivashina, and Lerner 2013). Will development returns sufficiently compensate for poor investment returns? It remains to be seen whether this pattern past will change. Until now, while SWFs have been continuing to develop the appropriate skillset, their strategy has often been to invest jointly with venture capital funds that they themselves have financed.

Second, recent years have seen the growth of new alliances between SWFs co-investing in venture capital. In 2013, the Abu Dhabi Investment Authority, the Alberta Investment Management Corporation, and the New Zealand Superannuation Fund created the Innovation Alliance. The Alliance will provide expansion capital to startups presented both by venture capital funds in which they hold stakes and by others. The Irish and Chinese governments have joined forces to create a $100 million joint sovereign venture capital fund to invest in Irish and Chinese startups. Switzerland has created the Sino-Swiss Venture Capital Fund, also with China.

Table 14.1 Leading investments by sovereign wealth funds in startups

Sovereign wealth fund	Company	Country	Year of investment	Size of investment (millions)	Equity
Abu Dhabi Investment Authority (UAE)	Spotify	Sweden	2015	N/A	N/A
Abu Dhabi Investment Corporation (UAE)	Coupons	United States	2014	N/A	N/A
Alaska Permanent Fund (U.S.)	Juno	United States	2013	$120	N/A
China Investment Corporation (China)	Alibaba	China	2012	$2,000	5.6%
Korean Investment Corporation (South Korea)	Tesla Motors	United States	2013	N/A	N/A
Kuwait Investment Authority (via subsidiary Impulse) (Kuwait)	Tyba	Spain	2014	$3.1[a]	N/A
Khazanah Nasional Berhad (Malaysia)	Alibaba	China	2013	$400	0.6%
Government of Singapore Investment Corporation (Singapore)	Netshoes	Brazil	2014	$170[a]	N/A
Government of Singapore Investment Corporation (Singapore)	Cheetah Mobile	China	2014	N/A	13%[a]
Government of Singapore Investment Corporation (Singapore)	iParadigms	United States	2014	$752[a]	N/A
Government of Singapore Investment Corporation (Singapore)	Lynx	Brazil	2014	N/A	N/A
Government of Singapore Investment Corporation (Singapore)	FlipKart	India	2014	$1,000[a]	N/A
Government of Singapore Investment Corporation (Singapore)	KKBOX	Taiwan	2014	$100[a]	N/A
Government of Singapore Investment Corporation (Singapore)	Square	United States	2014	$200[a]	N/A
Government of Singapore Investment Corporation (Singapore)	Xiaomi	China	2014	$1,000[a]	N/A
Mubadalla (UAE)	Prodea Systems	United States	2010	N/A	5.0%
Mubadalla (UAE)	Damballa	United States	2011	N/A	5.4%
Qatar Holding (Qatar)	Vente-privée	France	2014	N/A	N/A
Qatar Holding (Qatar)	Uber	United States	2014	$1,200[a]	N/A

(continued)

Table 14.1 (continued)

Sovereign wealth fund	Company	Country	Year of investment	Size of investment (millions)	Equity
Temasek Holdings (Singapore)	Alibaba	China	2012	$37 million	1.03%[b]
Temasek Holdings (Singapore)	Evonik	Germany	2013	€600	4.5%
Temasek Holdings (Singapore)	Markit	United Kingdom	2013	$500	10%
Temasek Holdings (Singapore)	Cloudery	China	2013	$110[a]	N/A
Temasek Holdings (Singapore)	Celtrion	South Korea	2013	N/A	10.5%
Temasek Holdings (Singapore)	Eros	India	2013	N/A	7.38%
Temasek Holdings (Singapore)	Tutor Group	China	2014	$100[a]	N/A
Temasek Holdings (Singapore)	Vancl	China	2014	$100[a]	N/A
Temasek Holdings (Singapore)	Yatra.com	India	2014	$23[a]	N/A
Temasek Holdings (Singapore)	GrabTaxi	Southeast Asia	2014	$10	N/A
Temasek Holdings (Singapore)	Virgin Mobile	Latin America	2014	$86[a]	N/A
Temasek Holdings (Singapore)	Snapdeal	India	2014	$100[a]	N/A
Temasek Holdings (Singapore)	Didi Dache	China	2014	$700[a]	N/A
Temasek Holdings (Singapore)	Lazada	Germany	2014	$250[a]	N/A
Temasek Holdings (Singapore)	Adyen	The Netherlands	2014	$250[a]	N/A
Temasek Holdings (Singapore)	Funding Circle	United Kingdom	2015	$150[a]	N/A
Temasek Holdings (Singapore)	17zuoye	China	2015	$100[a]	N/A
Temasek Holdings (Singapore)	SVB India Finance	India	2015	$47	100%

Abbreviations: N/A, not available; UAE, United Arab Emirates.

[a] Investment round with other participants.

[b] Equity as of November 2014.

Source: Santiso 2015.

Third, there is a tendency toward establishing small, dedicated offices in locations that place SWFs at the geographic coalface of venture investment. A clear example of this is Malaysia's Khazanah's decision to open an international office in San Francisco in 2013, which at the time was an unprecedented move for an SWF. This move was soon followed by similar initiatives; for example, Samruk Innovation, a subsidiary of Kazakhstan's Samruk-Kazyna, in Silicon Valley. In effect, "these funds are expanding geographically, moving their organizations into the markets they find appealing, rather than waiting for intermediaries to come to them, reflecting a broader trend towards the professionalization of pension and sovereign fund investment organizations" (Al-Kharusi, Dixon, and Monk 2014).

From the preceding discussion, three future trends may be anticipated. The first is the continuation of the investment boom by sovereign investors in venture capital (directly and through funds), startup ecosystems, and even startup accelerators. The second is that the startups, particularly those backed by sovereign venture funds from emerging markets, will continue to make their presence felt outside of the United States in Europe, Asia, and Latin America. The third trend involves a number of potential changes in sovereign venture funds' investment strategies and operational models, such as the following:

- Greater collaborative enterprises at the state level for investing in startups or venture capital funds, with emerging markets continuing to lead the initiatives, significantly strengthening domestic and regional venture capital ecosystems.
- More direct investments in venture capital, made by dedicated and highly skilled in-house teams.
- The wider use of investment platforms, a compromise between total insourcing and total outsourcing: combining the investor and capital strengths of the SWFs with the operational strength of the industrials. An example is CEPSA (Compañía Española de Petróleo S.A.), acquired by the International Petroleum Investment Company of Abu Dhabi, which now uses the Spanish operator for rolling out international investments. Long-term sovereign investors are reintermediating, allying themselves with industrial operators who contribute the know-how and capacity to scale up and support the operations.
- A larger number of SWFs entering the initial financing rounds around private-market deals (A-, B-, and C-series), allowing them access to

higher risk–return exposure than their traditional D-, E-, and F-series involvement (i.e., late-stage capital raising preceding a possible exit through an initial public offering or acquisition). Temasek is a good example of an SWF increasingly entering earlier investment rounds (mostly through B-series investments), but more will follow.

POLICY IMPLICATIONS AND RISKS FOR SOVEREIGN VENTURE FUNDS

There are two defining features of the emerging sovereign venture fund phenomenon, both with clear implications and risks for governments in general and sovereign investors more specifically. First, sovereign venture funds are sovereign players—they are public institutions with a commitment to fulfill public needs. The citizenry of a given country is ultimately the owner of the resources managed by its sovereign venture funds, typically being the proceeds from tax, national savings, or natural resource revenues. Therefore, sovereign venture funds are expected to behave transparently, to a greater or lesser degree, depending on how democratically its government functions, and demonstrate at least some form of contextually determined accountability.

The second feature of sovereign venture funds is that, despite their varied investment models and background, they remain investment funds. As investment funds, they distinguish themselves from regular trading corporations engaged in daily operations selling equities and bonds. They can take the form of a holding company, owning a portfolio of companies (e.g., Temasek, Khazanah, and Mubadala), and may operate in various legal settings (as a unit of a central bank, ministry of finance, or independent institution), but ultimately they have a similar structure to an investment firm. The common objective of SWFs, of which sovereign venture funds are a nascent subgrouping, is to look for long-term risk-adjusted returns.

How do these two features map into a set of policy implications? Venture capital is a very particularly risky asset class: nearly 80 percent of investments made by venture capitalists fail, while investors hope that the 20 percent successes will, over time, compensate for the failure. Legitimate concerns can be raised about the appropriateness of public funds entering this risky arena; for example, is it prudent to expose the capital of a general capital-scarce emerging market to this degree of loss probability?

On the other hand, SWFs do have characteristics that should, under the right circumstances, enable them to take some exposure to venture capital. Given the illiquid nature of startups, owing to their need for capital over a long period of time (average venture capital–backed startups take four to seven years from the dates of its first funding round and initial public offering), investors must be able to wait for long periods to access returns. Sovereign wealth funds, as long-term investors by nature, fit this profile—whereas most other institutional investors do not. Being in this minority position, SWFs should at least consider attempting to capture illiquidity, duration, and volatility premiums—which are all factors driving returns in venture capital, innovation, and technology.

The challenge is to integrate the traditional long-term strategies followed by SWFs with a new set of investment strategies relevant to venture capital. Paradoxically, investing in startups is a way to hedge against secular trends and sectors. Banks, airlines, and telecommunications companies are traditional sectors that have yielded stable returns to institutional investors, including SWFs. However, they have recently been under attack by startups disrupting the status quo. Thus, when sovereign venture funds invest in startups, it may not be only for return purposes, but also to hedge their own risks and portfolios relying heavily on these three traditional sectors. By not investing in startups, SWFs can actually increase risk to their portfolios, given the often intergenerational length of their investment horizons. It is interesting to note that many SWF investments in startups and venture are exactly in the same sectors where they tend to already hold significant traditional investments (e.g., telecommunications, retail, financial services, hospitality, entertainment) that are most at risk from disruption.

Investing in startups requires an exceptionally high degree of investment expertise and insights into underlying sectors. Venture capital is not only an illiquid and volatile asset class, but is also very demanding in terms of investment processes and skills (which is why fees for third-party services tend to be among the highest in the financial sector, as also discussed in chapter 4 and 13). Venture capital also tends to require rather speedy operations and investment decisions. An A-series decision typically takes less than five weeks, whereas the decision process for SWFs can take five months (or perhaps even five years!). The challenge is to change the investment processes and operational culture—if not of the whole institution, then more prudently of the unit (or subfunds) dedicated to venture financing, innovation, and technology.

Temasek is the most advanced in the field, and its processes for venture capital investment are particularly insightful. It currently invests mainly in the late-stage financing rounds, thereby reducing illiquidity and other risks, but, as mentioned, it is moving toward B- and even A-series funding. Further, Temasek's investment process for the asset class is streamlined relative to that its larger investments in other asset classes: Deals above $1 billion require board approval, whereas deals below that threshold are managed in Temasek's investment committee at the level of the managing directors. Investment committee meetings regarding venture investments are held twice monthly, in line with the world of startups. Despite this already advanced process, Temasek is considering the establishment of a "fast-track mode" so it can tap into A- and B-series funding.

A more general concern is how well equipped SWFs are to invest in such complex assets from a human resources perspective. As noted, in order to address this concern, many SWFs are hiring in expertise and investment teams, building in-house capacities. This trend indicates a move toward the required sophistication required—however, it does require greater flexibility around compensation schemes than those that typically apply to public sector institutions (and that are often extended to SWFs) and the ability to compensate top talent and expertise more generously (as also discussed in chapters 4 and 13).

Finally, it is important to note that in spite of the surge in activity, the world of sovereign venture funds is still relatively small: the money that SWFs engage in this asset class is marginal relative to the size of their overall assets—a rough estimate is that it accounts for less than 1 percent of their capital globally (Santiso 2015). A constraint for SWFs is the size of their overall portfolios. They suffer from the "liability of size," or the need to find enough suitable, risk-adjusted investment opportunities into which to deploy capital. Consider this example: an SWF looking to allocate, say, $5 billion to venture investments, would need to make around 1,000 transactions to deploy that capital, if industry-standard average ticket sizes of $5 million for A- and B-series funding applied. Even going on much larger stakes of $50 million (e.g., in later-stage funding) would imply closing 100 transactions for a $5 billion allocation. The implication is that it is very hard to "scale up" these types of investments in a major way.

REFERENCES

Al-Hassan, A., M. G. Papaioannou, M. Skancke, and C. C. Sung. 2013. "Sovereign Wealth Funds: Aspects of Governance Structures and Investment Management," IMF Working Paper 13/231. Washington, DC: International Monetary Fund.

Al-Kharusi, Q. A., A. D. Dixon, and A. H. B. Monk. 2014. "Getting Closer to the Action: Why Pension and Sovereign Funds are Expanding Geographically," Global Projects Center Working Paper. Stanford, CA: Stanford University.

Bachher, J. S., G. L. Clark, A. H. B. Monk, and K. Sridhar. 2014. "'The Valley of Opportunity' Rethinking Venture Capital for Long-Term Institutional Investors," Global Projects Center Working Paper. Stanford, CA: Stanford University.

Cohan, P. 2013. "Samsung Beats Apple in U.S. Smartphone Market, For Now." *Forbes,* June 6. www.forbes.com/sites/petercohan/2013/06/06/samsung-beats-apple-in-u-s-smartphone-market-for-now/#2715e4857a0b53d4277f5c09.

Dyck, A., and A. Morse. 2011. "Sovereign Wealth Fund Portfolios," Chicago Booth Research Paper No. 11–15. Chicago: Booth School of Business, University of Chicago.

Fang, L., V. Ivashina, and J. Lerner. 2013. "The Disintermediation of Financial Markets: Direct Investing in Private Equity," *Journal of Financial Economics* 116, no. 1: 160–178.

———. 2009. *Boulevard of Broken Dreams: Why Public Efforts to Boost Entrepreneurship and Venture Capital Have Failed—and What to Do About It.* Princeton, NJ: Princeton University Press.

Mazzucato, M. 2013. *The Entrepreneurial State: Debunking Public vs Private Sector Myths.* London: Anthem.

Musacchio, A., and S. Lazzarini. 2015. *Reinventing State Capitalism.* Cambridge, MA: Harvard University Press.

———. 2015. *España 3.0: Necesitamos resetear el país.* Barcelona: Planeta.

Senor, D., and S. Singer. 2009. *Start-up Nation: The Story of Israel's Economic Miracle.* New York: Hachette.

CHAPTER 15

Conclusion

Malan Rietveld and Perrine Toledano

Columbia Center on Sustainable Investment

Sovereign wealth funds (SWFs) have grown immensely in both number and size over the past decade and a half. The decade preceding the dramatic collapse in global oil prices in the fourth quarter of 2014 was a golden era for SWFs, whose growth was buoyed by a combination of rising global commodity prices, new resource discoveries, and swelling trade surpluses in many large emerging markets, coupled with many years of exceptional financial market returns. Particularly in resource-rich economies, there has been a growing (and sometimes uncritical) acceptance that SWFs are part of the "best-practice" toolkit for managing large, finite, and volatile revenue windfalls.

Judged in the context of some of the lowest points in the commodity cycle seen in decades and the low-to-no-growth economic environment that has followed from ultra-loose monetary and fiscal policies in the wake of the global financial crisis, the outlook for the coming decade of SWFs appears less promising. Lower investment expectations and economic dynamism in SWFs' traditional investment destinations, the prospect of a multiyear slump in commodities, and, not least, growing evidence of political and economic pressure on the management and asset base of SWFs to help fund fiscal shortfalls in the wake of the global financial crisis are the defining features of the new frontier of sovereign investment. The emerging challenges pertain to a number of dimensions, including macroeconomic policies, investment operations, investment strategies, and the internal and external governance of SWFs.

Yet, at the same time, the new frontier offers significant opportunities to sovereign investors. While the core of the global financial system remains, at least for the time being, in a stability-focused mindset, the continued geographic expansion of finance and market-based economies is creating historic opportunities for innovative, catalytic investors of the kind that an increasing number of SWFs aspire to be. At a more strategic level, a number of SWFs are part of a growing trend toward direct investing by asset owners that increasingly involve partnership platforms and co-investments by groups of sovereign investors.

THE RISE OF SOVEREIGN DEVELOPMENT FUNDS

As noted in the introduction to this volume, one development that has caused a considerable degree of confusion around the definitional boundaries of SWFs is the emergence of public investment institutions with a mandate to invest in the domestic economy, in pursuit of both commercial and noncommercial objectives. Are these institutions still SWFs? Or should they be regarded as completely distinct institutions, analyzed in an entirely different manner? In recent years, the literature has increasingly embraced the idea of "sovereign development funds" as distinct from the traditional SWF model. However, the distinctions are often blurred in practice, as the responsibilities for the management of domestic assets, portfolios, and funds are co-mingled with those of established SWFs with a more traditional emphasis on foreign investment.

How might we understand the trend toward a more developmental agenda for sovereign investors, characterized most apparently by the rise of sovereign development funds? A number of observers view the shifting role and mandates of SWFs as part of the current resurfacing of age-old debates around "state capitalism." Proponents of state capitalism argue that free-market reforms in the post-war era have led to regulatory failures and decline in economic dynamism in the West, while having at best a mixed record in terms of enabling economic growth in developing countries and emerging-market economies. It is further argued that the "guiding hand of the state" played a major role in the economic emergence of the advanced economies, historically and specifically in the aftermath of the Second World War, and particularly in a series of "growth miracles" since the 1960s, notably in Asia (Bremmer 2010; Ferguson 2012; Musacchio and Lazzarini 2014).

Cast against this background, many view sovereign funds—particularly those of a sovereign development variety—as instruments of state capitalism. As such, they form part of the government apparatus that advocates large-scale public investment programs; interventionist forms of industrial policy; state-led efforts to catalyze economic development, targeted growth sectors, and diversification; and seeks to cultivate an "innovation ecosystem" through state-sponsored investments in venture capital and technology (Lyons 2007; Santiso 2008; Schwartz 2012). Sovereign development funds are a departure from the earlier conception of SWFs, which placed a greater emphasis on "prudence-first" principles.

It should be noted that, despite the rising clout of sovereign development funds, the overwhelming share of SWF assets are still managed according to prudence-first principles: providing economic and fiscal stability in the face of resource volatility, transforming a share of finite revenues from a depleting asset into a permanent financial endowment, and saving unmanageably large and often anticipated revenue windfalls. For the majority of SWFs, the execution of such mandates involves investment policies and strategies that remain fairly conservative and simple to execute: Stabilization funds place surplus assets in highly liquid assets, with low risk of default and volatility, whereas savings and investment income funds typically have varying degree of portfolio diversification but ultimately largely mimic the investment strategies of other long-term institutional investors.

This is not to say that the more traditional SWFs do not also face considerable challenges in the current economic and financial environment. For resource-rich countries, the dominance of the more traditional, prudence-first model continues to reflect a desire to avoid the pitfalls of previous commodities booms, during which revenue windfalls were largely consumed without any consideration for future generations (Bauer, Rietveld, and Toledano 2014).

OTHER EXPLANATIONS FOR THE RISE OF SOVEREIGN DEVELOPMENT FUNDS

There are a number of complementary developments, alongside a perceived rebirth of enthusiasm for state capitalism, that explain the rise of sovereign development funds. As chapter 7, by Gratcheva and Anasashvili, underlines, the sovereign development fund landscape is in fact varied and has developed according to different countries' trajectories and strategies. There is significant variation, for example, in the sectors and assets these funds target: physical infrastructure, power generation, hospitality, real estate, technology, financial services, and so forth. Moreover, there are considerable differences with respect to the financial and nonfinancial criteria underlying investment decisions (implicitly or explicitly) and the extent to which these investments are executed directly or through intermediated third parties. A number of chapters in this volume help clarify these distinctions.

Some of this variation is explained by the fact that the embrace of the sovereign development model is arising in countries at opposite ends of the spectrum in terms of the track record, size, and internal expertise of their SWFs. At one end of the spectrum are the world's largest and most established SWFs—Singapore's Government Investment Corporation and Temasek, the China Investment Corporation, the United Arab Emirates' Mubadala and Malaysia's Khazanah. The majority of these funds are at the vanguard of efforts to devote state resources to strategic bets in the adventurous world of high-end investments in innovation, technology, and venture capital. As the chapters by Dixon and Monk (chapter 6), Ohrenstein and White (chapter 4), and Santiso (chapter 14) argue, many of these funds have historically eschewed these investments owing to the high cost of third-party investments in these asset classes, the high levels of risk and complexity, the demand they place on internal investment capacity (particularly if conducted directly), and the satisfactory returns on traditional, listed asset classes.

In the aftermath of the global financial crisis, a number of these funds have made more significant forays into these more adventurous areas (although it bears repeating that for most it remains at very small levels of their overall portfolios). The reasons for this development include expectations of lower returns on traditional SWF assets and a sense of rising opportunities for direct investments by patient SWFs as banks and other end investors have increased their risk aversion. Certainly, for most of these funds, the long-term strategic interest in these asset classes aligns with the ambition to disintermediate much of the investment process in order to make economies on the cost of these investments and influence the strategic direction of investee companies. Readers should be left with little doubt that this form of sovereign investment is not for the faint hearted: it is being pursued by SWFs with a track record of investment expertise and political support for developing world-class specialist internal investment teams (and the potentially significant costs associated with building that internal expertise and infrastructure).

At the other end of the spectrum are sovereign development funds from essentially poor countries with low levels of current and historic public investment and infrastructure. These include funds like the Nigeria Infrastructure Fund, managed by the Nigeria Sovereign Investment Authority, which have been granted a mandate to direct capital to areas that would be more commonly associated with public investment through the budget. However, given some of the political obstacles to long-term capital investment through the budget process, these sovereign development funds have emerged as pragmatic, "second-best" solutions. However, as Andrew Bauer notes in chapter 5, this could risk simply transferring problems of political patronage, wasteful investment, and a lack of accountability from the budget to the sovereign development fund. If the sovereign development funds' investments "are not subject to the same reporting or public procurement requirements as those financed out of the normal budget process," he warns, they may be used "to avoid public scrutiny, facilitating billions of dollars in wasteful spending." Relatedly, the International Monetary Fund and the World Bank have warned that the failure to coordinate the investments of the sovereign development fund with more traditional channels for public investments risks inefficiency owing to coordination failures, duplication, and the absence of complementarities.

Clearly, a considerable amount of research needs to be conducted—and practical experienced gained—in order for the sovereign development fund model, particularly as applied in the context of infrastructure-poor developing countries, to codify a set of working principles and practices. A number of chapters in this volume directly address these issues: In chapter 8, Gelb, Tordo, and Halland focus on the articulation of investment criteria for these funds; in chapter 6, Dixon and Monk discuss the matching of broad developmental mandates to the fund's expertise and track record; and in chapter 7, Gratcheva and Anasashvili's survey provides a comparative perspective on the critical policy, governance, and operational issues surrounding sovereign development funds.

CHALLENGES FACING MORE TRADITIONAL SOVEREIGN WEALTH FUNDS

The growing interest in and size of sovereign development funds should not distract from the fact that the more traditional SWF model—focused on purely commercial investments in pursuit of macroeconomic stability, saving, and income generation—remains a much bigger part of the story. While the traditional model remains popular, there are a number of reasons to suspect that the coming decade will be more challenging than the past one. Lower commodity prices and smaller trade surpluses from export-orientated Asian economies have been significantly subduing the underlying drivers of SWF asset growth since the turn of the century. In some of the worst-case scenarios, SWFs might not just see their asset growth stall—but even decline, if fund assets are not sufficiently ring-fenced, thus exposing them to asset grabs to close fiscal holes. Moreover, a number of stabilization funds that were designed to provide exactly this kind of budgetary support in tough times could find themselves depleted faster than anticipated, given the magnitude of emerging fiscal pressures.

On the investment side, traditional SWFs—particularly savings and investment income funds with long-term horizons—face the challenge of diversifying into new asset classes, as a consequence of the anticipated decline in returns and economic dynamism in traditional investment destinations and their own increasing maturity and sophistication. In this context, some of the world's most established and sophisticated sovereign investment authorities, which manage the likes of the New Zealand Superannuation Fund and the Alberta Heritage Savings Trust Fund, stand out and are increasingly emerging as leaders in investment excellence and responsible investment—setting the global standard for private and public investors alike on issues ranging from "insourcing" investment expertise, risk factor–based asset allocation, investments in alternative asset classes, co-investments, and sustainability (incorporating environmental, social, and governance [ESG] criteria).

THE EMERGING FRONTIER OF SOVEREIGN INVESTMENT

This volume features contributors from a multitude of disciplines and brings together complementary perspectives from the four groups of stakeholders—academia, the international financial institutions, the private sector, and government and SWF practitioners—on the continued evolution of SWFs in the face of new opportunities and challenges. This new frontier of sovereign investment requires reforms and changes across of a number of dimensions, including macroeconomic policies, investment strategies and operations, and internal and external forms of governance. While details and circumstance differ greatly from country to country and fund to fund, the contributors to this volume suggest that the most pressing issues confronting SWFs as a whole over the coming decade can be summarized as follows:

- **Macroeconomic policies:** Particularly for countries and subnational jurisdictions with resource-based SWFs, there will be an urgent need in the coming decade—most obviously if commodities remain subdued for a number of years (as they have done on a number of occasions in the past)—to improve and clarify the fiscal rules. Many funds have either ad hoc, informal rules or crude and procyclical savings rules, coupled with poorly designed policies for withdrawing SWF assets. Improved fiscal rules for SWFs will ensure that fund assets intended to be held for future generations are not depleted and/or provide adequate and sustainable support to their owners' compromised fiscal positions.
- **Investment strategies and policy:** Most critically, a number of SWFs need to take greater ownership of the most important determinant of long-term investment performance: strategic asset allocation. While this is less an issue for the most advanced SWFs, younger and less sophisticated funds tend to exhibit an overreliance on external consultants who sometimes provide "solutions" to asset allocation that are not sufficiently tailored to the specific needs of individual SWFs. Almost all SWFs, regardless of their starting positions, face the challenge of gradually increasing exposures to new asset classes to enhance portfolio diversification and increase expected returns (commensurate with the fund's expertise and risk tolerance).
- **Investment operations:** Many SWFs have acknowledged the urgent need to tighten up on inadequate risk assessment and management processes, which has become apparent during periods of financial stress in recent years. A more medium- to long-term strategic priority for many SWFs is developing in-house investment expertise and capabilities and reassessing the magnitude of fees paid to external fund managers. Managing a large share of the portfolio internally will reinforce the need for operational improvements—particularly if, as expected, SWFs move toward a more direct model of investing.
- **Internal governance:** As SWFs become more ingrained and accepted, a number of funds need to clarify the distinct roles and responsibilities of the board versus management. More specifically, there is a need to retool the governance and decision-making processes if and when funds pursue more direct (disintermediated) investment strategies—quite simply, direct investment models raise the bar considerably in terms of internal governance processes (in addition to requiring a differentiated approach compared with more intermediated investment models).

- **External governance:** There is widespread recognition of the need to continue improving transparency and external accountability. Sovereign wealth funds have come a long way in this respect over the past decade, as evidenced by improving scores almost across the board in third-party assessments and by the SWF community's historic establishment of the Santiago Principles. That said, progress along these lines should continue, as should pressure to increase compliance with the Santiago Principles. More generally, as increasingly significant and mature asset owners and capital allocators, SWFs need to keep enhancing their communication and dialogue with the public, regulators, and politicians and engage more constructively with investees, particularly on increasingly accepted expectations around sustainability and ESG issues.

The academic and policy literature has not fully captured and analyzed the significant differences in objectives, governance structures, investment strategies, and operational practices of SWFs, tending rather to treat these funds as a more or less homogeneous group. Yet, these differences are important to legislators and policymakers operating in diverse social, political, and economic contexts. This book casts new light on the range of governance, investment, and operational models available in establishing and reforming SWFs—presenting a much more nuanced and context-sensitive perspective on what is ultimately a highly differentiated group of investors. Both new and established SWFs are confronting a daunting set of challenges.

REFERENCES

Bauer, A., M. Rietveld, and P. Toledano. 2014. "Managing the Public Trust: How to Make Natural Resource Funds Work for Citizens," edited by A. Bauer. New York: Columbia Center on Sustainable Investment and Natural Resource Governance Institute. http://ccsi.columbia.edu/files/2014/09/NRF_Complete_Report_EN.pdf.

Bremmer, I. 2010. *The End of the Free Market: Who Wins the War Between States and Corporations?* London: Penguin.

Ferguson, N. 2012. "We're All State Capitalists Now," *Foreign Policy*, February 9.

Lyons, G. 2007. "State Capitalism: The Rise of Sovereign Wealth Funds," *Journal of Management Research* 7, no. 3: 119–146.

Musacchio, A., and G. Lazzarini. 2014. *Reinventing State Capitalism: Leviathan in Business, Brazil and Beyond.* Cambridge, MA: Harvard University Press.

Santiso, J. 2008. "Sovereign Development Funds: Key Financial Actors of the Shifting Wealth of Nations," OECD Emerging Markets Network Working Paper. Paris: Organisation for Economic Co-operation and Development.

Schwartz, H. 2012. "Political Capitalism and the Rise of Sovereign Wealth Funds," *Globalizations* 9, no. 4: 517–530.

Nikoloz Anasashvili is an analyst in the Financial Advisory & Banking team at the World Bank Treasury. Nikoloz provides research and analysis for the World Bank Treasury senior management on infrastructure finance, reserves management, and sovereign wealth fund investments. Prior to joining the World Bank in 2014, Nikoloz worked on the implementation and monitoring of United States Agency for International Development (USAID) projects at the University Research Company and Deloitte. He holds a B.A. in political science from the University of Chicago and an M.P.P. in public policy, international trade, and finance from the Harvard Kennedy School of Government, where he wrote his thesis on sovereign wealth fund investments in emerging market infrastructure.

Andrew Bauer is senior economic analyst at the Natural Resource Governance Institute (NRGI). At NRGI, he advises government officials and parliamentarians on macroeconomic management, natural resource revenue sharing, and public financial management and accountability. Andrew has advised on sovereign wealth fund governance in Canada, Ghana, Indonesia, Libya, Mexico, Mongolia, Myanmar, Timor-Leste, and Uganda, among others. Prior to joining NRGI, he served on the government of Canada's G8 and G20 teams as an international economist at the Department of Finance. He has also worked for several governmental, private sector, academic and nonprofit organizations. He holds a B.A. in economics and international development studies from McGill University and an M.Sc. in economics for development from the University of Oxford.

Corinne Deléchat is the deputy division chief in the African and Western Hemisphere Departments of the International Monetary Fund (IMF). She has covered natural resources management and sovereign wealth fund design in a number of countries, including Burkina Faso, Liberia, Panama, and Venezuela. Prior to joining the IMF, she coordinated bilateral assistance to a group of low-income countries at the Swiss Ministry of Economy and has also worked as an economist at the Organisation for Economic Co-operation and Development (OECD). Her research interests and publications focus on development, natural resource management, and banking. Corinne holds an M.A. and Ph.D. in economics from Georgetown University and a Masters in international economics from the Graduate Institute of International Studies in Geneva.

Adam D. Dixon is Reader in Economic Geography at the University of Bristol. He is also a research affiliate at Stanford University's Global Projects Center, the European Centre for Corporate Engagement at Maastricht University in the Netherlands, and IE Business School's Sovereign Investment Lab. He has served as a consultant for the OECD Development Centre on its work related to natural resource–based development. He holds a B.A. in international affairs from George Washington University, a Masters in finance from the Institut d'études politiques de Paris, and a Ph.D. in economic geography from the University of Oxford.

Alan Gelb is a senior fellow at the Center for Global Development in Washington, D.C. He was previously with the World Bank in a number of positions, including director of development policy and chief economist for the Africa region. His research areas include the management of resource-rich economies, African economic development, results-based financing, and the use of digital identification technology for development. He has written a number of books and papers for scholarly journals. He earned a B.Sc. in applied mathematics from the University of Natal and a B.Phil. and Ph.D. in economics from the University of Oxford.

Ekaterina Gratcheva is Lead Financial Officer at the World Bank Treasury's Reserve Asset Management Program (RAMP). Since joining the World Bank Treasury in 1998, she has held various positions in the organization, including in Investment Management, Quantitative Strategy Risk and Analytics, Banking and Debt Management, and Financial Advisory and Banking. Prior to assuming client management responsibilities in 2008, Ekaterina's primary responsibility was the development of investment policy and strategic asset allocation for the World Bank Group's own assets and for other clients' portfolios. She has led client engagements with sovereign wealth funds, ministries of finance, central banks, and other public financial and development institutions in numerous countries, including Azerbaijan, Egypt, Indonesia, Kazakhstan, Libya, Mozambique, the Pacific Island States, Panama, Poland, Romania, Russia, South Africa, South Korea, Tanzania, Turkey, Ukraine, among other countries. She holds a Master's of Public Administration from the Harvard Kennedy School, a D.Sc. from George Washington University, and an M.Sc. from Moscow State University.

Håvard Halland is a senior economist in the Investment Funds Group at the World Bank's Finance and Markets Global Practice. His research and advisory work focus on sovereign wealth funds and strategic investment funds. In particular, his work has focused on fund mandates, governance frameworks, and the economic and policy implications of SWFs' domestic investment. He is the author of several academic and policy research papers and book chapters and regularly presents at international conferences and seminars. He earned a Ph.D. in economics from the University of Cambridge.

Ashby H. B. Monk is executive director of the Global Projects Center at Stanford University. He is also a senior research associate at the University of Oxford and a senior adviser to the chief investment officer of the University of California. He was named by *aiCIO* magazine as one of the most influential academics in the institutional investing world. He has been an advisory and consultant to several sovereign wealth funds and has played a leading role in the establishment of various partnership and co-investment platforms for sovereign funds and other institutional investors globally. He holds a B.A. in economics from Princeton University, a Masters in international economics from the Université de Paris 1 Panthéon Sorbonne, and a Ph.D. in economic geography from the University of Oxford.

Robert Ohrenstein has over twenty years' experience advising direct investors on transactions. He currently leads KPMG's Global Private Equity practice, which delivers a full range of services to the firm's private equity clients and their portfolio companies. These range from merger-and-acquisition deal origination, buy- and sell-side deal execution, and a broad range of strategic and operational consulting services to enable fast and effective creation and realization of value within portfolio companies. Robert is KPMG's lead partner for a number of larger global clients and is also responsible for overseeing KPMG teams working with their investee companies. He has worked on numerous complex global and cross-border transactions on both the buy and sell side across a variety of industries. In addition to his private equity clients, Robert also works for other direct investment clients, particularly sovereign wealth funds, large pension funds, and family offices. Robert is a graduate of the London School of Economics and holds an M.B.A. from Warwick Business School. He trained and was made a partner at Arthur Andersen before joining Deloitte and subsequently KPMG in 2004.

Stella Ojekwe-Onyejeli is chief risk officer and executive director at the Nigeria Sovereign Investment Authority (NSIA). She joined the NSIA after serving as director and head of Operational Risk & Control at Barclays, covering emerging markets and Africa. She also served as vice-president and head of quality assurance for Africa at Citibank, with direct oversight of the enterprise risk and control environment of fourteen countries across Africa. She had a decade-long career at professional services firms Arthur Andersen and KPMG in Nigeria and South Africa, providing financial advisory and business assurance services. Stella was a Federal Government of Nigeria Scholar and an Institute of Chartered Accountants of Nigeria Prize winner. She is also a qualified chartered financial and tax accountant. Stella holds a first degree in chemistry from the University of Lagos and an M.B.A. from Cranfield School of Management.

Uche Orji is managing director and chief executive officer of the Nigeria Sovereign Investment Authority. He joined the NSIA as CEO in October 2012 from Switzerland's largest bank, UBS Securities, where he was managing director of the New York branch of its Equities Division. Prior to his UBS experience, he spent six years at JPMorgan in London, including as vice-president and managing director within the bank's Equities Division. Prior to JPMorgan, he worked for Goldman Sachs Asset Management in London. His first banking financial industry experiences were with Diamond Bank and Arthur Andersen in Nigeria. Uche studied chemical engineering at the University of Port Harcourt and obtained an M.B.A. from Harvard Business School.

Adrian Orr is chief executive officer of the Guardians of the New Zealand Superannuation Fund. Adrian joined the Guardians in February 2007 from the Reserve

Bank of New Zealand, where he was deputy governor. Adrian has also held the positions of chief economist at Westpac Banking Corporation, chief manager of the Economics Department of the Reserve Bank of New Zealand, and chief economist at the National Bank of New Zealand. He has also worked at the New Zealand Treasury and the OECD, based in Paris. Adrian is chair of the International Forum of Sovereign Wealth Funds, board member of the Pacific Pension Institute, and a member of the Expert Advisory Group for the World Bank's Treasury. He is also a board member of the Emory Center for Alternative Investments at Emory University.

Arunma Oteh joined the World Bank as vice-president and treasurer in 2015. She manages a team responsible for managing more than $150 billion in assets and borrowing in more than twenty currencies. Before joining the World Bank, she served as director general of the Securities and Exchange Commission of Nigeria. She was a member of the board of the International Organization of Securities Commissions (IOSCO) and Chairperson of the Africa Middle East Regional Committee of IOSCO. Prior to joining SEC Nigeria, Arunma was group vice-president, from 2006 to 2009, and group treasurer, from 2001 to 2006, at the African Development Bank Group. She holds a B.Sc. in computer science from the University of Nigeria and an M.B.A. from Harvard Business School. In 2011, in recognition of her contribution to economic development and to transforming the Nigerian capital markets, Arunma was awarded the Officer of the Order of the Niger national honor.

Sanjay Peters is an associate research scholar at the Committee for Global Thought at Columbia University and associate professor of economics at the Department of International Economics and Management at Copenhagen Business School. He has also worked as an economic adviser to the British foreign office and as a consultant to the World Bank and the United Nations Development Programme. Sanjay serves on the editorial board of several scholarly journals and as an economic adviser to a number of multinational companies and governments. He was previously an associate professor of economics at IESE Business School and ESADE Business School. His current research focuses on sovereign wealth funds and long-term investment in infrastructure and development in Africa and other transition economies. He received an M.Phil. and Ph.D. in economics from the University of Cambridge.

Malan Rietveld is a fellow at the Columbia Center on Sustainable Investment (CCSI) at Columbia University. Malan's specific areas of expertise are sovereign wealth funds, fiscal policies for the management of natural resource revenues, and the governance of large public investors. He previously served as director of the Investec Institute, a client research team of Investec Asset Management. Malan has edited four books and numerous academic papers on sovereign wealth funds. He has consulted for the World Bank, the Asian Development Bank, the government of Alaska, and a number of sovereign wealth funds and public pension funds. He has an M.Sc. in economics from the University of Leuven, an M.Sc. in economic history from the London School of Economics, and a Ph.D. in economics from the University of Stellenbosch. He was previously a fellow at the Center for International Development at the Harvard Kennedy School.

Javier Santiso is Professor of Economics at IE Business School. He previously held positions at Johns Hopkins University and ESADE Business School. Javier has also served as chief economist of Banco Bilbao Vizcaya Argentaria (BBVA) in charge of emerging markets and as director general and chief economist of the OECD Development Center. He has advised the government of Colombia on the creation of its sovereign wealth fund. Javier is the editor and director of the Annual Report on Sovereign Wealth Funds, published by IE Business School. He is the founder of Amerigo, the $350 million venture capital fund network in Europe and Latin America, powered by Telefónica, and the founder of Spain Startup, the leading platform for startups and ventures, powered in cooperation with the Rafael del Pino Foundation. Javier completed his doctoral studies at the University of Oxford and also holds an M.B.A. from the HEC School of Management and an executive M.B.A. from the IESE Business School.

Alison Schneider is director of responsible investing at the Alberta Investment Management Corporation (AIMCo). She sits on various responsible investing committees including the Pension Investment Association of Canada, the Canadian Coalition for Good Governance, and the International Corporate Governance Network. Alison recently cochaired the investor group that founded GRESB Infrastructure, an industry-driven organization committed to assessing the environmental, social, and governance (ESG) performance of real assets globally, including real estate portfolios and infrastructure assets. She currently serves on the advisory board for GRESB Infrastructure, which has more than 200 members, including 60 pension funds and their fiduciaries. She holds an M.B.A. in international business from the University of Alberta.

Perrine Toledano heads the Columbia Center on Sustainable Investment's focus on extractive industries and sustainable development. She leads research, training, and advisory projects on fiscal regimes; financial modeling; leveraging extractive industry investments in rail, port, telecommunications, water, and energy infrastructure for broader development needs; local content; revenue management; and optimal legal provisions for development benefits. Prior to joining CCSI, she worked as a consultant for several nonprofit organizations, including the World Bank, the U.K.'s Department for International Development and Revenue Watch Institute and private sector companies, including Natixis Corporate and Investment Banking and Ernst and Young. She has an M.B.A. from ESSEC Business School and a Master's of Public Administration from Columbia University.

Silvana Tordo is a lead energy economist at the World Bank's Energy and Extractives Global Practice, Extractives Group. She focuses on extractive-sector legal and contractual frameworks, taxation, and sovereign wealth funds. Her advisory work, research, and publications include value creation by national oil companies, auction design in oil and gas, extractives-led productive policies, petroleum taxation, resource revenue frameworks, and sovereign wealth management, with a particular focus on governance arrangements and policies for domestic investment. Prior to joining the World Bank in 2003, Silvana held various senior management positions in new ventures, negotiations, legal affairs, finance, and mergers and acquisitions.

Mauricio Villafuerte has been deputy division chief in the African and Fiscal Affairs Departments of the International Monetary Fund. He specializes in fiscal monetary policy issues in natural resource–dependent countries and has worked extensively with oil-producing countries, including Chad, Nigeria, Norway, and Venezuela, and in technical assistance missions linked to the design and set-up of sovereign wealth funds in Nigeria, Panama, and Papua New Guinea. Mauricio has produced several publications on fiscal policy management, including fiscal institutions for resource-rich countries, fiscal consolidation strategies, and the management of sovereign balance sheet risks.

James White has specialized in advising direct investors for over fifteen years across a wide variety of transactions from large pan-global and European leveraged buyouts through midmarket management buyouts to early-stage technology venture funding. He has also advised funds in connection with restructuring to achieve independence from former sponsoring financial institutions or governments. In recent years, James has also been involved with developing and coordinating KPMG's global teams servicing private equity and sovereign wealth clients. James ran KPMG's Private Equity Research initiative in conjunction with a leading British business school, benchmarking best-practice techniques in the various private equity value creation processes. He speaks on private equity and sovereign wealth in a number of forums including conferences, client workshops, business schools, and trade bodies. He is currently a member of an M.B.A. jury panel at a leading European business school. James joined KPMG in 1994 and spent a number of years in Hong Kong before returning to London.

Shu-Chun S. Yang is a senior economist in the Research Department of the International Monetary Fund. Before joining the IMF, she was a principal analyst at the Congressional Budget Office. She has also worked as an assistant research fellow at Academia Sinica as an economist at the Congressional Joint Committee on Taxation and as an assistant professor at John Carroll University. Her main research interest is the macroeconomic effects of fiscal policy.

Page numbers in italics indicate figures or tables.